Classes and Elites in Democracy and Democratization
A Collection of Readings

Edited by
Eva Etzioni-Halevy

GARLAND PUBLISHING, INC.
New York & London
1997

Library of Congress Cataloging-in-Publication Data

Classes and elites in democracy and democratization : a collection of
    readings / edited by Eva Etzioni-Halevy.
        p.   cm. — (Garland reference library of social science ; v. 1083)
    Includes index.
    ISBN 0-8153-2204-6 (alk. paper). — ISBN 0-8153-2864-8 (pbk. :
alk. paper)
    1. Social classes.   2. Elite (Social sciences)   3. Democracy.
I. Etzioni-Halevy, Eva.   II. Series.
HN90.S6C56   1997
305.5—dc21   97–11283
                                                                                  CIP

Printed on acid-free, 250-year-life paper
Manufactured in the United States of America

To Danielle with love

History has thrust upon our generation an indescribably important destiny—to complete a process of democratization.

—Martin Luther King Jr.

Contents

Foreword	xv
Preface	xix
Introduction	xxiii

**PART I: Classes in Democracy and
Democratization—Classical Analyses** 3

Ruling Class, Proletariat, and Bourgeois Democracy 7
Selections from the Works of
Karl Marx and Friedrich Engels

**Intellectuals and the Hegemony of the Dominant
Class in Modern Western Democracies** 12
Selections from the Work of
Antonio Gramsci

Repressive Tolerance in Contemporary Democracy 18
Selections from the Work of
Herbert Marcuse

**The Reproduction of Working-Class Exploitation
in Capitalist Democracies** 24
Selections from the Work of
Louis Althusser

The Democratic Route to Modern Society 30
Selections from the Work of
Barrington Moore

Some Social Requisites of Democracy 37
Seymour Martin Lipset

**PART II: Elites in Democracy and
Democratization—Classical Analyses**   43

The Governing Élite in Present-Day Democracy   47
Selections from the Work of
Vilfredo Pareto

The Ruling Class in Representative Democracy   53
Selections from the Work of
Gaetano Mosca

**Democracy and the Countervailing Powers
of Bureaucracy, Charisma, and Parliament**   63
Selections from the Work of
Max Weber

The Power Elite   71
C. Wright Mills

An Elite Theory of Democracy   78
Selections from the Work of
Joseph A. Schumpeter

The Ruling Minorities in Western Societies   86
Selections from the Work of
Raymond Aron

**PART III: Classes in Democracy and
Democratization—New Analyses**   93

**The Relative Autonomy of the Capitalist
State, Democracy, and Dominant Class
Hegemony**   97
Selections from the Work of
Nicos Poulantzas

**Democratic Sovereignty, the Bourgeoisie's
Dominance, and Disciplinary Power in the West**   103
Selections from the Work of
Michel Foucault

Democracy and Capitalism
[*Contradiction, Accommodation,*
and Instability]   111
Selections from the Work of
Samuel Bowles and Herbert Gintis

Rediscovering the American Democratic Dream   120
John F. Manley

Transition to Capitalist Democracy as
Class Compromise   128
Selections from the Work of
Adam Przeworski

The Rule of Capital and the Rise of Democracy   134
Göran Therborn

Economic Development and Democracy
[*The Role of Subordinate Classes*]   142
Selections from the Work of
Evelyne Huber, Dietrich Rueschemeyer,
and John D. Stephens

PART IV: Elites in Democracy and
Democratization—New Analyses   151

The Irony of Democracy   155
Thomas Dye and Harmon Zeigler

Prospects for Pluralism
[*Linkages Between Leaders and Followers in the*
American Democracy]   160
Selections from the Work of
Nelson W. Polsby

Democratic Government by Leading Minorities,
Responsiveness, and Responsibility   168
Selections from the Work of
Giovanni Sartori

**National Elite Configurations and Transition
to Democracy**   174
Selections from the Work of
G. Lowell Field, John Higley, and Michael G. Burton

**Modes of Transition and the Emergence
of Democracy in Latin America and
Southern Europe**   185
Selections from the Work of
Terry Lynn Karl and Philippe C. Schmitter

**South Korea's Elite Settlement and
Democratic Consolidation**   194
Michael G. Burton and Jai P. Ryu

**Party Elites and Democratic Consolidation
in Southern Europe**   205
Leonardo Morlino

Delegative Democracy   214
Guillermo O'Donnell

**Elites' Political Values and Democratic
Consolidation in Brazil**   222
Elisa P. Reis and Zairo B. Cheibub

**The Role of Political Elites in the
Transition from Communism to Democracy**
The Case of Poland   230
Wlodzimierz Wesolowski

**PART V: Classes and Elites in
Democracy and Democratization**   239

**The Oligarchical Tendencies of Working-
Class Organizations**   243
Selections from the Work of
Robert Michels

**State Leaders as Promoters of Capitalist
Interests in Democracies**   251
Selections from the Work of
Ralph Miliband

The Ruling Class Does Not Rule
[*State Managers, Capitalists, and the Working Class
in Capitalist Democracies*]   259
Selections from the Work of
Fred Block

The Dilemma of Pluralist Democracy
[*Autonomy Versus Equality*]   267
Selections from the Work of
Robert A. Dahl

**The Top-down and Bottom-up
Construction of Democracy**   275
Selections from the Work of
Charles Tilly

The Third Wave
[*Economic Development, Expansion of the Middle Class,
Elite Compromises, and Democratization in the
Late Twentieth Century*]   285
Selections from the Work of
Samuel P. Huntington

**Class Inequalities, Elite Patterns, and
Transition to Democracy in Latin America**   293
Selections from the Work of
Larry Diamond and Juan Linz

**Capitalism by Democratic Design in
East/Central Europe**   302
Selections from the Work of
Claus Offe

Elites and the Working Class
On Coupling, Uncoupling, Democracy, and
(In)equalities in the West   310
Eva Etzioni-Halevy

Conclusion   327

Indexes   331

Foreword

Recent (actual or attempted) transitions to democracy in various parts of the world have focused widespread interest on this type of regime. Attention has focused on the conditions that foster its emergence and consolidation, versus those that lead to its abortion or breakdown. Attention has also focused on its achievements and shortcomings, and on the social forces and actors that are to be held responsible for these. These issues have been addressed most prominently by two schools of thought: class theory, which has been concerned with the role of classes in either blocking, subverting, or fostering democracy, and elite theory, which has done the same for elites.[1]

This collection of readings has been compiled on the assumption that for an adequate explanation of the success and failure, the strengths and weaknesses, of democracy, it is necessary to resort to both class and elite theories, and to strive for the further development of the extant beginnings of a synthesis between them. For this purpose, it presents the most central and intellectually outstanding readings that illustrate the manner in which the two theories have analyzed democracy, as well as democratization, in various parts of the world. The readings range from those of the most prominent classical thinkers, beginning with Karl Marx, Friedrich Engels, Max Weber, Vilfredo Pareto, and Gaetano Mosca, to the best known later and contemporary scholars such as C. Wright Mills, Joseph Schumpeter, Barrington Moore, Seymour Martin Lipset, Juan Linz, Philippe Schmitter, Michael Burton, John Higley and Dietrich Rueschemeyer, to mention but a few. In this manner, the volume provides a grounding in both the origins of and the "state of the art" in the field.

In addition, the volume attempts something to which insufficient attention has been paid before—exploring the role of classes versus that of elites in democracy and democratization. It does so by presenting some analyses (still scant at the moment) which address themselves to both these issues. It concludes with an evaluation of what such analyses have and have not accomplished. In this manner it paves the way for the further convergence of class and elite theories of democracy.

Overall, the volume brings an innovative yet balanced perspective to bear on a topic that is now at the center of interest of the intellectual community, and of the social sciences in particular. For this reason it should be of interest to scholars in various disciplines, including sociologists and political scientists; to those confining their analyses to one particular country or geographical area; as well as to comparativists. Also, because of the wide range it covers, the core readings it includes, and the prominent authors it presents, it should be suitable as a text or as a collection of supplementary readings for a variety of courses at various (both graduate and undergraduate) levels in several disciplines. Courses for which this reader would be suitable include those on social and political theory, democracy and democratization, comparative politics or comparative political regimes, courses in political sociology, and the like.

To make the reader suitable for such courses, key readings have been selected which are intellectually powerful yet brief (or that could be excerpted without being distorted),[2] and whose ideas are presented in a straightforward and easily comprehensible way. For this purpose, too, the preface, introductions, and conclusion have been written in a clear style and special efforts have been made to minimize jargon and to present all ideas as concisely as possible. This has been done on the assumption that there is no positive correlation between the intellectual power of ideas and the convoluted manner in which they are expressed, that even complex ideas can be expressed in simple terms, that ideas that cannot be expressed lucidly are themselves muddled, and, therefore, not worth expressing at all.

An attempt has also been made to present the material in a manner which does not render it tedious to students. This task has not been onerous, for the topic itself is so fascinating that special efforts would have been required to make it boring. It is hoped that the intellectual excitement which the editor has felt in compiling this volume will come through to students. The editor hopes that this will make them all the more eager to grasp what democracy is all about, how it came into being, what is wrong with it today, how classes and elites can be seen to be responsible for what it is and is not, and what agents can be made to be responsible for further democratization in the future.

Notes

1. In its broad sense, elite theory also includes writings that are known as state-centered and corporatist theories. There are other theories as well, notably pluralist and participatory theories of democracy. However, pluralist theory which was popular in the 1950s and 1960s has recently fallen from grace and many of its erstwhile proponents (such as Robert Dahl) have changed their views in a way which brings them close to either class theory (neo-pluralism) or elite theory (pluralist-elitism). Their recent analyses are therefore easily accommodated in the respective sections of this volume. As for participatory theory, although it is extremely valuable as a normative or prescriptive theory, it has had little to say on the conditions, forces, and manner in which democracy emerged in the West, and on transitions to democracy in other parts of the world today.

2. All omissions are marked in the text by ellipses. To make the material more easily comprehensible, some of the headings have been supplied by the editor; these headings are enclosed in brackets.

Preface

A movement toward democracy seems to be in progress in various areas of the world today. It began with the toppling of Western Europe's last remaining dictatorships in Greece, Portugal, and Spain in the 1970s. It then crossed over to Latin America, where most military dictatorships were dismantled in the 1980s. A movement toward democracy was evident in East Asia as well: in the Philippines, in South Korea, and (to some extent) in Taiwan. Even more dramatic has been the collapse of the communist regimes in Eastern Europe, and the attempts of the erstwhile autocracies to grapple with democracy, since the end of the 1980s. Last but not least has been the dismantling of apartheid and the general election in South Africa, in 1994.

These overtures toward democracy have been variable in their success, but they have had at least one common result: they have led to renewed concern with democracy among intellectuals; they have brought about a surge of scholarly interest not only in the transitions to democracy, but also in what democracy as a regime is all about. Not so many years ago, the issue of democracy was widely considered as passé. The ideas of the new left, and later those of the new right, were at the hub of the intellectual debate, and this caused a sagging of interest in other topics, including that of democracy.

Recently, however, all this has changed. The new left and the new right are no longer as new as they used to be. The social movements which spearheaded the new left have shriveled and many of their activists have become part of the establishment; and the Reaganite-Thatcherist regimes which aimed to implement the ideas of the new right, have suffered an eclipse. Thus, both ideologies have lost some of their lustre and the controversies they raised are no longer as intellectually exciting as they were before.

To be sure, some of the controversies that surround democracy are not new either. But the attempted transitions to democracy in so many geographically distant and culturally divergent countries all over the world, have led scholars to consider democracy and its evolution from hitherto unexplored angles. These processes have given rise to the idea that perhaps there is more to democracy than has previously met the (scholarly) eye. Whether for this reason or because previous intellectual debates have exhausted themselves, in any case, considering democracy as passé is now itself passé, and the discourse on democracy is "in" again.

The renewed interest in democracy might have been short-lived had the recently celebrated idea of Francis Fukuyama that the collapse of the autocratic regimes in Eastern Europe heralds the triumph of democracy, and the ensuing "end of history," proved to be valid. Following the movement toward democracy in so many countries all over the world, it did in fact seem for a while that democracy was celebrating a resounding victory, that its future was well assured, and that, indeed, there was little left to argue about. It soon became clear, however, that this was but an optical illusion. This is so, not only because the recently embarked upon transitions to democracy have not all been successful and because there is no guarantee that the more successful of these transitions will not be reversed. It is so, not merely (and not chiefly) because Islamic fundamentalism may now replace the Communist regimes as a formidable world rival to Western democracy.

Rather, it is so, because the main threats to democracy spring primarily not from external enemies, but from inside itself. The already eclipsed idea of Francis Fukuyama makes even less sense, if we consider that democracy's problems have always sprung first and foremost from domestic subversions of its own principles. Today, these subversions are rife not only in the newly emerging democracies, but also (albeit in different forms) in the older ones in the West. All over the world, then, democracy has not yet "arrived." It may not be all at sea, but it certainly has not reached safe harbor yet.

To help it do so, a fuller understanding of this type of regime is required. This is not easy, since democracy is a seemingly simple, but actually intricate phenomenon. In some respects, democracy is straightforward: it is unexceptionable, enjoys universal support (or so it would seem), and even those who do not practice it themselves pay lip service to it. In other respects, democracy is very complex: even those who do not practice it claim that they do, and it is not always patently clear whether they practice democracy or pseudodemocracy. Further, the causes that lead to the emergence of democracy are uncertain and as yet have not been fully explored. The intricacies of democracy are the topic of this volume.

Introduction

This volume is about democracy: how it comes about, how it is sustained, why it may break down, and how it affects economic inequalities. But what do we mean when we say "democracy"?

What Is Democracy?

As numerous writers on this topic have not failed to remind us, the word *democracy* (derived from the Greek: *demos*—the people; *kratein*—to rule) means rule by the people. Abraham Lincoln characterized democracy as "rule of the people by the people for the people." Both the original term and this—or similar—characterizations are of great value as an ideal; but, taken literally, they cannot be used as yardsticks for existing reality. For if we were to do so, we would be hard put to find a democracy in the world today (or indeed at any other time in history). Yet we still use the term *democracy* as an epitaph for a certain type of actually existing regime. What sort of regime is this? And if it is not rule by the people, how does it differ from other regimes?

As most commonly understood among social scientists today, the term *democracy* denotes a regime in which the authority to govern derives from the consent of the majority of the people. In practice such consent is expressed through arrangements whereby certain people acquire and exercise government power on the basis of regular, free, competitive elections by all adults, whose votes have equal value. The electoral principle of democracy is intertwined with basic liberal principles, that is, civil liberties—including freedom of speech, of information, of association, and of participation in the contest for power—without which free elections would not be possible.

For most observers, then, democracy is a political rather than an economic system, while the relationship that this polity may bear to economic patterns and to degrees of economic inequality versus equality is left open for investigation. Also, for many observers, the political arrangements included in the definition of democracy are its minimal requirements. Beyond this baseline, there are qualitative differences between democracies. For instance, democracies may differ by the extent to which they have channels of public influence on the government in between elections, and by the extent to which they have fair campaigning opportunities for all contestants. However, most observers use the previously listed definition as the minimal criterion for classifying a country as a democracy even if, beyond that bare minimum, there are many imperfections in its implementation of democratic principles.

The Heroes and Villains of Democracy: Classes and Elites

Democracy, even by the above minimal definition, is a unique phenomenon in human history. As such, it did not just happen to appear; rather, it is the outcome of power struggles between holders of clashing interests, between proponents and opponents, and of the various alliances they made with and against each other. In the West, its emergence was the result of protracted contests which lasted over several centuries, and of the eventual coalitions to which these gave rise. In other parts of the world, the collisions and collusion over the emergence and stabilization of democracy are still going on today. Even in the West democracy is a fragile regime, which various powerful interests threaten to disrupt and whose persistence into the future is by no means ensured.

The confrontations over the emergence, persistence, and occasional breakdown of democracy may thus be seen as a drama. But who are its heroes and its villains? Who brings about democracy and sustains it? Who opposes it, and if it falls apart who is responsible for this? This volume has been compiled on the assumption that there are basically two types of agents that are both the heroes and villains of democracy: classes and elites. So, to understand democracy, we also have to clarify what we mean by classes and elites.

What Are Classes and What Are Elites?

In all known societies, as George Orwell put it, "some are more equal than others," meaning that some are better off than others. And, as Ralph Miliband added, "some are more plural than others." By this he meant that while a plurality of groups may have an impact on the political process, some are more powerful and more influential than others. To put it differently, in all known societies there are two dimensions of inequality: classes, differentiated primarily by their command of economic means, and elites, differentiated from the public by the extent of their power and influence.

Based on a combination of theoretical perspectives we may say, then, that classes are distinguished from each other by their members' ownership and control of material/economic resources: means of production, capital, and other means (including skills) that determine their market position (or "life chances"). In modern capitalist societies they range from the capitalist, dominant class, which owns and controls the means of production and exchange, to the subordinate working class, whose market position rests on the sale of its labor power (though part of it also possesses practical skills). In between there is the middle class, including the "old" middle class: the owners of small-scale means of production and exchange, and the "new" middle class: those with knowledge-related skills, the "intelligentsia." There are also the (inappropriately termed) "underclass": the chronically unemployed and welfare dependent and the (rapidly vanishing) peasant class.

As commonly viewed, elites may be distinguished from the rank and file or the public by their exertion of substantial power and influence over that public and over political outcomes. As distinct from class position which is seen as based on economic resources (although these may derive from, and give rise to, other resources) elite position is seen as based on various overlapping resources. These include, besides economic means, organizational resources (control of organizations), political resources (public support), symbolic resources (knowledge and ability to manipulate symbols), and personal resources (such as charisma, time, motivation, and energy). Some elites—especially those whose positions are based on public support and on charisma—are usually also referred to as leaders.

On this basis, elites in modern capitalist societies are commonly divided into state and nonstate elites. The state elites include political leaders, whose power flows primarily from political and organizational resources, and the heads of large-scale state-based organizations, such as the government bureaucracy, the military, and the police, whose power is based primarily on that of their organizations. The nonstate elites include the economic elite (or the captains of business and industry), whose power rests primarily on the control of economic enterprises and thus of economic resources; the elite of the media and the academic and cultural elites, whose influence lies in their command of symbols; trade union leaders, who rely for their power on political and organizational resources, and leaders of social movements, where personal resources (which are important for the other elites as well), in conjunction with political resources of popular support, most clearly come into play.

Class Theory and Elite Theory: Why We Need a Convergence

In view of the two dimensions of inequality—between classes and between elites and the public—two strategies have been devised in the social sciences for mapping out social structure. One strategy is known as class theory, the second as elite theory.

If both classes and elites are the heroes and villains of democracy, then, to understand democracy, we need to understand the role of classes versus that of elites in it. Yet, so far, not enough effort has been invested in the project of analyzing the two phenomena in conjunction with each other, and both together in conjunction with democracy. Mostly, class and elite theories have gone their separate ways, each paying but scant attention to the phenomenon that is central to the other (as will be seen in the first four parts of this volume).

To be sure, there have been some beginnings of a theoretical convergence: some analysts have dissected the role of both classes and elites in the emergence and persistence of democracy (as can be seen in the fifth part of this volume). Overall, however, the analytical crop from this theoretical crossbreeding is still slim. It is still the case that most of class theory has not been sufficiently concerned with elites in relation to democracy and most of elite theory has not had enough to say about the role of classes in democracy. This has led to the prominence of two partial conceptions of democracy. Each of these is valuable on its own and has made a major contribution to our understanding of democracy. But, being incomplete, each is also responsible for some deficiencies in our understanding of democracy and of democratization.

Why Class Theory on Democracy on Its Own Is Inadequate

Class theory is usually divided into two major strands: Marxist and Weberian. Of the two, it is Marxist class theory that has most prominently used its conception of economic class inequalities as a basis for branching out into an analysis of politics, the state, and democracy in capitalist regimes (the only type of regime in which democracy has so far developed). Hence it is this branch of the theory that is most relevant for our understanding of democracy.

And it is a large part of this strand that also raises some problems in this respect. This does not go for all of Marxist theory, since it is by no means a chorus that sings in unison. A few proponents of this school of thought have offered sophisticated analyses of the relationship between classes and elites, and of the impact of this relationship on democracy (as several of the writings in Part V of the volume will show).

In spite of this, it is still the case that most Marxist writings (the most prominent of which are presented in Parts I and III of this volume) explain the bulk of social phenomena chiefly in terms of class interests and class action. Thereby they have made a unique contribution to unmasking the inequalities inherent in all hitherto existing societies, and particularly in capitalist regimes. This contribution has been widely acclaimed and is not in question. The question, however, is whether they have not focused excessively on classes, attributing to them both demonic and heroic deeds, which, by themselves, classes could not possibly have perpetrated or accomplished. And while such theorists recognize the existence of a plurality of social forces, the query is whether they have not viewed these forces (including those of the state and its elites) as more closely connected with social classes than is warranted by actual reality. And if so, it must be asked if (as part of this tendency) they have not belittled the independent role of the state and of state elites; and further, whether this has not led them, perhaps inadvertently, also to belittle democracy.

For, using Marx's ideas as a point of departure, several class theorists regard the modern capitalist state—no matter how much relative autonomy it may have gained—as ultimately acting on behalf
of the capitalist ruling class. They recognize that the state and those
who staff it (the state elites or the state apparatus) necessarily have
an indigenous interest that does not emanate from any particular
class—that of exercising and perpetuating power and accumulating
more of it. But mostly they then argue that in order to perpetuate
such power, state elites have no choice but to back capitalist class
interests, to the disadvantage of the working class (see for instance
Poulantzas, Miliband, and Block in this volume).

Hence Marxist class theory shows much concern with class exploitation, and with state power which serves the interests of such
exploitation. But several of its major proponents show a lesser sensitivity to the danger of self-propelled state oppression. This raises the
question of whether they pay sufficient attention to the issue (which
is at the core of liberal thought) of the state on its own—and not
merely in alignment with class rule—encroaching on human rights
and liberties. And it raises the further question of whether they place
sufficient theoretical emphasis on the importance of the mechanisms
of democracy (such as free elections, civil liberties, and the separation of powers) for limiting the oppressive might of the state and its
rulers, the state elites, however imperfectly such mechanisms may
be implemented in actual reality.

Doubts thus arise as to whether such Marxist analysts are capable of offering a systematic analysis of what it is that—despite
whatever may be wrong with them—still makes the mechanisms of
liberal democracy preferable to the devices that channel power in
autocratic regimes. Such doubts certainly do not arise with respect
to all Marxist scholars. Przeworski for one, and also Bowles and Gintis
(in this volume), offer precisely this kind of theory of the mechanisms of democracy, and of the manner in which they curb (even
though they do not eliminate) both capitalist and state power. But
these scholars are still in the minority within their own camp.

Thus, such doubts do arise with respect to the more numerous
class theorists (such as Marcuse, Althusser, or Miliband in this volume) who hold democracy in capitalist regimes to embody but the
rule of capital through the instrument of liberal/democratic proce-

dures, including freedom of speech and free multiparty elections. In the work of such authors, these democratic processes are cast in the role of instruments of ruling-class hegemony. They are viewed as designed to divert the attention of the exploited classes from the true role of the state, as standing in league with the capitalist class, and to convince them that the state is serving them too.

Even these Marxist scholars do not dismiss democracy as a mere sham, and they praise it as being preferable to dictatorial regimes. But they still lay themselves open to the critique that—being overly concerned with class exploitation, being insufficiently concerned with independent state/elite oppression, having no theory of their own on the mechanisms that may curb it, and holding the actually existing mechanisms of democracy to be mere instruments of class rule— they display an ambivalent or even a skeptical view of democracy and its liberal devices, which are there in order to curb state oppression. They lay themselves open to the critique that they not merely (and justifiably) take to task the many inequities and iniquities which arise from the cohabitation of capitalism and democracy, but that they also undervalue democracy itself or, at the very least, help mystify the issue of democracy.

Why Elite Theory on Democracy on Its Own Is Inadequate

A similar critique may also be leveled at elite theory. Like class theory, elite theory is far from homogeneous. It may be roughly divided into two variants: the first may be referred to as mainstream elite theory, and it includes the writings of Pareto, Mosca, Michels, Mills, and several contemporary scholars, such as Dye and Zeigler and Field, Higley, and Burton. The other may be referred to as democratic elite theory; it has its roots in liberal thought, and includes writers such as Weber, Schumpeter, and Aron. More recently, it has been taken up by Etzioni-Halevy. Both variants have contributed to our understanding of power and politics. Yet (like much of class theory) they, too, have been lopsided in their conception of democracy (as some of the writings in Parts II and IV of this volume quite clearly indicate).

Several mainstream elite theorists from Pareto and Mosca onward have been as skeptical as class theorists in their view of democratic regimes. The ideal of democracy is upheld, but extant democracy is shown to fall far short of the ideal. Democracy—the classical elite theorists say—is usually presented as a regime in which majorities rule minorities. In actually existing democracies, however, as in all other regimes, the few rule and the many are ruled. And those who rule invariably find ways of explaining why it is proper, just, and beneficial for them to do so.

Some of these theorists (such as Mills) have further posited the existence of a concerted power elite (made up of a few interlocking groups of power holders) that rules in democracies, particularly in the American one. The public, or the masses, have no choice but to acquiesce in this arrangement; they are virtually devoid of power and have little impact on government policies that affect their lives. Like several Marxist class theorists, then, some (though not all) writers of this brand of elite theory have but a low regard for democracy as it evolved in actual reality, and they, too, display a cynical attitude toward it.

Unlike these mainstream elite theorists, democratic elite theorists put greater stress on the uniqueness of democracy, even in the imperfect form in which it evolved in actual reality. They follow liberal thought in their claim that unrestrained state power forms a threat to human rights and liberties, and must be limited in the interest of these rights. For them, such curbing of state power must occur through its dispersion among different agents and by means of their institutionalized separation from each other. They add that in liberal democracies an (albeit only relative) degree of such separation has in fact evolved.

Although democracies are not ruled by the people but by elites, democracies are seen to have some features which set them apart from other regimes. These include not only free elections, the assumption of the power to govern on the basis of such elections, and the government and would-be government elites' competition for the people's vote. They also include the fact that in them several other elites (for instance the business elite, the elite of the media, the academic elite, and the leaders of trade unions) have gained a degree of autonomy from the state, which enables them to countervail and restrain state power.

However, as can be seen from this brief overview (and even more so from the pertinent readings in this volume), both variants of elite theory have something in common: they have little to say about classes and class-based economic inequalities in democratic regimes. As critics have pointed out, this theory has insufficiently emphasized that in practice in democracy, as in other regimes, those who already have the most, get the most; the lion's share usually goes to the lion. To be sure, some elite theorists—especially Michels and Mills—are greatly concerned with inequality. But what concerns them is basically the inequality between leaders and the rank and file, between the power-elite and the masses, in what purport to be democratic countries or organizations. For these theorists, then, it is the inequality of power and not the—class-based—inequality of economic life chances, which obviates democracy.

Liberal democratic elite theorists have been criticized along similar lines. They have been taken to task for their stress on liberty at the expense of economic equality, for forgetting that capitalist-style liberty merely means that the poor, no less than the rich, are free to sleep under the bridge. Because of their underemphasis on the injustices of economic inequality in democratic regimes, democratic elite theorists have also been denigrated for evincing an overly complacent view of democracy. Or, as Carole Pateman (1970, p. 16) put it, according to most of these theorists "the system that we ought to have is the very one that we do in fact have."

Like many class theorists, many elite theorists have thus presented one-sided views of democracy: some are overly cynical, others overly complacent with respect to that regime. And many writers of both variants of elite theory have turned a blind eye to class-based economic inequalities that, in all hitherto existing democratic regimes, have been very much in evidence.

Why Each Theory on the Transition to Democracy on Its Own Is Inadequate

Just as large parts of both theories are instructive yet one-sided with respect to their understanding of democracy, so they are also incomplete with respect to their analyses of the transition to democracy (as should also come through from the pertinent readings in the first four parts of this volume). Some class theorists do indeed juxtapose the role of classes to that of elites in the transition to democracy (see the fifth part of this volume) but they are not many. More numerous are the class theorists who attribute not only exploitation and suppression, but also struggles to abolish it and further democracy, almost exclusively to social classes. An overbearing, rigid aristocracy is held to be responsible for the persistence of autocracy, while the bourgeoisie, the middle class, and the working class are variously viewed as being responsible for the advent of democracy.

In placing the onus of democracy so heavily on social classes, these class theorists only glance at one of the most important aspects of democratization: the double-edged role of elites in this process. They have little to say on the self-induced role of some elites in preserving state oppression, in crushing liberation movements, and in opposing democratization. And they have equally little to say on the role of other elites in struggling for liberty and the advent of democracy. Through their insufficient emphasis on the despotism-preserving potential of some elites and on the democracy-generating potential of others, they have also been led to underestimate the liberating and democratizing potential of the struggles and alliances between and within them.

The same, in reverse, is true of elite theory: several of its representatives attribute democratic developments almost exclusively to elites. Such developments are attributed to pacts or consensual agreements between elites; or else they are attributed to struggles leading to elite imposition of democracy, or to the attainment of some elites' relative autonomy from the state. Thereby these elite theorists underestimate the role of classes in either maintaining autocracy or promoting democracy.

Elites, to be sure, are the ones that conduct the actual struggles to block or foster democracy. But their positions depend to a considerable extent on the interests they represent, and on the support they can therefore gain among different social classes. Hence elite analyses that neglect these interests afford but an imperfect understanding of the social forces that contend with each other in the struggle for democratization and the stabilization of democracy.

Does All This Really Matter?

Both class- and elite theories count among their representatives some of the finest minds in the social sciences, and we are indebted to them for the better part of what we do comprehend about democracy today. Yet, when we look at the writings that represent both theories, we must conclude that mostly—though with some notable exceptions—they, each on their own, fall short of offering a comprehensive and balanced view of this type of regime and of the forces that confront each other in its emergence and implementation. At the same time, what both theories have accomplished in unison is still sparse. Should the partial "apartheid" of the two theories be of concern to scholars and students? I say that it should.

This is so, because (unlike their image in the eyes of many students) social and political theories are not divorced from reality, but quite the contrary. Theories on the nature of society and politics are inspired by values and contain certain worldviews. At one time, to be sure, many social scientists believed that the social sciences should be value-neutral. Today, however, most scholars realize that whether or not the theories which form part of the social sciences *should* be value-neutral, the fact is that most of them are not. For evidence of this, we may go as far back as the theories of the founding fathers, including Marx, Weber, and Durkheim, or as far forward as to the critical and feminist theories today. Indeed, we need only go as far as the writings in this volume, most of which have certain *Weltanschauungen* (worldviews) or even ideologies implied in them.

Such worldviews, moreover, are not incarcerated in the ivory tower of academia. In fact, some of them exert a great deal of influence on the intellectual climate of their societies. There is no point in deluding ourselves into thinking that those who are active in the political arena sit down to peruse the writings of sociopolitical theorists before they set out to implement their programs of social and political action. But it would be equally naive not to realize that the ideas contained in prominent theories seep through into widely adhered-to interpretations of political realities. And frequently they have the effect of helping either to legitimize or to delegitimize such realities.

Further, as many of the writings in this volume also illustrate, the worldviews emanating from social and political theories often include implicit guidelines for action (or inaction), which, in turn, shapes social and political forces and realities. And eventually some of these guidelines exert a certain, even if only an indirect, influence on such action (or lack thereof) and thereby on the resulting realities themselves. Hence it should be of concern that many proponents of class theory, and some of those of elite theory, have been ambivalent, uncertain, or even cynical concerning the value of democracy as it exists today. Thus they have failed to furnish the theoretical basis for its defense. By default, this may well lay the theoretical and ideological groundwork for its delegitimation, and for the legitimation of undemocratic practices and regimes.

Equally, it should be of concern that most advocates of elite theory have been insufficiently adamant as to the inequity of economic class inequality, and as to the onus on democracy to lead to its decrease or elimination. Thus they have furnished no theoretical basis for a push toward greater class equality; and some of them may even have furnished the theoretical basis for the legitimation of inequality. It should be of no less concern that some major representatives of one of the above theories have overrated the role of classes and underrated the role of elites in the advent of democracy, and that major representatives of the other have been beset by the opposite bias. Thus, such representatives of these theories have shared responsibility for conceptions each of which, on its own, would make but an imperfect guide for democratization.

Encouraging the Convergence
This being the case, it follows that class theory and elite theory have each made a major contribution to our understanding of democracy and democratization—a contribution that is well worth studying on its own. But, to the extent that major representatives of each theory have paid insufficient attention to the other, each on its own is insufficient.

Would it make much difference, then, if, where the analysis of democracy is concerned, there were to be a fuller development of the extant beginnings of a convergence between those two theories? I argue that it would, that the further convergence of class and elite theories might lead not only to a fuller and more balanced understanding of the emergence of democracy and of present democracy and its discontents, but also to a better understanding and to an encouragement of the forces that could bring about a more equitable democracy in the future.

In view of this, the aim of this volume is to encourage such a convergence between the two theories. It does so not only by presenting excerpts from the writings of the most prominent class and elite theorists that clearly stand on one or the other side of the fence, but also by devoting its final part to writings in which a convergence is noticeable. This includes contributions from some outstanding Marxist writers, who recognize the importance of elites for democracy, and from some elite theorists, who also pay attention to social classes in relation to democracy. It also includes contributions from those analysts who cannot be classified as either class or elite theorists, inasmuch as they take equal account of the role of both classes and elites vis-à-vis democracy. Finally it includes contributions (from all camps)—however few they may be—that pay special attention to the relationship between classes and elites, and to its implications for democracy.

By bringing class and elite analyses together, and by highlighting in particular those analyses that combine elements from both, an attempt is made to see whether such a theoretical wedding cannot produce a more incisive understanding and more fruitful guidelines for democracy and democratization than each theory is capable of producing on its own.

Plan of the Book

In view of all this, the first four parts of this volume are devoted to presenting both views: Parts I and III, respectively, present classical and contemporary class analyses of democracy and democratization and Parts II and IV present classical and contemporary elite analyses of this regime and the transitions to it. Particularly in Parts III and IV, which are devoted to contemporary analyses, theoretical perspectives are interspersed with, or followed by, empirical ones; the latter confront the theories with reality and illustrate the actual problems of democracy and of transitions to it. Then, Part V presents the presently still thin harvest of writings that combine the two perspectives, in the hope that they may open a new analytical pathway for future analyses.

References

Pateman, Carole. 1970. *Participation and Democratic Theory,* Cambridge: Cambridge University Press.

Classes and Elites in
Democracy and Democratization

Part I

Classes in Democracy and Democratization— Classical Analyses

Introduction

This first part of the volume presents the most notable classical class analyses of democracy. They are classical in that they are of relatively old vintage but have aged well, having withstood the test of time. To be sure: the dividing line between classical and new analyses is to some extent arbitrary. Still, many observers would probably agree that a good litmus test for being of old vintage is that a piece of writing stem from a previous generation of thinkers; that is to say, that it be *at least* twenty-five years of age (it may, of course, be much older).

The litmus test for a contribution having withstood the test of time is that it is still widely referred to and considered worthy of attention today. This is not to say that it is always referred to favorably. Indeed, sustained critique is the greatest tribute that can be paid to any piece of writing in the social sciences. If some older analyses have not attracted much critique, this is because they have not attracted much attention. Being unimportant, they have been disregarded and speedily forgotten, only to join uncountable previously forgotten writings in the garbage can of (intellectual) history. Only those theories that have served as landmarks in the evolution of the discipline have been singled out for repeated onslaughts; and only those that have been the targets of such onslaughts have survived.

The pieces included in this part of the volume are clear cases in point: they all continue to be the focus of critical attention. Apart from the fact that they are all both *classical* and *class* analyses of democracy, and that they all share wide-ranging attention and critique, there is little that they all have in common. Marx opened up this field of thought and investigation; and his contribution, the most classical of all class analyses, opens this volume. Gramsci, Marcuse, and Althusser in one way or another follow in his footsteps by emphasizing the hegemonic role of the ruling class in capitalist democracy, while the analyses by Moore and Lipset follow a somewhat different bent, as explained below.

Marx, writing on these topics from around the middle of the nineteenth century onward, made only brief comments on the state and on democracy and these are scattered over several of his writings. In them, Marx puts forward the now-famous claims that political power is an offshoot of economic power, that the modern capitalist state represents the interests of the bourgeoisie—the capitalist ruling class—and that this class, which controls the means of material production, also controls the means of mental production. Thus it rules not only economically but also ideologically and politically.

Marx also denounces capitalist democracy (as distinct from that of the short-lived Paris Commune of 1871), as nothing but a repressive form of bourgeois rule since, in it, elections merely determine which members of the ruling class are to exercise power. Yet he admits that democracy wrests some power, and the assurance of power, from the hands of the bourgeoisie. Not surprisingly, Marx has been taken to task for his ambivalence with respect to democracy: his statements beg the question of how it is that democracy, which merely enables the ruling class to rule more effectively, nevertheless wrests from it the assurance of its power. To this question we find no answer in Marx's writings.

Gramsci's contribution—written during his sojourn in a fascist Italian prison—contains an idea that is reminiscent of Marx's notion on the ideological rule of the ruling class. But Gramsci pushes this idea further by suggesting that in modern democracy the dominant class exercises what he terms hegemony through intellectuals and a variety of cultural and other institutions which disseminate its ideology. Thereby the dominant class succeeds in obtaining a large degree of consent from the subjected class, and it can therefore reduce coercion to situations of crisis in which hegemony-induced consent breaks down.

The idea of ruling class hegemony finds further advocates among postwar Marxist writers, notably Marcuse, the guru of the New Left in the 1960s. In his contribution, Marcuse presents what is probably his best-known idea, that of repressive tolerance. In advanced democracy, argues Marcuse, even tolerance plays an hegemonic, repressive role. Freedom of expression is allowed, but in various ways is rendered innocuous. Thereby people gain the illusion of democratic liberties, and this is used to entrench repression in the predominant class interests.

Althusser, a most influential figure in European Marxism, sees the reproduction of the relations of production—and thereby of ruling-class hegemony—as proceeding through the exercise of state power. He not merely designates the state as the general perpetrator of this rule, but also identifies the repressive state apparatuses—including the military, the police—and the ideological state apparatuses—including parliamentary-democratic institutions and most prominently education—as the executors of such rule.

If, as the idea of ideological rule and hegemony implies, the ruling class rules by imposing its ideology on society, it follows that the people accept such ideological rule, even though it works to their disadvantage. This gives rise to the query of how it is that in democratic societies, where communication from a variety of sources (such as that from Marxist writings, which promulgate the idea of ruling class hegemony) is freely available, people are so easily duped into docility. Thus, the very popularity of the notion of hegemony must itself cast doubt on its validity.

Marx and Marxist writers consider the bourgeoisie, or the ruling class, as the villain that uses democracy to further its own rule. Yet Moore considers the bourgeoisie as democracy's hero. He attributes the evolution of democracy to an unsettling of a dominant coalition of labor-repressive landlords and a powerful state. This is but the other side of the coin of the rise of a strong bourgeoisie, which fulfills a central role in bringing about democracy. Or, as he so forcefully put it: "no bourgeois—no democracy."

Whereas Marxists pay little attention to the role of the middle class in generating or sustaining democracy, Lipset makes this class both the focus of his attention and the chief pillar of this regime. Lipset points to a correlation between economic development and democracy; this is so because such development leads to increased wealth and education and to decreased inequality; these are associated with moderate lower and upper classes and with a larger middle class. Since this class is generally moderate, the larger its size, the better the chances for democratic consolidation.

Moore's and Lipset's theses are among the most widely cited in this area of the social sciences. Still, others point out that both the bourgeoisie and the middle class further democracy only as long as it tallies with their own interests. When it does not, they abandon democracy to its fate, or even oppose it. There is but one class that invariably benefits from democracy and hence invariably promotes it. To find out which class this is, it is necessary turn to the new class analyses in Part III of this volume. First, however, the classical thinkers presented in the first two parts of the volume must be allowed to speak for themselves.

Ruling Class, Proletariat, and Bourgeois Democracy

Selections from the Works of
Karl Marx and Friedrich Engels

[Ruling Class, Ruling Ideas]*

The ideas of the ruling class are in every epoch the ruling ideas: i.e., the class which is the ruling *material* force of society, is at the same time its ruling *intellectual* force. The class which has the means of material production at its disposal, consequently also controls the means of mental production, so that the ideas of those who lack the means of mental production are on the whole subject to it. The ruling ideas are nothing more than the ideal expression of the dominant material relations, the dominant material relations grasped as ideas; hence of the relations which make the one class the ruling one, therefore, the ideas of its dominance.

The individuals composing the ruling class possess among other things consciousness, and therefore think. Insofar, therefore, as they rule as a class and determine the extent and compass of an historical epoch, it is self-evident that they do this in its whole range, hence among other things rule also as thinkers, as producers of ideas, and regulate the production and distribution of the ideas of their age: thus their ideas are the ruling ideas of the epoch. For instance, in an age and in a country where royal power, aristocracy, and bourgeoisie are contending for domination and where, therefore, domination is shared, the doctrine of the separation of powers proves to be the dominant idea and is expressed as an "eternal law" . . .

* Excerpts from Karl Marx and Friedrich Engels, *The German Ideology* (1845–1846). In Karl Marx and Friedrich Engels, *Collected Works*, vol. 5 (London: Lawrence R. Wishart, 1965; New York: International Publishers, 1976), pp. 59, 89–90. Reprinted by permission of both publishers. Bracketed headings have been created by the editor of this volume.

[The Bourgeoisie and the State]

In the case of the nations which grew out of the Middle Ages, tribal property evolved through various stages—feudal landed property, corporative movable property, capital invested in manufacture—to modern capital, determined by large-scale industry and universal competition, i.e. pure private property, which has cast off all semblance of a communal institution and has shut out the state from any influence on the development of property. To this modern private property corresponds the modern state, which, purchased gradually by the owners of property by means of taxation, has fallen entirely into their hands through the national debt, and its existence has become wholly dependent on the commercial credit which the owners of property, the bourgeois, extend to it, as reflected in the rise and fall of government securities on the stock exchange. By the mere fact that it is a *class* and no longer an *estate*, the bourgeoisie is forced to organise itself no longer locally, but nationally, and to give a general form to its average interests. Through the emancipation of private property from the community, the state has become a separate entity, alongside and outside civil society; but it is nothing more than the form of organisation which the bourgeois are compelled to adopt both for internal and external purposes, for the mutual guarantee of their property and interests . . .

[Class Struggle and the State]†

The history of all hitherto existing society is the history of class struggles. Freeman and slave, patrician and plebeian, lord and serf, guild master and journeyman, in a word, oppressor and oppressed, stood in constant opposition to one another, carried on an uninterrupted, now hidden, now open fight, a fight that each time ended either in a revolutionary reconstitution of society at large, or in the common ruin of the contending classes . . .

The modern bourgeois society that has sprouted from the ruins of feudal society has not done away with class antagonisms. It has but established new classes, new conditions of oppression, new forms

---

† Excerpts from Karl Marx and Friedrich Engels, *The Manifesto of the Communist Party* (1848). In Karl Marx, *Selected Works*, vol. 1 of 2 (New York: International Publishers, 1933), 204–207. Reprinted by permission of the publisher. Bracketed headings have been created by the editor of this volume.

of struggle in place of the old ones. Our epoch, the epoch of the bourgeoisie, possesses, however, this distinctive feature: it has simplified the class antagonisms. Society as a whole is more and more splitting up into two great hostile camps, into two great classes directly facing each other: bourgeoisie and proletariat . . .

Each step in the development of the bourgeoisie was accompanied by a corresponding political advance of that class. An oppressed class under the sway of the feudal nobility, an armed and self-governing association in the medieval commune; here independent urban republic (as in Italy and Germany), there taxable "third estate" of the monarchy (as in France); afterwards, in the period of manufacture proper, serving either the semi-feudal or the absolute monarchy as a counterpoise against the nobility, and, in fact, cornerstone of the great monarchies in general, the bourgeoisie has at last, since the establishment of modern industry and of the world market, conquered for itself, in the modern representative state, exclusive political sway. The executive of the modern state is but a committee for managing the common affairs of the whole bourgeoisie . . .

[The Contradiction of Bourgeois Democracy]‡

February 25, 1848, had granted the *republic* to France . . . The June fight had been led by the *republican* faction of the bourgeoisie; with victory, political power inevitably fell to its share . . . After the June days the Constituent Assembly remained the *exclusive representative of bourgeois republicanism* . . . And the "great organic work" of the Constituent National Assembly consisted in . . . producing a republican *constitution* . . . The most comprehensive contradiction of this constitution, however, consisted in the following: The classes whose social slavery the constitution is to perpetuate, proletariat, peasantry, petty bourgeois, it puts in possession of political power through universal suffrage. And from the class whose old social power it sanctions, the bourgeoisie, it withdraws the political guarantees of this power. It forces its political rule into democratic conditions, which at every moment help the hostile classes to victory and jeopardise

‡ Excerpts from Karl Marx, *The Class Struggles in France* (1848–1850). In Karl Marx *Selected Works,* vol. 2 of 2 (New York: International Publishers, 1933), 221–232. Reprinted by permission of the publisher. Bracketed headings have been created by the editor of this volume.

the very foundations of bourgeois society. From the former classes it demands that they should not go forward from political to social emancipation; from the others that they should not go back from social to political restoration . . .

[Proletarian Democracy, Bourgeois Democracy]§

On the dawn of the eighteenth of March, Paris arose to the thunderburst of *"Vive la Commune!"* What is the Commune, that sphinx so tantalising to the bourgeois mind? . . .

The Commune was formed of the municipal councillors, chosen by universal suffrage in the various wards of the town, responsible and revocable at short terms. The majority of its members were naturally workingmen, or acknowledged representatives of the working class. The Commune was to be a working, not a parliamentary, body, executive and legislative at the same time. Instead of continuing to be the agent of the central government the police was at once stripped of its political attributes and turned into the responsible and at all times revocable agent of the Commune. So were the officials of all other branches of the Administration . . . The judicial functionaries were to be divested of that sham independence which had but served to mask their abject subserviency to all succeeding governments to which, in turn, they had taken, and broken, the oaths of allegiance. Like the rest of public servants, magistrates and judges were to be elective, responsible, and revocable . . .

The unity of the nation was not to be broken, but, on the contrary, to be organised by the Communal Constitution, and to become a reality by the destruction of the state power which claimed to be the embodiment of that unity independent of and superior to, the nation itself, from which it was but a parasitic excrescence. While the merely repressive organs of the old government power were to be amputated, its legitimate functions were to be wrested from an authority usurping pre-eminence over society itself and restored to the responsible agents of society. Instead of *deciding once in three or six years which member of the ruling class was to*

---

§ Excerpts from Karl Marx, *The Civil War in France* (1871). In Karl Marx, *Selected Works*, vol. 2 of 2 (New York: International Publishers, 1933), 494, 498–502. Reprinted by permission of the publisher. Bracketed headings have been created by the editor of this volume.

misrepresent the people in Parliament [italics supplied], universal suffrage was to serve the people, constituted in communes . . .

The communal constitution would have restored to the social body all the forces hitherto absorbed by the state parasite feeding upon, and clogging the free movement of, society. By this one act it would have initiated the regeneration of France . . . It supplied the republic with the basis of really democratic institutions . . .

Intellectuals and the Hegemony of the Dominant Class in Modern Western Democracies

Selections from the Work of
Antonio Gramsci

[Social Classes and Their Intellectuals]

Every social group, coming into existence on the original terrain of an essential function in the world of economic production, creates together with itself, organically, one or more strata of intellectuals which give it homogeneity and an awareness of its own function not only in the economic but also in the social and political fields. The capitalist entrepreneur creates alongside himself the industrial technician, the specialist in political economy, the organisers of a new culture, of a new legal system, etc. . . .

However, every "essential" social group which emerges into history out of the preceding economic structure, and as an expression of a development of this structure, has [also] found (at least in all of history up to the present) categories of intellectuals already in existence and which seemed indeed to represent an historical continuity uninterrupted even by the most complicated and radical changes in political and social forms.

The most typical of these categories of intellectuals is that of the ecclesiastics, who for a long time (for a whole phase of history, which is partly characterised by this very monopoly) held a monopoly of a number of important services: religious ideology, that is the philosophy and science of the age, together with schools, education, morality, justice, charity, good works, etc. The category of ecclesiastics can be considered the category of intellectuals organically bound to the

Excerpts from Antonio Gramsci, *Selections from the Prison Notebooks of Antonio Gramsci*, ed. and trans. by Quintin Hoare and Geoffrey Nowell-Smith (London: Lawrence and Wishart, 1971), 5–18. Reprinted by permission of Lawrence and Wishart and of International Publishers. Bracketed headings have been created by the editor of this volume.

landed aristocracy. It had equal status juridically with the aristocracy, with which it shared the exercise of feudal ownership of land, and the use of state privileges connected with property. But the monopoly held by the ecclesiastics in the superstructural field was not exercised without a struggle or without limitations, and hence there took place the birth, in various forms, . . . of other categories, favoured and enabled to expand by the growing strength of the central power of the monarch, right up to absolutism. Thus we find the formation of the *noblesse de robe*, with its own privileges, a stratum of administrators, etc., scholars and scientists, theorists, non-ecclesiastical philosophers, etc.

Since these various categories of traditional intellectuals experience through an "*esprit de corps*" their uninterrupted historical continuity and their special qualification, they thus put themselves forward as autonomous and independent of the dominant social group. This self-assessment is not without consequences in the ideological and political field, consequences of wide-ranging import. The whole of idealist philosophy can easily be connected with this position assumed by the social complex of intellectuals and can be defined as the expression of that social utopia by which the intellectuals think of themselves as "independent", autonomous, endowed with a character of their own, etc. . . .

The traditional . . . type of the intellectual is given by the man of letters, the philosopher, the artist. Therefore journalists, who claim to be men of letters, philosophers, artists, also regard themselves as the "true" intellectuals. In the modern world, technical education, closely bound to industrial labour even at the most primitive and unqualified level, must form the basis of the new type of intellectual . . . The mode of being of the new intellectual can no longer consist in eloquence, which is an exterior and momentary mover of feelings and passions, but in active participation in practical life, as constructor, organiser, "permanent persuader" and not just a simple orator (but superior at the same time to the abstract mathematical spirit); from technique-as-work one proceeds to technique-as-science and to the humanistic conception of history, without which one remains "specialised" and does not become "directive" (specialised and political).

[Intellectuals as Dominant Class Deputies in the Exercise of Hegemony]

Thus there are historically formed specialised categories for the exercise of the intellectual function. They are formed in connection with all social groups, but especially in connection with the more important, and they undergo more extensive and complex elaboration in connection with the dominant social group. One of the most important characteristics of any group that is developing towards dominance is its struggle to assimilate and to conquer "ideologically" the traditional intellectuals, but this assimilation and conquest is made quicker and more efficacious the more the group in question succeeds in simultaneously elaborating its own organic intellectuals.

The enormous development of activity and organisation of education in the broad sense in the societies that emerged from the medieval world is an index of the importance assumed in the modern world by intellectual functions and categories. Parallel with the attempt to deepen and to broaden the "intellectuality" of each individual, there has also been an attempt to multiply and narrow the various specialisations. This can be seen from educational institutions at all levels, up to and including the organisms that exist to promote so-called "high culture" in all fields of science and technology . . .

It is worth noting that the elaboration of intellectual strata in concrete reality does not take place on the terrain of abstract democracy but in accordance with very concrete traditional historical processes. Strata have grown up which traditionally "produce" intellectuals and these strata coincide with those which have specialised in "saving," i.e. the petty and middle landed bourgeoisie and certain strata of the petty and middle urban bourgeoisie. The varying distribution of different types of school (classical and professional) over the "economic" territory and the varying aspirations of different categories within these strata determine, or give form to, the production of various branches of intellectual specialisation . . .

The relationship between the intellectuals and the world of production is not as direct as it is with the fundamental social groups but is, in varying degrees, "mediated" by the whole fabric of society and by the complex of superstructures, of which the intellectuals are, precisely, the "functionaries." It should be possible both to measure the "organic quality" of the various intellectual strata and their degree of connection with a fundamental social group, and to establish a gradation of their functions and of the superstructures from the bottom to the top (from the structural base upwards).

What we can do, for the moment, is to fix two major superstructural "levels": the one that can be called "civil society," that is the ensemble of organisms commonly called "private," and that of "political society" or "the State." These two levels correspond on the one hand to the function of *"hegemony" which the dominant group exercises throughout society* and on the other hand to that of "direct domination" or command exercised through the State and "juridical" government. The functions in question are precisely organisational and connective. *The Intellectuals are the dominant group's "deputies" exercising the subaltern functions of social hegemony and political government* [italics supplied]. These comprise:

1. The "spontaneous" consent given by the great masses of the population to the general direction imposed on social life by the dominant fundamental group; this consent is "historically" caused by the prestige (and consequent confidence) which the dominant group enjoys because of its position and function in the world of production.
2. The apparatus of state coercive power which "legally" enforces discipline on those groups who do not "consent" either actively or passively. This apparatus is, however, constituted for the whole of society in anticipation of moments of crisis of command and direction when spontaneous consent has failed.

This way of posing the problem has as a result a considerable extension of the concept of intellectual, but it is the only way which enables one to reach a concrete approximation of reality. It also clashes with preconceptions of caste. The function of organising social hegemony and state domination certainly gives rise to a particular division of labour and therefore to a whole hierarchy of qualifications in some of which there is no apparent attribution of directive or organisational functions. For example, in the apparatus of social and state direction there exist a whole series of jobs of a manual and instrumental character (non-executive work, agents rather than officials or functionaries). It is obvious that such a distinction has to be made just as it is obvious that other distinctions have to be made as well. Indeed, intellectual activity must also be distinguished in terms of its intrinsic characteristics, according to levels which in moments of extreme opposition represent a real qualitative difference—at the highest level would be the creators of the various sciences, philosophy, art, etc., at the lowest the most humble "administrators" and divulgators of pre-existing, traditional, accumulated intellectual wealth.

In the modern world the category of intellectuals, understood in this sense, has undergone an unprecedented expansion. The democratic-bureaucratic system has given rise to a great mass of functions which are not all justified by the social necessities of production, though they are justified by the political necessities of the dominant fundamental group . . .

[Intellectuals and Hegemony in Western Democracies: Some Examples]

France offers the example of an accomplished form of harmonious development of the energies of the nation and of the intellectual categories in particular. When in 1789 a new social grouping makes its political appearance on the historical stage, it is already completely equipped for all its social functions and can therefore struggle for total dominion of the nation. It does not have to make any essential compromises with the old classes but instead can subordinate them to its own ends. The first intellectual cells of the new type are born along with their first economic counterparts. Even ecclesiastical organisation is influenced (gallicanism, precocious struggles between Church and State). This massive intellectual construction explains the function of culture in France in the eighteenth and nineteenth centuries. It was a function of international and cosmopolitan outward radiation and of imperialistic and hegemonic expansion in an organic fashion, very different therefore from the Italian experience, which was founded on scattered personal migration and did not react on the national base to potentiate it but on the contrary contributed to rendering the constitution of a solid national base impossible.

In England the development is very different from France. The new social grouping that grew up on the basis of modern industrialism shows a remarkable economic-corporate development but advances only gropingly in the intellectual-political field. There is a very extensive category of organic intellectuals—those, that is, who come into existence on the same industrial terrain as the economic group—but in the higher sphere we find that the old land-owning class preserves its position of virtual monopoly. It loses its economic supremacy but maintains for a long time a politico-intellectual supremacy and is assimilated as "traditional intellectuals" and as directive group by the new group in power . . .

Repressive Tolerance in Contemporary Democracy

Selections from the Work of
Herbert Marcuse

This essay examines the idea of tolerance in our advanced industrial society. The conclusion reached is that . . . what is proclaimed and practiced as tolerance today, is in many of its most effective manifestations serving the cause of oppression . . .

According to a dialectical proposition it is the whole which determines the truth—not in the sense that the whole is prior or superior to its parts—but in the sense that its structure and function determine every particular condition and relation. Thus, within a repressive society, even progressive movements threaten to turn into their opposite to the degree to which they accept the rules of the game. To take a most controversial case: the exercise of political rights (such as voting, letter-writing to the press, to Senators, etc., protest-demonstrations with a priori renunciation of counterviolence) in a society of total administration serves to strengthen this administration by testifying to the existence of democratic liberties which, in reality, have changed their content and lost their effectiveness. In such a case, freedom (of opinion, of assembly, of speech) becomes an instrument for absolving servitude. And yet (and only here the dialectical proposition shows its full intent) the existence and practice of these liberties remain a precondition for the restoration of their original oppositional function, provided that the effort to transcend their (often self-imposed) limitations is intensified.

[Tolerance and Class Inequalities]

Generally, the function and value of tolerance depend on the equality prevalent in the society in which tolerance is practiced . . . In other words, tolerance is an end in itself only when it is truly universal, practiced by the rulers as well as by the ruled, by the lords as well as by the peasants, by the sheriffs as well as by their victims . . . As long as these conditions do not prevail, the conditions of tolerance are "loaded": they are determined and defined by the institutionalized inequality (which is certainly compatible with constitutional equality), i.e., by the class structure of society. In such a society, tolerance is *de facto* limited on the dual ground of legalized violence or suppression (police, armed forces, guards of all sorts) and of the privileged position held by the predominant interests and their "connections" . . .

Within the framework of such a social structure, tolerance can be safely practiced and proclaimed. It is of two kinds: (1) the passive toleration of entrenched and established attitudes and ideas even if their damaging effect on man and nature is evident; and (2) the active, official tolerance granted to the Right as well as to the Left . . . I call this non-partisan tolerance "abstract" or "pure" inasmuch as it refrains from taking sides—but in doing so it actually protects the already established machinery of discrimination . . .

Under a system of constitutionally guaranteed and (generally and without too many and too glaring exceptions) practiced civil rights and liberties, opposition and dissent are tolerated unless they issue in violence and/or in exhortation to and organization of violent subversion. The underlying assumption is that the established society is free, and that any improvement, even a change in the social structure and social values, would come about in the normal course of events, prepared, defined, and tested in free and equal discussion, on the open marketplace of ideas and goods. Now . . . free and equal discussion can fulfill the function attributed to it only if it is [a] *rational*—expression and development of independent thinking, free from indoctrination, manipulation, extraneous authority.

The notion of pluralism and countervailing powers is no substitute for this requirement. One might in theory construct a state in which a multitude of different pressures, interests, and authorities balance each other out and result in a truly general and rational interest. However, such a construct badly fits a society in which powers are and remain unequal and even increase their unequal weight when they run their own course. It fits even worse when the variety of pressures unifies and coagulates into an overwhelming whole, integrating the particular countervailing powers by virtue of an increasing standard of living and an increasing concentration of power. Then, the laborer, whose real interest conflicts with that of management, the common consumer whose real interest conflicts with that of the producer, the intellectual whose vocation conflicts with that of his employer find themselves submitting to a system against which they are powerless and appear unreasonable. The ideas of the available alternatives evaporate into an utterly utopian dimension in which it is at home, for a free society is indeed unrealistically and undefinably different from the existing ones. Under these circumstances, whatever improvement may occur "in the normal course of events" and without subversion is likely to be improvement in the direction determined by the particular interests which control the whole.

By the same token, those minorities which strive for a change of the whole itself will, under optimal conditions which rarely prevail, be left free to deliberate and discuss, to speak and to assemble—and will be left harmless and helpless in the face of the overwhelming majority, which militates against qualitative social change. This majority is firmly grounded in the increasing satisfaction of needs, and technological and mental coordination, which testify to the general helplessness of radical groups in a well-functioning social system . . .

[Tolerance as Repression]

In the contemporary period, the democratic argument for abstract tolerance tends to be invalidated by the invalidation of the democratic process itself. The liberating force of democracy was the chance it gave to effective dissent, on the individual as well as social scale, its openness to qualitatively different forms of government, of culture, education, work—of the human existence in general. The toleration of free discussion and the equal right of opposites was to define and clarify the different forms of dissent: their direction, content, prospect. But with the concentration of economic and political power and the integration of opposites in a society which uses technology as an instrument of domination, effective dissent is blocked where it could freely emerge: in the formation of opinion, in information and communication, in speech and assembly.

Under the rule of monopolistic media—themselves the mere instruments of economic and political power—a mentality is created for which right and wrong, true and false are predefined wherever they affect the vital interests of the society. This is, prior to all expression and communication, a matter of semantics: the blocking of effective dissent, of the recognition of that which is not of the Establishment which begins in the language that is publicized and administered. The meaning of words is rigidly stabilized. Rational persuasion, persuasion to the opposite is all but precluded. The avenues of entrance are closed to the meaning of words and ideas other than the established one—established by the publicity of the powers that be, and verified in their practices. Other words can be spoken and heard, other ideas can be expressed, but, at the massive scale of the conservative majority (outside such enclaves as the intelligentsia), they are immediately "evaluated" (i.e., automatically understood) in terms of the public language—a language which determines "a priori" the direction in which the thought process moves.

Thus the process of reflection ends where it started: in the given conditions and relations. Self-validating, the argument of the discussion repels the contradiction because the antithesis is redefined in terms of the thesis. For example, thesis: we work for peace; antithesis: we prepare for war; . . . unification of opposites: preparing for war *is* working for peace. Peace is redefined as necessarily, in the prevailing situation, including preparation for war . . . and in this Orwellian form, the meaning of the word "peace" is stabilized. Thus, the basic vocabulary of the Orwellian language operates as a priori categories of understanding: preforming all content. These conditions invalidate the logic of tolerance which involves the rational development of meaning and precludes the closing of meaning. Consequently, persuasion through discussion and the equal presentation of opposites (even where it is really equal) easily lose their liberating force as factors of understanding and learning; they are far more likely to strengthen the established thesis and to repel the alternatives.

Impartiality to the utmost, equal treatment of competing and conflicting issues is indeed a basic requirement for decision-making in the democratic process—it is an equally basic requirement for defining the limits of tolerance. But in a democracy with totalitarian organization, objectivity may fulfill a very different function, namely, to foster a mental attitude which tends to obliterate the difference between true and false, information and indoctrination, right and wrong. In fact, the decision between opposed opinions has been made before the presentation and discussion get under way—made, not by a conspiracy or a sponsor or a publisher, not by any dictatorship, but rather by the "normal course of events," which is the course of administered events, and by the mentality shaped in this course. Here, too, it is the whole which determines the truth. Then the decision asserts itself, without any open violation of objectivity, in such things as the make-up of a newspaper (with the breaking up of vital information into bits interspersed between extraneous material, irrelevant items, relegating of some radically negative news to an obscure place), in the juxtaposition of gorgeous ads with unmitigated horrors, in the introduction and interruption of the broadcasting of facts by overwhelming commercials. The result is a *neutralization* of opposites, a neutralization, however, which takes place on the firm grounds of the structural limitation of tolerance and within a preformed mentality . . .

[The Search for an Alternative]

The factual barriers which totalitarian democracy erects against the efficacy of qualitative dissent are weak and pleasant enough compared with the practices of a dictatorship which claims to educate the people in the truth. With all its limitations and distortions, democratic tolerance is under all circumstances more humane than an institutionalized intolerance which sacrifices the rights and liberties of the living generations for the sake of future generations. The question is whether this is the only alternative . . .

The break through the false consciousness may provide the Archimedean point for a larger emancipation—at an infinitesimally small spot, to be sure, but it is on the enlargement of such small spots that the chance of change depends. The forces of emancipation cannot be identified with any social class which, by virtue of its material condition, is free from false consciousness. Today, they are hopelessly dispersed throughout the society, and the fighting minorities and isolated groups are often in opposition to their own leadership. In the society at large, the mental space for denial and reflection must first be recreated . . .

[Conclusion]

I have tried to show how the changes in advanced democratic societies, which have undermined the basis of economic and political liberalism, have also altered the liberal function of tolerance. The tolerance which was the great achievement of the liberal era is still professed and (with strong qualifications) practiced, while the economic and political process is subjected to an ubiquitous and effective administration in accordance with the predominant interests . . . The altered social structure tends to weaken the effectiveness of tolerance toward dissenting and oppositional movements and to strengthen conservative and reactionary forces . . . And on the firm foundations of a coordinated society all but closed against qualitative change, tolerance itself serves to contain such change rather than to promote it . . .

A redressing seems to be tantamount to the establishment of a "right of resistance" to the point of subversion. There is not, there cannot be, any such right for any group or individual against a constitutional government sustained by a majority of the population. But I believe that there is a "natural right" of resistance for oppressed and overpowered minorities to use extralegal means if the legal ones have proved to be inadequate. Law and order are always and everywhere the law and order which protect the established hierarchy; it is nonsensical to invoke the absolute authority of this law and this order against those who suffer from it and struggle against it—not for personal advantages and revenge, but for their share of humanity. There is no other judge over them than the constituted authorities, the police, and their own conscience. If they use violence, they do not start a new chain of violence but try to break an established one. Since they will be punished, they know the risk, and when they are willing to take it, no third person, and least of all the educator and intellectual has the right to preach them abstention.

The Reproduction of Working-Class Exploitation in Capitalist Democracies

Selections from the Work of
Louis Althusser

Every social formation must reproduce the conditions of its production at the same time that it produces, and in order to be able to produce. It must therefore reproduce: 1. the productive forces 2. the existing relations of production . . .

The *reproduction of the relations of production* . . . is a *crucial question* for the Marxist theory of the mode of production . . . I shall give a short analysis of . . . the State *from this point of view* . . . The definition of the State as a class State, existing in the repressive State apparatus, casts a brilliant light on all the facts observable in the various orders of repression whatever their domains . . . It casts light on the subtle everyday domination beneath which can be glimpsed, in the forms of political democracy, for example, what Lenin, following Marx, called the dictatorship of the bourgeoisie. And yet . . . I think it is indispensable to add something to the . . . Marxist theory of the State.

[Repressive and Ideological State Apparatuses]

In order to advance the theory of the State it is indispensable to take into account . . . also another reality which is clearly on the side of the (repressive) State apparatus, but must not be confused with it. I shall call this reality by its concept: *the ideological State Apparatuses.* What are ideological State apparatuses (ISAs)? They must not be confused with the (repressive) State apparatus (RSA). Remember

Excerpts from Louis Althusser, "Ideology and Ideological State Apparatuses" in *Lenin and Philosophy and Other Essays*, trans. Ben Brewster, 127–186. Copyright © 1971 by Verso. Reprinted by permission of the Monthly Review Foundation. Bracketed headings have been created by the editor of this volume.

that in Marxist theory, the State Apparatus (SA) contains: the Government, the Administration, the Army, the Police, the Courts, the Prisons, etc., which constitute what I . . . call the RSA . . .

[In distinction to these] we can for the moment regard the following institutions as ideological State apparatuses: the religious ISA (the system of the different Churches), the educational ISA (the system of the different public and private "Schools"), the family ISA, the legal ISA, the political ISA (the political system, including the different parties), the trade-union ISA, the communications ISA (press, radio and television, etc.), the cultural ISA (Literature, the Arts, sports, etc.). I have said that the ISAs must not be confused with the RSA. What constitutes the difference? . . .

It is clear that whereas the RSA belongs entirely to the *public* domain, much the larger part of the ISAs are part, on the contrary, of the *private* domain. Churches, Parties, Trade Unions, families, some schools, most newspapers, cultural ventures, etc., etc., are private . . . But someone is bound to ask me by what right I regard as ideological *State* apparatuses, institutions which for the most part do not possess public status, but are quite simply *private* institutions.

As a conscious Marxist, Gramsci already forestalled this objection in one sentence. The distinction between the public and the private is a distinction internal to bourgeois law, and valid in the (subordinate) domains in which bourgeois law exercises "authority." The domain of the State escapes it because the latter is "above the law": the State, which is the State of the ruling class, is neither public nor private; on the contrary, it is the precondition for any distinction between public and private. The same thing can be said from the starting point of our State Ideological Apparatuses. It is unimportant whether the institutions in which they are realized are "public" or "private." What matters is how they function. Private institutions can very well "function" as Ideological State Apparatuses. A reasonably thorough analysis of any one of the ISAs proves it.

But now for what is essential . . . I shall say that every State Apparatus, whether Repressive or Ideological, "functions" both by violence and by ideology, but with one very important distinction which makes it imperative not to confuse the ISAs with the RSA. This is the fact that the RSA functions massively and predominantly *by repression* (including physical repression), while functioning secondarily by ideology. (There is no such thing as a purely repressive apparatus.) For example, the Army and the Police also function by ideology both to ensure their own cohesion and reproduction, and in the "values" they propound externally.

In the same way, but inversely, it is essential to say that for their part the ISAs function massively and predominantly *by ideology*, but they also function secondarily by repression, even if ultimately, but only ultimately, this is very attenuated and concealed, even symbolic. (There is no such thing as a purely ideological apparatus.) Thus Schools and Churches use suitable methods of punishment, expulsion, selection, etc., to "discipline" not only their shepherds, but also their flocks. The same is true of the family, etc. . . .

If the ISAs "function" massively and predominantly by ideology, the ideology by which they function is always . . . *the ruling ideology*, which is the ideology of "the ruling class." Given the fact that the "ruling class" in principle holds State power (openly or more often by means of alliances between classes or class fractions) and therefore has at its disposal the RSA, we can accept the fact that this same ruling class is active in the ISAs insofar as it is ultimately the ruling ideology which is realized in the ISAs . . . To my knowledge, *no class can hold State power over a long period without at the same time exercising its hegemony over and in the ISAs . . .*

[ISAs and the Reproduction of the Relations of Production in Capitalist Democracies]

I can now answer the central question which I have left in suspense: . . . *how is the reproduction of the relations of production secured?* . . . I shall say: for the most part, it is secured by the exercise of State power in the State Apparatuses, on the one hand the RSA, on the other the ISAs . . . The role of the RSA, insofar as it is a repressive apparatus, consists essentially of securing by force (physical or otherwise) the political conditions of the reproduction of the relations of production which are in the last resort relations of exploitation. Not only does the State apparatus contribute generously to its own reproduction (the capitalist State contains political dynasties, military dynasties, etc.), but also, and above all, the State apparatus secures by repression (from the most brutal physical force, via mere administrative commands and interdictions, to open and tacit censorship) the political conditions for the action of the ISAs. In fact, it is the latter which largely secure the reproduction specifically of the relations of production, behind a "shield" provided by the RSA . . .

In the pre-capitalist historical period, . . . *there was one dominant ISA, the Church,* which concentrated within it not only religious functions, but also educational ones, and a large proportion of the function of communications and "culture" . . . The foremost objective and achievement of the French Revolution was not just to transfer State power from the feudal aristocracy to the merchant-capitalist bourgeoisie, to break part of the former repressive RSA and replace it with a new one (e.g., the national popular Army)—but also to attack the number one ISA: the Church. Hence the civil constitution of the clergy, the confiscation of ecclesiastical wealth, and the creation of new ISAs to replace the religious ISA in its dominant role.

Naturally, these things did not happen automatically: witness the Concordat, the Restoration and the long class struggle between the landed aristocracy and the industrial bourgeoisie throughout the nineteenth century for the establishment of bourgeois hegemony over functions formerly fulfilled by the Church: above all over the Schools. It can be said that *the bourgeoisie relied on the new political parliamentary-democratic, ISA,* installed in the earliest years of the revolution, then restored after long and violent struggles, for a few months in 1848 and for decades after the fall of the Second Empire, in order to conduct its struggle against the Church and wrest its ideological functions away from it, in other words, *to ensure not only its own political hegemony, but also the ideological hegemony indispensable to the reproduction of capitalist relations of production* [italics supplied].

That is why I believe that I am justified in advancing the following thesis, however precarious it is. I believe that the ISA which has been installed in the *dominant* position in mature capitalist social formations as a result of a violent political and ideological class struggle against the old dominant ISA, is the *educational ideological apparatus.* This thesis may seem paradoxical, given that for everyone, i.e. in the ideological representation that the bourgeoisie has tried to give itself and the classes it exploits, it really seems that the dominant ISA in capitalist social formations is not the Schools, but the political ISA, i.e. the regime of parliamentary democracy combining universal suffrage and party struggle. However, history, even recent history, shows that the bourgeoisie has been and still is able to accommodate itself to political State apparatuses other than parliamentary democracy . . .

Hence I believe that I have good reasons for thinking that behind the scenes of its political ISA which occupies the front stage, what the bourgeoisie has installed as its number-one, i.e. as its dominant ISA, is the educational apparatus, which has in fact replaced in its functions the previously dominant ISA, the Church . . . Why is the educational apparatus in fact the dominant ISA in capitalist formations, and how does it function? . . .

1. All ISAs, whatever they are, contribute to the same result: the reproduction of the relations of production, i.e., of capitalist relations of exploitation.

2. Each of them contributes towards this single result in the way proper to it. The political apparatus by subjecting individuals to the political State ideology, the "indirect" (parliamentary) or direct (plebiscitary or fascist) "democratic" ideology. The communications apparatus by cramming every "citizen" with daily doses of nationalism, chauvinism, liberalism, moralism, etc. by means of the press, the radio and television. The same goes for the cultural apparatus (the role of sport in chauvinism is of the first importance), etc. The religious apparatus by recalling in sermons and the other great ceremonies of Birth, Marriage and Death, that man is only ashes, unless he loves his neighbour to the extent of turning the other cheek to whoever strikes first. The family apparatus . . . but there is no need to go on . . .

3. Nevertheless, in this concert, one ISA certainly has the dominant role, although hardly anyone lends an ear to its music: it is so silent! This is the School. It takes children from every class at infant-school age, and then for years, the years in which the child is most "vulnerable," . . . it drums into them a certain amount of "know-how" wrapped in the ruling ideology (French, arithmetic, natural history, the sciences, literature) or simply the ruling ideology in its pure state (ethics, civic instruction, philosophy).

Somewhere around the age of sixteen, a huge mass of children are ejected "into production": these are the workers or small peasants. Another portion of the scholastically adapted youth carries on: and for better or worse, it goes somewhat further, until it falls by the wayside and fills the posts of small and middle technicians, white collar workers, small and middle executives, petty bourgeois of all kinds. A last portion reaches the summit, either to fall into intellectual semi-employment, or to provide, as well as the "intellectuals of the collective labourer," the agents of exploitation (capitalists, managers), the agents of repression (soldiers, policemen, politicians, administrators, etc.) and the professional ideologists (priests of all sorts, most of whom are convinced "laymen").

Each mass ejected *en route* is practically provided with the ideology which suits the role it has to fulfil in class society: the role of exploited (with a "highly developed" "professional," "ethical," "civic," "national" and a-political consciousness); the role of the agent of exploitation (ability to give . . . orders and enforce obedience, . . . or ability to manipulate the demagogy of a political leader's rhetoric), or of the professional ideologist (ability to treat consciousness with the respect, i.e., with the contempt, blackmail and demagogy they deserve, adapted to the accents of Morality, of Virtue, of . . . the Nation, etc.) . . .

Of course, many of these contrasting Virtues . . . are also taught in the family, in the Church, in the Army, in Good Books, in films and even in the football stadium. But no other ISA has the obligatory . . . audience of the totality of the children in the capitalist social formation, eight hours a day for five or six days out of seven . . .

[Conclusion]

Let me summarize: . . . the ideology of the ruling class does not become the ruling ideology by the grace of God, nor even by virtue of the seizure of state power alone. It is by the installation of the ISAs in which this ideology is realized and realizes itself that it becomes the ruling ideology . . .

The Democratic Route
to Modern Society

Selections from the Work of
Barrington Moore

From our present perspective we might sketch . . . three routes to the modern world. The earliest one combined capitalism and parliamentary democracy after a series of revolutions: the Puritan Revolution, the French Revolution, and the American Civil War . . . I have called this the route of bourgeois revolution, a route that England, France, and the United States entered at succeeding points in time with profoundly different societies at the starting point. The second path was also a capitalist one, but, in the absence of a strong revolutionary surge, it passed through reactionary political forms to culminate in fascism . . . The third course is of course the communist one . . .

[The Crown, the Aristocracy, and the Bourgeoisie]

In early modern times . . . a decisive precondition for modern democracy has been the emergence of a rough balance between the crown and the nobility, in which the royal power predominated but left a substantial degree of independence to the nobility. The pluralist notion that an independent nobility is an essential ingredient in the growth of democracy has a firm basis in historical fact . . . The ways in which this independence has been hammered out are equally important. In England, the *locus classicus* for positive evidence, the Wars of the Roses decimated the landed aristocracy, making considerably easier the establishment of a form of royal absolutism rather milder than that in France. It is wise to recall that the achievement of such a balance, so dear to the liberal and pluralist tradition, has

Excerpts from Barrington Moore, *The Social Origins of Dictatorship and Democracy* (Boston: Beacon Press, 1966), 413–432. Copyright © 1966 by Barrington Moore Jr. Reprinted by permission of Beacon Press. Bracketed headings have been created by the editor of this volume.

been the fruit of violent and occasionally revolutionary methods that contemporary liberals generally reject.

At this point one may ask what happens when and if the landed aristocracy tries to shake free from royal controls in the absence of a numerous and politically vigorous class of town dwellers. To put the question in less exact form, what may happen if the nobility seeks freedom in the absence of a bourgeois revolution? I think it is safe to say that the outcome is highly unfavorable to the Western version of democracy. In Russia during the eighteenth century the service nobility managed to have its obligations to the tsarist autocracy rescinded, while at the same time it retained and even increased its land holdings as well as its power over the serfs. The whole development was highly unfavorable to democracy.

German history is in some respects even more revealing. There the nobility carried on its struggle against the Great Elector for the most part separately from the towns. Many of the aristocratic demands of the time resemble those made in England: for a voice in the government and especially in the government's ways of raising money. But the outcome was not parliamentary democracy. The weakness of the towns has been a constant feature in German history subsequent to their efflorescence in southern and western Germany in the late Middle Ages, after which they went into a decline. Without going into the evidence further, . . . we may simply register strong agreement with the Marxist thesis that a vigorous and independent class of town dwellers has been an indispensable element in the growth of parliamentary democracy. *No bourgeois, no democracy* [italics supplied].

[The Aristocracy and the Peasantry]

The principal actor would not appear on the stage if we confined our attention strictly to the agrarian sector. Still the actors in the countryside have played a sufficiently important part to deserve careful inquiry. And if one wishes to write history with heroes and villains, a position the present writer repudiates, the totalitarian villain sometimes has lived in the country, and the democratic hero of the towns has had important allies there.

Such, for example, was the case in England. While absolutism was growing stronger in France, in a large section of Germany, and

in Russia, it met its first major check on English soil, where to be
sure the attempt to establish it was much feebler. In very large measure this was true because the English landed aristocracy at an early
date began to acquire commercial traits. Among the most decisive
determinants influencing the course of subsequent political evolution are whether or not a landed aristocracy has turned to commercial agriculture and, if so, the form that this commercialization has
taken. Let us try to perceive this transformation in its major con-
tours . . .

The advance of commerce in the towns and the demands of
absolutist rulers for taxes had among their many consequences the
result that the overlord needed more and more cash . . . [In response,]
the English landed aristocracy turned to a form of commercial farming that involved setting the peasants free to shift for themselves as
best they could. The French landed élite generally left the peasants
in *de facto* possession of the soil. In the areas where they turned
toward commerce they did so by compelling the peasants to turn
over a share of the produce which the nobles then marketed . . .

In England, . . . the turn toward commercial farming by the landed
aristocracy removed much of what remained of its dependence on the
crown and generated a great deal of its hostility to fumbling Stuart
attempts at absolutism. Likewise the form commercial farming took
in England . . . created a considerable community of interest with the
towns. Both factors were important causes of the Civil War and the
ultimate victory of the parliamentary cause . . .

The consequences appear even more clearly if we set the English experience alongside other varieties. Broadly speaking, there
are two other possibilities. The commercial impulse may be quite
weak among the landed upper classes. Where that happens, the result will be the survival of a huge peasant mass that is at best a tremendous problem for democracy and at worst the reservoir for a
peasant revolution leading to a communist dictatorship. The other
possibility is that the landed upper class will use a variety of political
and social levers to hold down a labor force on the land and make its
transition to commercial farming in this fashion. Combined with a
substantial amount of industrial growth, the result is likely to be
what we recognize as fascism . . .

The failure of appropriate forms of commercial agriculture to take hold at an early point in time still left open another route to modern democratic institutions. Both features are apparent in French and American history. In parts of France, commercial agriculture left peasant society largely intact but took more out of the peasantry, thereby making a contribution to revolutionary forces. Over most of France the impulse among the nobility toward commercial agriculture was weak compared with England. But the Revolution crippled the aristocracy and opened the way toward parliamentary democracy.

In the United States plantation slavery was an important aspect of capitalist growth. On the other hand, to put it mildly, this was an institution unfavorable to democracy. The Civil War overcame this obstacle, though only partially. Generally speaking, plantation slavery is only the most extreme form of repressive adaptations to capitalism. Three factors make it unfavorable to democracy. The landed upper class is likely to need a state with a powerful repressive apparatus and thus one that imposes a whole climate of political and social opinion unfavorable to human freedom. Further, it encourages the preponderance of the countryside over the towns, which are likely to become mere transshipment depots for export to distant markets. Finally, there are the brutalizing consequences of the élite's relationship to its work force, especially severe in those plantation economies where the laborers belong to a different race . . .

[The Aristocracy and the Bourgeoisie]

So far the discussion has concentrated upon two major variables, the relationships of the landed upper classes with the monarchy and their response to the requirements of production for the market. There is a third major variable that has already crept into the discussion: the relationship of the landed upper classes with the town dwellers, mainly the upper stratum that we may loosely call the bourgeoisie . . . Where the interests of the upper strata in town and country converge against the peasants and workers, the outcome is likely to be unfavorable to democracy. However, a great deal depends on the historical circumstances within which this alignment arises.

A very important instance of convergent interests between major segments of the landed aristocracy and the upper ranks of the town dwellers occurred in Tudor and Stuart England. There the convergence arose at an early stage in the course of modernization and under circumstances that led both groups to oppose the royal authority. These aspects are of crucial importance in explaining the democratic consequences. In contrast to the situation in France of the same period, where manufacturers were largely engaged in producing arms and luxury goods for the king and court aristocracy, the English bourgeoisie was vigorous and independent with far-flung interests in an export trade.

On the side of the landed nobility and the gentry, there was also a series of favorable factors. The wool trade had affected the countryside during the sixteenth century and before, leading to enclosures for sheep pasturing. The English sheep-raising upper class, a minority but an influential one, needed the towns which exported the wool, a situation quite different from that in eastern Germany where grain growing in Junker hands bypassed the declining towns.

The convergence between the landed and urban upper classes in England before the Civil War in such a way as to favor the cause of freedom was, among the major countries, a unique configuration. Perhaps the larger situation of which it was a part could occur only once in human history: the English bourgeoisie from the seventeenth through much of the nineteenth century had a maximum material stake in human freedom because it was the first bourgeoisie and had not yet brought its foreign and domestic rivals to their full powers. Nevertheless it may be useful to express certain inferences from the English experience in the form of tentative general hypotheses about the conditions under which collaboration between important sections of the upper classes in the towns and the countryside could be favorable to the growth of parliamentary democracy . . . It is important that the fusion take place in opposition to the royal bureaucracy.

A second condition appears to be that the commercial and industrial leaders must be on their way to becoming the dominant element in society. Under these conditions the landed upper classes are able to develop bourgeois economic habits. This takes place not by mere copying, but as a response to general conditions and their own life circumstances. All these things can happen, it seems, only at an early stage in economic development. That they will be repeated anywhere in the twentieth century also seems highly unlikely . . .

Finally I would suggest that the landed élite must be able to transmit some of its aristocratic outlook to the commercial and industrial classes. There is more to this transmission than the intermarriage in which an ancient estate may preserve itself by forming an alliance with new money. Many subtle changes in attitude are involved that are at present only very imperfectly understood. We only know the consequence: that bourgeois attitudes have to become stronger, rather than the other way around, as happened in Germany . . .

[The Taming of the Agrarian Sector and the Bourgeois Revolutions]

A brief glance at the fate of the English peasantry suggests one more condition of democratic growth that may well be decisive in its own right. Though England's "final solution of the peasant question" through the enclosures may not have been as brutal or as thorough as some earlier writers have led us to think, there can be little doubt that the enclosures as part of the industrial revolution eliminated the peasant question from English politics. Hence there was no massive reservoir of peasants to serve the reactionary ends of the landed upper classes, as in Germany and Japan. Nor was there the mass basis for peasant revolutions as in Russia and China. For quite different reasons, the United States too escaped from the political plague of a peasant question. France did not escape, and the instability of French democracy during the nineteenth and twentieth centuries is partly due to this fact.

The admitted brutality of the enclosures confronts us with the limitations on the possibility of peaceful transitions to democracy and reminds us of the open and violent conflicts that have preceded its establishment. It is time to restore the dialectic, to remind ourselves of the role of revolutionary violence. A great deal of this violence, perhaps its most important features, had its origins in the agrarian problems that arose along the road that has led to Western democracy. The English Civil War checked royal absolutism and gave the commercially minded big landlords a free hand to play their part during the eighteenth and early nineteenth centuries in destroying peasant society. The French Revolution broke the power of a landed élite that was still mainly precommercial, though sections of it had begun to go over to new forms requiring repressive mechanisms to maintain its labor force. In this sense, as already noted, the French Revolution constituted an alternative way of creating institutions eventually favorable to democracy. Finally, the American Civil War likewise broke the power of a landed élite that was an obstacle in the way of democratic advance but, in this case, one that had grown up as part of capitalism.

Whether one believes that these three violent upheavals aided or hindered the development of liberal and bourgeois democracy, it remains necessary to recognize that they were an important part of the whole process. In itself this fact provides considerable justification for designating them as bourgeois or, if one prefers, liberal revolutions . . . [They] were quite violent upheavals in a long process of political change leading up to what we recognize as modern Western democracy . . .

The taming of the agrarian sector has been a decisive feature of the whole historical process that produced such a society. It was just as important as the better-known disciplining of the working class and of course closely related to it. Indeed the English experience tempts one to say that getting rid of agriculture as a major social activity is one prerequisite for successful democracy. The political hegemony of the landed upper class had to be broken or transformed. The peasant had to be turned into a farmer producing for the market instead of for his own consumption and that of the overlord. In this process the landed upper classes either became an important part of the capitalist and democratic tide, as in England, or, if they came to oppose it, they were swept aside in the convulsions of revolution or civil war. In a word, the landed upper classes either helped to make the bourgeois revolution or were destroyed by it . . .

Some Social Requisites of Democracy

Seymour Martin Lipset

This paper is primarily concerned with explicating the social conditions which serve to *support* a democratic political system . . . In order to test [some] generalizations bearing on the differences between countries which rank high or low in possession of the attributes associated with democracy, it is necessary to establish some empirical measures of the type of political system. Individual deviations from a particular aspect of democracy are not too important, as long as the definitions unambiguously cover the great majority of nations which are located as democratic or undemocratic. The precise dividing line between "more democratic" and "less democratic" is also not a basic problem, since presumably democracy is *not* a quality of a social system which either does or does not exist, but is rather a complex of characteristics which may be ranked in many different ways. For this reason it was decided to divide the countries under consideration into two groups, rather than to attempt to rank them from highest to lowest. Ranking *individual* countries from the most to the least democratic is much more difficult than splitting the countries into two classes, "more" or "less" democratic, although even here borderline cases such as Mexico pose problems.

Efforts to classify all countries raise a number of problems. Most countries which lack an enduring tradition of political democracy lie in the traditionally underdeveloped sections of the world . . . Some of the complications introduced by the sharp variations in political practices in different parts of the earth can be reduced by dealing

Excerpts from Seymour Martin Lipset, "Some Social Requisites of Democracy," *American Political Science Review* 53 (1959): 71–85. Bracketed headings have been created by the editor of this volume.

with differences among countries within political culture areas. The two best areas for such internal comparison are Latin America as one, and Europe and the English-speaking countries as the other . . .

The main criteria used in this paper to locate European democracies are the uninterrupted continuation of political democracy since World War I, *and* the absence over the past 25 years of a major political movement opposed to the democratic "rules of the game." The somewhat less stringent criterion employed for Latin America is whether a given country has had a history of more or less free elections for most of the post-World War I period. Where in Europe we look for stable democracies, in South America we look for countries which have not had fairly constant dictatorial rule . . .[1]

Economic Development and Democracy

Perhaps the most widespread generalization linking political systems to other aspects of society has been that democracy is related to the state of economic development. Concretely, this means that the more well-to-do a nation, the greater the chances that it will sustain democracy. From Aristotle down to the present, men have argued that only in a wealthy society in which relatively few citizens lived in real poverty could a situation exist in which the mass of the population could intelligently participate in politics and could develop the self-restraint necessary to avoid succumbing to the appeals of irresponsible demagogues. A society divided between a large impoverished mass and a small favored elite would result either in oligarchy . . . or in tyranny . . .

As a means of concretely testing this hypothesis, [two] indices of economic development—wealth . . . and education—have been defined, and averages (means) have been computed for the countries which have been classified as more or less democratic in the Anglo-Saxon world and Europe and Latin America. In each case, the average wealth . . . and level of education is much higher for the more democratic countries . . . The differences are striking on every score. In the more democratic European countries, there are 17 persons per motor vehicle compared to 143 for the less democratic countries. In the less dictatorial Latin American countries there are 99 persons per motor vehicle, as against 274 for the more dictatorial ones. Income differences for the groups are also sharp, drop-

ping from an average per capita income of $695 for the more demo-
cratic countries of Europe to $308 for the less democratic ones; the
corresponding difference for Latin America is from $171 to 119[2] . . .

Many have suggested that the better educated the population,
the better the chances for democracy, and the comparative data available support this proposition. The "more democratic" countries of
Europe are almost entirely literate: the lowest has a rate of 96 per
cent, while the "less democratic" nations have an average literacy
rate of 85 per cent. In Latin America, the difference is between an
average rate of 74 per cent for the "less dictatorial" countries and 46
per cent for the "more dictatorial." The educational enrollment per
thousand total population at primary [and] post-primary [levels] is
equally consistently related to the degree of democracy . . .

The relationship between education and democracy is worth
more extensive treatment since an entire philosophy of democratic
government has seen in increased education the spread of the basic
requirement of democracy . . . Education presumably broadens men's
outlooks, enables them to understand the need for norms of tolerance, restrains them from adhering to extremist and monistic doctrines, and increases their capacity to make rational electoral choices.

The evidence bearing on the contribution of education to democracy is even more direct and strong in connection with individual behavior *within* countries, than it is in cross-national correlations. Data gathered by public opinion research agencies which have
questioned people in different countries with regard to their belief
in various democratic norms of tolerance for opposition . . . and with
regard to their belief in multi-party as against one-party systems have
found that *the most important single factor differentiating those giving
democratic responses from others has been education.* The higher one's
education, the more likely one is to believe in democratic values and
support democratic practices. All the relevant studies indicate that
education is far more significant than income or occupation . . . If
we cannot say that a "high" level of education is a sufficient condition for democracy, the available evidence does suggest that it comes
close to being a necessary condition in the modern world. Thus if
we turn to Latin America . . . we find that of all the nations in which
more than half the population is illiterate, only one, Brazil, can be
included in the "more democratic" group . . .

[Economic Development, the Class Structure and Democracy]

In addition to the effect, already discussed, of a high level of education and literacy in creating or sustaining belief in democratic norms, perhaps most important is the relationship between modernization and the form of the "class struggle." For the lower strata, economic development, which means increased income, greater economic security, and higher education, permits those in this status to develop longer time perspectives and more complex and gradualist views of politics. A belief in secular reformist gradualism can only be the ideology of a relatively well-to-do lower class. Increased wealth and education also serve democracy by increasing the extent to which the lower strata are exposed to cross pressures which will reduce the intensity of their commitment to given ideologies and make them less receptive to supporting extremist ones . . .

This process . . . essentially functions through enlarging their involvement in an integrated national culture as distinct from an isolated lower-class one, and hence increasing their exposure to middle-class values. Marx argued that the proletariat were a revolutionary force because they have nothing to lose but their chains . . . Tocqueville, in analyzing the reasons why the lower strata in America supported the system, paraphrased and transposed Marx before Marx ever made this analysis, by pointing out that only those who have nothing to lose ever revolt.

Increased wealth is not only related causally to the development of democracy by changing the social conditions of the workers, but it also affects the political role of the middle class through changing the shape of the stratification structure so that it shifts from an elongated pyramid, with a large lower-class base, to a diamond with a growing middle class. *A large middle class plays a mitigating role in moderating conflict since it is able to reward moderate and democratic parties and penalize extremist groups* [italics supplied].

National income is also related to the political values and style of the upper class. The poorer a country, and the lower the absolute standard of living of the lower classes, the greater the pressure on the upper strata to treat the lower classes as . . . vulgar, as innately inferior, as a lower caste. The sharp difference in the style of living between those at the top and those at the bottom makes this psychologically necessary. Consequently, the upper strata also tend to regard political rights for the lower strata, particularly the right to share in power, as essentially absurd and immoral. The upper strata not only resist democracy themselves, but their often arrogant political behavior serves to intensify extremist reactions on the part of the lower classes.

The general income level of a nation will also affect its receptivity to democratic political tolerance norms. The values which imply that it does not matter greatly which side rules, that error can be tolerated even in the governing party can best develop where (a) the government has little power to affect the crucial life chances of most powerful groups, or (b) there is enough wealth in the country so that it actually does not make too much difference if some redistribution does take place. If loss of office is seen as meaning serious loss for major power groups, then they will be readier to resort to more drastic measures in seeking to retain or secure office . . .

Notes from the Editor

1. In Europe and among English-speaking countries, those classified by the author as stable democracies are Australia, Belgium, Canada, Denmark, Ireland, Luxembourg, The Netherlands, New Zealand, Norway, Sweden, Switzerland, United Kingdom, United States. Those classified as unstable democracies and dictatorships are Austria, Bulgaria, Czechoslovakia, Finland, France, Germany (West), Greece, Hungary, Iceland, Italy, Poland, Portugal, Rumania, Spain, Yugoslavia. In Latin America the countries classified as democracies and unstable dictatorships are: Argentina, Brazil, Chile, Colombia, Costa Rica, Mexico, Uruguay. Those classified as stable dictatorships are Bolivia, Cuba, Dominican Republic, Ecuador, El Salvador, Guatemala, Haiti, Honduras, Nicaragua, Panama, Paraguay, Peru, Venezuela.
2. Compiled from data furnished by International Urban Research, University of California, Berkeley.

Part II

Elites in Democracy and Democratization— Classical Analyses

Introduction

The earliest class analysis of democracy—presented in the previous part of this volume—stems from the middle of the nineteenth century. By contrast, elite theory in general, and the elite conception of democracy in particular, did not make its appearance until the turn of that century. Once it appeared on the scene, however, it did so with triple strength: the three founding fathers of the mainstream of this school of thought—Pareto, Mosca, and Michels—made their appearance almost simultaneously. The contributions by Pareto and Mosca open this part of the volume, while (for reasons that will become clear further on) that by Michels has been reserved for Part V.

Having made their appearance virtually at the same time, Pareto and Mosca fell into a dispute over the paternity of elite theory (which Mosca lost). They need not have done so, however, for their ideas, while displaying some similarities, also show that each of them has been a highly original (and influential) thinker.

Pareto distinguishes between a governing and a nongoverning elite, adding that, although in principle, elites (including governing elites) are made up of people who excel, this is not always so in practice. As long as a governing elite, or class, is composed of people with the proper qualities of excellence, and is open to absorb into its ranks the most talented people from the nonelite—while shedding the more degenerate of its own members—this ensures a circulation of elites that keeps society in a state of equilibrium and gradual change. When, however, this circulation is impeded, the social equilibrium is upset, and society becomes prone to violent upheavals. In all this, so-called democracy—as Pareto refers to it—makes little difference. It does not spell popular representation within the governing elite or class, but merely leads that governing class to use different ways of manipulating the people.

Where Pareto refers to those who govern as a governing elite or class, Mosca dubs them the ruling class.[1] In all societies, including democracies, there is a small organized class that rules and a large unorganized one that is ruled. According to democratic theory, majorities rule minorities. In fact, even in a democracy, the domination of an organized minority over an unorganized majority is inevitable.

According to critics, Pareto's and Mosca's notion—that in all societies there are those who govern and those who are governed—is self-evident. To transcend this platitude, it would have to be shown that the governing elite/class has some internal unity, which exacerbates its power. This, in fact, is the thesis of the prominent postwar elite theorist, Mills. Mills sees democratic (especially American) society, as dominated by the upper political, military, and corporate economic personnel. These three groups are in a perpetual though uneasy coalition with each other, and together they form a conglomeration of power, or a power elite. Members of congress, trade unions, and interest group leaders make up the middle levels of power. And at the bottom there are the masses, the mostly passive and powerless receiving end of the power elite's manipulation and rule.

Overall, these classical elite theorists—known as mainstream elite theorists—have a common focus in viewing extant democracies, no less than nondemocracies, as divided into the wielders of power and those who are subject to it, who have little power of their own. Thus they have little to say on what it is that still makes democracy (with all its iniquities) a distinctive regime.

It fell to the lot of other classical theorists—known as liberal, democratic elite theorists—to fill this void. These include Weber, Schumpeter, Aron, and (surprisingly) also Mosca in some later developments of his thought. Foremost among these is Weber, a contemporary of Pareto and Mosca. He, too, admits that even in a democracy the demos itself never governs. But democracy (embodied in elected charismatic leaders and parliaments) is still of prime importance as a counterbalance to the expanding, frightening, practically indestructible, rule of bureaucracy. No less frightening is the prospect that democracy may give rise to leaders who gain the faith of the masses, hence power, by means of demagogy. But a properly working parliament can restrain the power of such leaders as well, even though, in the end, democracy must make concessions to them.

This brings us back to Mosca who, despite losing out to Pareto in his paternity suit over elite theory, still has an advantage over Pareto. For he alone may be regarded as both a mainstream and a democratic elite theorist. While he sees a ruling class as inevitable in a democracy, in his later ideas he also stresses that democracy divides that class into separate branches: that derived from bureaucratic appointment, and that derived from popular suffrage, the popularly elected assembly. Like Weber he believes that parliamentary assemblies curb what would otherwise be the pernicious power of bureaucracy. Importantly, however, he also believes that the bureaucratic and judicial branches of the ruling class, if autonomous, fulfill an equally essential democratic role in curbing the corrupting power of elected politicians. With all its faults, democracy thus accords some liberty and some influence to the public.

During and in the wake of the Second World War, some prominent thinkers expressed like-minded ideas. Rejecting the notion that democracy ensures popular participation in the decision-making process, Schumpeter sees its essence in the arrangement whereby leaders gain the power to make decisions through a competition for the people's votes. This implies considerable freedom of discussion, but it lends the electors only limited control over the elected. Hence the latter's power, together with the range of political decisions, must be (and in fact is) limited through independent agencies or elites. These include—besides the judiciary, the top of the state bureaucracy, and the central bank—universities, or academic elites.

Similarly, for Aron, what most clearly distinguishes Western democratic from autocratic regimes is the dissociation and independence of leading minorities, or elites. Also distinctive to democracy is the free and legitimate mutual competition of the claimants to such positions, based on free elections and on consensus over the rules of the game. All this cannot ensure effective participation in the decision-making process for all, but it ensures some elite response to the needs and demands of the public.

Democratic elite theorists thus share the idea that the distinctiveness of democracy lies not only in free competitive elections, but also in the autonomy of elites from each other, which enables them to countervail each other's power. Thereby power restrains power, increasing the liberty of the public and the elites' responsiveness to its demands. In opposition to this it has been argued that these supposed virtues of democracy are more fiction than reality, that those who believe in them are overly complacent with respect to democracy. Further, the argument is that these theorists have offered not merely an elite but an *elitist* theory of democracy, one which applauds elite rule, while paying insufficient attention to the democratic role of the public. As well, they are said to have disregarded the exploitative nature of capitalism—the economic system in which democracy prevails—and its persistent economic inequalities. Before deciding in favor or against these critiques, those against whom they are leveled must be allowed to have their say.

Note

1.   Mosca's concept of the ruling class differs substantially from the Marxist conception of this class, as evident from the pertinent writings in Part I of this volume.

The Governing Élite
in Present-Day Democracy

Selections from the Work of
Vilfredo Pareto

[Élites and Non-élites]

Let us assume that in every branch of human activity each individual is given an index which stands as a sign of his capacity, very much the way grades are given in the various subjects in examinations in school. The highest type of lawyer, for instance, will be given 10. The man who does not get a client will be given 1—reserving zero for the man who is an out-and-out idiot. To the man who has made his millions—honestly or dishonestly as the case may be—we will give 10. To the man who has earned his thousands we will give 6; to such as just manage to keep out of the poor house, 1, keeping zero for those who get in . . .

So let us make a class of the people who have the highest indices in their branch of activity, and to that class give the name of *élite* . . . It will help if we further divide that class into two classes: a *governing elite*, comprising individuals who directly or indirectly play some considerable part in government, and a *non-governing elite*, comprising the rest. So we get two strata in a population: (1) A lower stratum, the *non-elite*, with whose possible influence on government we are not just here concerned; then (2) a higher stratum, the *elite*, which is divided into two: (a) a governing *elite*; (b) a non-governing *elite* . . .

[The Circulation of Élites]

The manner in which the various groups in a population intermix has to be considered. In moving from one group to another an indi-

Excerpts from Vilfredo Pareto, *The Mind and Society,* trans. A. Bongiorno and A. Livingston (New York: Dover Publications, 1935), 1422–1432, 1568–1592. Bracketed headings have been created by the editor of this volume.

vidual generally brings with him certain inclinations, sentiments, attitudes, that he has acquired in the group from which he comes, and that circumstance cannot be ignored. To this mixing, in the particular case in which only two groups, the *élite* and the *non-élite*, are envisaged, the term "circulation of *élites*" has been applied . . . We must pay special attention (1) in the case of one single group, to the proportions between the total of the group and the number of individuals who are nominally members of it but do not possess the qualities requisite for effective membership; and then (2) in the case of various groups, to the ways in which transitions from one group to the other occur, and to the intensity of that movement—that is to say, to the velocity of the circulation . . .

The upper stratum of society, the *élite*, nominally contains certain groups of people, not always very sharply defined, that are called aristocracies. There are cases in which the majority of individuals belonging to such aristocracies actually possess the qualities requisite for remaining there; and then again there are cases where considerable numbers of the individuals making up the class do not possess those requisites . . .

Aristocracies do not last. It is an incontestable fact that after a certain length of time they pass away. History is a graveyard of aristocracies . . . Where, in France, are the descendants of the Frankish conquerors? The genealogies of the English nobility have been very exactly kept; and they show that very few families still remain to claim descent from the comrades of William the Conqueror. The rest have vanished. In Germany the aristocracy of the present day is very largely made up of descendants of vassals of the lords of old. The populations of European countries have increased enormously during the past few centuries. It is as certain as certain can be that the aristocracies have not increased in proportion.

They decay not in numbers only. They decay also in quality, in the sense that they lose their vigour, that there is a decline in the proportions of the residues[1] which enabled them to win their power and hold it. The governing class is restored not only in numbers, but—and that is the more important thing—in quality, by families rising from the lower classes and bringing with them the vigour and the proportions of residues necessary for keeping themselves in power. It is also restored by the loss of its more degenerate members . . .

In virtue of class-circulation, the governing *élite* is always in a state of slow and continuous transformation. It flows on like a river, never being today what it was yesterday. From time to time sudden and violent disturbances occur. There is a flood—the river overflows its banks. Afterwards, the new governing *élite* again resumes its slow transformation. The flood has subsided, the river is again flowing normally in its wonted bed.

Revolutions come about through accumulations in the higher strata of society—either because of a slowing-down in class-circulation or from other causes—of decadent elements no longer possessing the residues suitable for keeping them in power, and shrinking from the use of force; while meantime in the lower strata of society elements of superior quality are coming to the fore, possessing residues suitable for exercising the functions of government and willing enough to use force . . .

[How the Governing Élite in a Democracy Bamboozles King Demos]

Everyone recognizes that in our day "democracy" is tending to become the political system of all civilized peoples. But what is the exact meaning of the term "democracy"? It is even more vague than that vaguest of terms, "religion." We must therefore leave it to one side and turn to the facts that it covers . . .

We need not linger on the fiction of "popular representation"— poppycock grinds no flour. Let us go on and see what substance underlies the various forms of power in the governing classes. Ignoring exceptions, which are few in number and of short duration, one finds everywhere a governing class of relatively few individuals that keeps itself in power partly by force and partly by the consent of the subject class, which is much more populous . . .

A governing class is present everywhere, even where there is a despot, but the forms under which it appears are widely variable. In absolute governments a sovereign occupies the stage alone. In so called democratic governments it is the parliament. But behind the scenes in both cases there are always people who play a very important role in actual government. To be sure they must now and again bend the knee to the whims of ignorant and domineering sovereigns or parliaments, but they are soon back at their tenacious, patient, never-ending work, which is of much the greater consequence . . .

King Demos, good soul, thinks he is following his own devices. In reality he is following the lead of his rulers. But that very often turns out to the advantage of his rulers only, for they, from the days of Aristotle down to our own, have made lavish use of the arts of bamboozling King Demos . . . Among the derivations[2] which they use to show that their rule is to the advantage of a country, interesting is the assertion that the public is better qualified to pass on general questions than on special ones. The fact, in reality, is the precise opposite. One has to talk only for a very brief time with an uneducated person to see that he grasps special questions, which are usually concrete, much more clearly than general questions, which as a rule are abstract. But abstract questions have the advantage for people in power that whatever the answers that are given them by the public, they will be able to draw any inference they choose from them . . .

[How the Governing Élite in a Democracy Maintains Its Power]

For purposes of maintaining its power the governing class uses individuals from the subject class, who may be grouped in two divisions corresponding to the two principal instruments for holding power secure. The one group uses force, and is made up of soldiers, police of one sort or another; . . . the other uses skill, and ranges in character and in time all the way from the clientage of the old Roman politicians to the clientèles of our contemporary politicians. Those two groups are always with us, but never in the same actual proportions, nor, much less, in the same visible proportions. One extreme is marked by the Rome of the praetorians, where the chief *de facto* instrument of governing, and even more so the visible instrument, was armed force. The other extreme is represented by the United States of America, where the chief actual instrument of governing, and to a somewhat lesser extent the apparent instrument, is the political "machine."

These cliques work in various ways. The principal way is the least conspicuous. The administration in power "looks after" the interests of the speculators,[3] and often without any explicit understanding with them. A protectionist government, for instance, gets the confidence and the support of the manufacturers it protects without having to come to explicit terms with all of them, though it may have some agreement with outstanding individuals. The situation is the same with public works, though agreement with the big contractors is becoming the rule.

Other ways are better known—they are less important from the social standpoint, but are commonly regarded as more important from the ethical standpoint. Among them is the bribery of voters, elected officials, government ministers, newspaper-owners, and other such persons, which has its counterpart under systems of absolutism in the bribery of courtiers, favourites, male and female, officials, generals, and so on—an old form of corruption that has not altogether disappeared. Such means have been employed in all periods of history, from the days of ancient Athens and republican Rome down to our own . . .

And that is why the numberless attempts which have been made to "purify" politics have been failures and still remain such. Witchgrass may be cut as often as one chooses, but it sprouts only the more rankly if the roots are left untouched. Our democracies in France, Italy, England, and the United States are tending more and more to become demagogic plutocracies and may be following that road on the way to one of those radical transformations that have been witnessed in the past . . .

Evolution towards "democracy" seems to stand in strict correlation with the increased use of that instrument of governing which involves resort to artifice and to the "machine," as against the instrument of force. In ancient times, that was clearly observable towards the end of the Republic in Rome, where there was a conflict between precisely those two instrumentalities, force winning the final victory in the Empire. It is even more apparent in our own day, when the régimes in many "democratic" countries might be defined as a sort of feudalism that is primarily economic and in which the principal instrument of governing is the manipulation of political followings, whereas the military feudalism of the Middle Ages used force primarily as embodied in vassalage.

[Conclusion: The Iniquities of Democracy]

A political system in which "the people" expresses its "will"—given but not granted that it has one—without cliques, intrigues, "com-bines," "gangs," exists only as a pious wish of theorists. It is not to be observed in reality, either in the past or in the present, either in our Western countries or in any others. Such phenomena, long the subject of remark, are usually described as aberrations, or "degenerations," of "democracy"; but when and where one may be introduced to the perfect, or even the merely decent, state from which said aberration or "degeneration" has occurred, no one ever manages to tell . . .

It is further to be noted that the defects in various systems of government may differ from each other, but, taking things as a whole, it cannot be held that one type of régime is very different in that respect from any other. The criticisms that are levelled at modern democracy are not greatly different from those that were levelled at ancient democracies, the Athenian, for instance; and if there are cases of corruption in democracies old and new, it would not be difficult to find cases just as bad in absolute and constitutional monarchies, in oligarchical governments, and in any other sort of régime . . .

Notes from the Editor

1.   Pareto conceives of residues as psychic states: manifestations of sentiments and instincts.
2.   Pareto conceives of derivations as representing the workings of the mind—reasoning, ideological justifications—which account for residues.
3.   By this Pareto means business people.

The Ruling Class in Representative Democracy

Selections from the Work of
Gaetano Mosca

[The Ubiquity of the Ruling Class]

Among the constant facts and tendencies that are to be found in all political organisms, one is so obvious that it is apparent to the most casual eye. In all societies—from societies that are very meagerly developed and have barely attained the dawning of civilization, down to the most advanced and powerful societies—two classes of people appear—a class that rules and a class that is ruled. The first class, always the less numerous, performs all political functions, monopolizes power and enjoys the advantages that power brings, whereas the second, the more numerous class, is directed and controlled by the first, in a manner that is now more or less legal, now more or less arbitrary and violent, and supplies the first, in appearance at least, with material means of subsistence and with the instrumentalities that are essential to the vitality of the political organism.

In practical life we all recognize the existence of this ruling class (or political class) . . . We all know that, in our own country, whichever it may be, the management of public affairs is in the hands of a minority of influential persons, to which management, willingly or unwillingly, the majority defer. We know that the same thing goes on in neighboring countries, and in fact we should be hard put to it to conceive of a real world otherwise organized—a world in which all men would be directly subject to a single person without relationships of superiority or subordination, or in which all men would share equally in the direction of political affairs. If we reason other-

Excerpts from Gaetano Mosca, *The Ruling Class*, trans. Hannah D. Kahn; ed. and rev. Arthur Livingston (New York: McGraw-Hill Book Company, 1939), 50–53, 153–156. Bracketed headings have been created by the editor of this volume.

wise in theory, that is due partly to inveterate habits that we follow in our thinking and partly to the exaggerated importance that we attach to two political facts that loom far larger in appearance than they are in reality.

The first of these facts—and one has only to open one's eyes to see it—is that in every political organism there is one individual who is chief among the leaders of the ruling class as a whole and stands, as we say, at the helm of the state . . . The second fact, too, is readily discernible. Whatever the type of political organization, pressures arising from the discontent of the masses who are governed, from the passions by which they are swayed, exert a certain amount of influence on the policies of the ruling, the political, class.

But the man who is at the head of the state would certainly not be able to govern without the support of a numerous class to enforce respect for his orders and to have them carried out; and granting that he can make one individual, or indeed many individuals, in the ruling class feel the weight of his power, he certainly cannot be at odds with the class as a whole or do away with it. Even if that were possible, he would at once be forced to create another class, without the support of which action on his part would be completely paralyzed. On the other hand, granting that the discontent of the masses might succeed in deposing a ruling class, inevitably there would have to be another organized minority within the masses themselves to discharge the functions of a ruling class. Otherwise all organization, and the whole social structure, would be destroyed . . .

[Why Even in Representative Democracy Minorities Rule Majorities]

We think it may be desirable, nevertheless, to reply at this point to an objection which might very readily be made to our point of view. If it is easy to understand that a single individual cannot command a group without finding within the group a minority to support him, it is rather difficult to grant, as a constant and natural fact, that minorities rule majorities, rather than majorities minorities. But that is one of the points—so numerous in all the other sciences—where the first impression one has of things is contrary to what they are in reality. In reality the dominion of an organized minority, obeying a single impulse, over the unorganized majority is inevitable. The power of any minority is irresistible as against each single individual in the majority, who stands alone before the totality of the organized minority. At the same time, the minority is organized for the very reason that it is a minority . . .

Many doctrines that advocate liberty and equality, as the latter terms are still commonly understood—doctrines which the eighteenth century thought out, which the nineteenth perfected and tried to apply and which the twentieth will probably dispense with or modify substantially—are summed up and given concrete form in the theory that views universal suffrage as the foundation of all sound government. It is commonly believed that the only free, equitable and legitimate government is a government that is based upon the will of the majority, the majority by its vote delegating its powers for a specified length of time to men who represent it . . .

[Yet] what happens in other forms of government—namely, that an organized minority imposes its will on the disorganized majority—happens also and to perfection, whatever the appearances to the contrary, under the representative system. When we say that the voters "choose" their representative, we are using a language that is very inexact. The truth is that the representative *has himself elected* by the voters, and, if that phrase should seem too inflexible and too harsh to fit some cases, we might qualify it by saying that *his friends have him elected.* In elections, as in all other manifestations of social life, those who have the will and, especially, the moral, intellectual and material means to force their will upon others take the lead over the others and command them.

The political mandate has been likened to the power of attorney that is familiar in private law. But in private relationships, delegations of powers and capacities always presuppose that the principal has the broadest freedom in choosing his representative. Now in practice, in popular elections, that freedom of choice, though complete theoretically, necessarily becomes null, not to say ludicrous. If each voter gave his vote to the candidate of his heart, we may be sure that in almost all cases the only result would be a wide scattering of votes. When very many wills are involved, choice is determined by the most various criteria, almost all of them subjective, and if such wills were not coordinated and organized it would be virtually impossible for them to coincide in the spontaneous choice of one individual. If his vote is to have any efficacy at all, therefore, each voter is forced to limit his choice to a very narrow field, in other words to a choice among the two or three persons who have some chance of succeeding; and the only ones who have any chance of succeeding are those whose candidacies are championed by groups, by committees, by *organized minorities* . . .

How do these organized minorities form about individual candidates or groups of candidates? As a rule they are based on considerations of property and taxation, on common material interests, on ties of family, class, religion, sect or political party. Whether their component personnels be good or bad, there can be no doubt that such committees—and the representatives who are now their tools, now their leaders or "bosses"—represent the organization of a considerable number of social values and forces. In practice, therefore, the representative system results not at all in government by the majority; it results in the participation of a certain number of social values in the guidance of the state, in the fact that many political forces which in an absolute state, a state ruled by a bureaucracy alone, would remain inert and without influence upon government become organized and so exert an influence on government . . .

[The Influence of the Voters]

The great majority of voters are passive, it is true, in the sense that they have not so much freedom to choose their representatives as a limited right to exercise an option among a number of candidates. Nevertheless, limited as it may be, that capacity has the effect of obliging candidates to try to win a weight of votes that will serve to tip the scales in their direction, so that they make every effort to flatter, wheedle and obtain the good will of the voters. In this way certain sentiments and passions of the "common herd" come to have their influence on the mental attitudes of the representatives themselves, and echoes of a widely disseminated opinion, or of any serious discontent, easily come to be heard in the highest spheres of government.

It may be objected that this influence of the majority of voters is necessarily confined to the broad lines of political policy and makes itself felt only on a very few topics of a very general character, and that within limits as narrow as that even in absolute governments the ruling classes are obliged to take account of mass sentiments. In fact the most despotic of governments has to proceed very cautiously when it comes to shocking the sentiments, convictions or prejudices of the majority of the governed, or to requiring of that majority pecuniary sacrifices to which they are not accustomed. But wariness about giving offense will be much greater when every single representative, whose vote may be useful or necessary to the executive branch of government, knows that the discontent of the masses may at almost any moment bring about the triumph of a rival . . .

[The Importance of Checks and Balances]

Many objections are now being urged against representative government in general, and especially against those forms of it in which the democratic ideal may be said to have been best realized, in view of a broad-based popular suffrage and the political preponderance that has been acquired by elective "lower houses." . . . The best founded of all, relates to the excessive interference, not so much by lower houses as political bodies as by individual members of lower houses, in the courts, in public administration, in the distribution of the large portion of the social wealth that is levied by the state in the form of duties and taxes and applied to various public services, and in the distribution of that portion, also large, of the social wealth that is concentrated in banks, in great industrial speculations and in public charities . . . Anyone can see that, in highly bureaucratized systems such as ours are, continuous pottering, interloping and officiousness on the part of members of lower houses must be an exceedingly baneful thing . . .

[But] the defects of parliamentary assemblies, and the evil consequences which their control of power and their participation in power produce in all representative systems, are merest trifles as compared with the harm that would inevitably result from abolishing them or stripping them of their influence. Under the conditions that prevail at present in society, the suppression of representative assemblies would inevitably be followed by a type of regime that is commonly called "absolute." We believe it might better be termed "exclusively bureaucratic," since its chief characteristic is that it alienates from public life all political forces, all social values, except such as are represented in the bureaucracy. At the very least, it completely subordinates all other forces and values to the bureaucratic element . . . We need give no long demonstration of that thesis . . . as to the dangers and drawbacks involved in giving absolute predominance to a single political force that is not subject to any limitation or discussion whatever . . .

People of our time have come to take for granted the advantages of a system in which all governmental acts are subject to public discussion. That alone can explain why superficial observers among our younger generations fail to realize at a glance the moral ruin that would result from the downfall of such a system. That ruin would take the form of a series of violations of juridical defense, of justice, of everything that we commonly call "liberty"; and those violations would be far more pernicious than any that can be laid to the charge of even the most dishonest of parliamentary governments, let alone of representative governments . . . It cannot be denied that the representative system provides a way for many different social forces to participate in the political system and, therefore, to balance and limit the influence of other social forces and the influence of bureaucracy in particular. If that were [its] only possible consequence, . . . it would clearly be advantageous to accept it on that ground alone . . .

The soundest point in the criticisms that for a good half century past have been leveled at representative governments is the excessive and exclusive power that is given by many of them . . . to the elected representatives. The prime and real root of the evils that are being so generally lamented lies in the facts that where parliamentarism is in force the ministry directing the vast and absorbing bureaucratic machine issues from the ranks of the elected chamber, and, more serious still, the fact that prime ministers and their cabinets stay in power as long, and only as long, as it pleases the majority of the elected chamber to retain them. Because of these two facts, discussion of governmental acts in our parliaments and the control that representatives should exercise over governmental acts almost always go astray under pressure of personal ambitions and party interests.

Because of the same facts, the natural desire of governors to govern well is continuously and effectively thwarted by their no less natural desire to serve their own personal interests, and the sense of professional duty in ministers and representatives is always balanced by all sorts of ambitions and vanities, justified and unjustified. Finally, the courts and the administrative departments become parts of a great electioneering agency with a corresponding cost in public money and in moral atmosphere; and a demand on the part of any important vote-getter upon the representative who needs him, or on the part of the minister who needs the representative, is often enough to silence any respect for equity and law. In a word, because of a constant, flagrant and manufactured contradiction between the duty and the interest of the man who governs, and of the man who should judge and limit governmental action, the bureaucracy and the elective elements, which should control and balance each other, end by corrupting and denaturing each other . . .

It is not hard to imagine modifications in present institutions that might effectively contribute toward attenuating the evils of parliamentarism. No one, for instance, can fail to see how helpful it would be to increase guarantees of the independence of the courts by assuring to magistrates in all countries that real permanency of tenure which is now established in only a few, and by raising the social position and prestige of judges in fact and not merely in words. No one can fail to see how advantageous it would be to France, for instance, and not to France alone, to introduce the system that prevailed in imperial Germany, whereby all public officials of high rank were responsible for their acts to really independent administrative tribunals, and at the same time were free from the jurisdiction of ministers, and therefore of representatives. Financial control also could be better organized by increasing the independence of our auditing departments . . .

It is a matter of common knowledge that the defects of parliamentary government in Europe almost all come down to improper interference with elections to central and local elective bodies by bureaucracies, acting mainly through prefects appointed by the ministries, and to equally improper interference with the bureaucracies by representatives elected to the national chambers. All this gives rise to a shameful and hypocritical traffic in reciprocal indulgences and mutual favors, which is a veritable running sore in most European countries . . .

All the same . . . specialization in the various political functions and cooperation and reciprocal control between bureaucratic and elective elements are two of the outstanding characteristics of the modern representative state . . . As for safeguarding against any excesses on the part of bureaucracy, it seemed sufficient to entrust to parliaments control over income and expenditure and the right to audit and criticize the state administration as a whole; and, in countries governed by parliamentary systems, to put the various branches of the bureaucratic machine in charge of men who came largely from the membership of the elective chamber itself, and who therefore issued indirectly from popular suffrage . . .

[Civil Liberties in Representative Democracies]

In modern Europe, and in all countries of European civilization in general, the conception of political liberty has not been applied solely by instituting representative government. Almost everywhere the latter has been supplemented to a greater or lesser extent by a series of institutions that assure individuals and groups of individuals not a few effective guarantees as against holders of public power. In countries that have so far rightly been reputed free, private property cannot be violated arbitrarily. A citizen cannot be arrested and condemned unless specified rules are observed. Each person can follow the religion of his choice without forfeiture of his civil and political rights. The press cannot be subjected to censorship and is free to discuss and criticize acts of government. Finally, if they conform with certain rules, citizens can meet to engage in discussions of a political character, and they can form associations for the attainment of moral, political or professional ends.

These liberties, and others like them, may be looked upon as real limitations which the state has imposed upon its own sovereign powers in its relations to individual citizens. They are largely imitations of laws that England had adopted at the end of the seventeenth century, after the "Glorious Revolution," or even at later dates. They are necessary complements to representative systems, which would function very badly if all free political activity on the part of individuals were suppressed, and if individuals were not fairly well protected against arbitrary acts on the part of the executive and judiciary powers. At the same time, those liberties find their maximum guarantee in the existence of the representative system, which provides that legislative power, which alone has the right to remove or restrict them, should emanate from the same political forces that are interested in conserving them. Far harder to put into practice has been the concept of equality, for equality is contrary to the nature of things, and is also less real, less concrete, than liberty in the sense just mentioned . . .

[Conclusion: The Achievements of Representative Democracy]

In conclusion . . . majority government and absolute political equality, two of the mottos that the century inscribed on its banners, were not achieved, because they could not be achieved, and the same may be said of fraternity. But the ranks of the ruling classes have been held open. The barriers that kept individuals of the lower classes from entering the higher have been either removed or lowered, and the development of the old absolutist state into the modern representative state has made it possible for almost all political forces, almost all social values, to participate in the political management of society.

This development, it should be noted, has divided the political class into two distinct branches, one issuing from popular suffrage, and the other from bureaucratic appointment. This . . . has made it possible to distribute the sovereign functions, or powers, of the state, and that distribution, whenever social conditions are such as to make it effective, constitutes the chief virtue of representative systems . . . Rousseau set himself an unattainable goal when he tried to show that the only form of legitimate government was one that was founded upon the express consent of the majority of citizens. Montesquieu stated a much more practical and profound idea when he maintained that if a nation is to be free, in other words governed according to law and not according to the arbitrary will of its rulers, it must have a political organization in which authority arrests and limits authority, and in which, therefore, no individual and no assembly has the power to make laws and at the same time the power to apply them. To make that doctrine complete, one need add that a controlling and limiting political institution can be effective only when it represents a section of the political class that is different from the section represented by the institution to be limited and controlled.

If, again, we take due account of the individual liberties that protect the citizen from possible arbitrary acts on the part of any or all of the powers of the state, especially of liberty of the press, which, along with liberty of parliamentary debate, serves to call public attention to all possible abuses on the part of those who govern, one readily sees the great superiority of the representative system. That system has permitted the establishment of a strong state, which has been able to canalize immense sums of individual energies toward purposes related to the collective interest. At the same time it has not trampled on those energies or suppressed them. It has left them with sufficient vitality to achieve remarkable results in other fields, notably in the scientific, literary and economic fields. If, therefore, the nations of European civilization have succeeded in maintaining their primacy in the world . . . the fact has been due in large part to the beneficent effects of their political system . . .

Democracy and the Countervailing Powers of Bureaucracy, Charisma, and Parliament

Selections from the Work of
Max Weber

[Bureaucratization and Democratization]

Bureaucracy inevitably accompanies modern mass democracy . . .
The progress of bureaucratization within the state administration
itself is a phenomenon paralleling the development of democracy, as
is quite obvious in France, North America, and now in England. Of
course, one must always remember that the term "democratization"
can be misleading. The demos itself, in the sense of a shapeless mass,
never "governs" larger associations, but rather is governed. What
changes is only the way in which the executive leaders are selected
and the measure of influence which the demos, or better, which social
circles from its midst, are able to exert upon the content and the direction of administrative activities by means of "public opinion" . . .

Once fully established, bureaucracy is among those social structures which are the hardest to destroy. Bureaucracy is *the* means of
transforming social action into rationally organized action. Therefore, as an instrument of rationally organizing authority relations,
bureaucracy was and is a power instrument of the first order for one
who controls the bureaucratic apparatus. [As] rationally organized
and directed action [it] is superior to every kind of collective behavior and also [to] social action opposing it. Where administration has
been completely bureaucratized, the resulting system of domination
is practically indestructible . . .

Excerpts from Max Weber, *Economy and Society,* 2 vols., trans. and ed. G. Roth and
C. Wittich (Berkeley: University of California Press, 1978): chapters X, XIV; appendix II.
Copyright © 1978 The Regents of the University of California. Reprinted by permission
of the Regents of the University of California and the University of California Press.
Bracketed headings have been created by the editor of this volume.

[Democratization of Charismatic Leadership]

In radical contrast to bureaucratic organization, charisma . . . is self-determined and sets its own limits. Its bearer seizes the task for which he is destined and demands that others obey and follow him by virtue of his mission. If those to whom he feels sent do not recognize him, his claim collapses; if they recognize it, he is their master as long as he "proves" himself. However, he does not derive his claims from the will of his followers, in the manner of an election; rather, it is their duty to recognize his charisma . . . The pure type of charismatic rulership is in a very specific sense unstable, and all its modifications have basically one and the same cause: The desire to transform charisma and charismatic blessing from a unique, transitory gift of grace of extraordinary times and persons into a permanent possession of everyday life . . .

For charismatic leadership, if it wants to transform itself into a perennial institution, the first basic problem is that of finding a successor to the prophet, hero, teacher or party leader. This problem inescapably channels charisma into the direction of legal regulation and tradition. Given the nature of charisma, a free election of a successor is originally not possible, only the acknowledgment that the pretender actually *has* charisma . . . However, charisma is not alien to all . . . democratic forms of election. Certainly the democratic system of so-called plebiscitarian rulership—the official theory of French caesarism—has essentially charismatic features, and the arguments of its proponents all emphasize this very quality . . .

[Also] acclamation by the ruled may develop into a regular electoral system, with standardized suffrage, direct or indirect election, majority or proportional method, electoral classes and districts. It is a long way to such a system. As far as the election of the supreme ruler is concerned, only the United States went all the way—and there, of course, the nominating campaign within each of the two parties is one of the most important parts of the election business. Elsewhere at most the parliamentary representatives are elected, who in turn determine the choice of the prime minister and his colleagues. The development from acclamation of the charismatic leader to popular election occurred at the most diverse cultural stages, and every advance toward a rational, emotionally detached consideration of the process could not help but to facilitate this transformation.

However, only in the Occident did the election of the ruler gradually develop into the representative system . . .

[Bureaucratic Rule and the Countervailing Power of Parliamentary/Political Leadership]

In a modern state the actual ruler is necessarily and unavoidably the bureaucracy, since power is exercised neither through parliamentary speeches nor monarchical enunciations but through the routines of administration. This is true of both the military and civilian officialdom. Even the modern higher-ranking officer fights battles from the "office." Just as the so-called progress toward capitalism has been the unequivocal criterion for the modernization of the economy since medieval times, so the progress toward bureaucratic officialdom—characterized by formal employment, salary, pension, promotion, specialized training and functional division of labor, well-defined areas of jurisdiction, documentary procedures, hierarchical sub- and super-ordination—has been the equally unambiguous yardstick for the modernization of the state, whether monarchic or democratic; at least if the state is not a small canton with rotating administration, but comprises masses of people. The democratic state no less than the absolute state eliminates administration by feudal, patrimonial, patrician or other notables holding office in honorary or hereditary fashion, in favor of employed civil servants. It is they who decide on all our everyday needs and problems . . .

Given the basic fact of the irresistible advance of bureaucratization, the question about the future forms of political organization can only be asked in the following way: (1) How can one possibly save any remnants of "individualist" freedom in any sense? After all, it is a gross self-deception to believe that without the achievements of the age of the Rights of Man any one of us, including the most conservative, can go on living his life. But this question shall not concern us here, for there is another one: (2) In view of the growing indispensability of the state bureaucracy and its corresponding increase in power, how can there be any guarantee that any powers will remain which can check and effectively control the tremendous influence of this stratum? How will democracy even in this limited sense be at all possible? . . .

This brings us straight to the discussion of [that] power which can be a controlling and directing force in the modern constitutional state, next to the all-encompassing officialdom: . . . the *parliament* . . . Modern parliaments are primarily representative bodies of those ruled with bureaucratic means. After all, a certain minimum of consent on the part of the ruled, at least of the socially important strata, is a precondition of the durability of every, even the best organized, domination. Parliaments are today the means of manifesting this minimum consent . . .

The control over the raising of revenues—the budget right—is the decisive power instrument of parliament, as it has been ever since the corporate privileges of the estates came into being. However, as long as a parliament can support the complaints of the citizens against the administration only by rejecting appropriations and other legislation or by introducing unenforceable motions, it is excluded from positive participation in the *direction* of political affairs. Then it can only engage in "negative politics," that means, it will confront the administrative chiefs as it if were a hostile power; as such it will be given only the indispensable minimum of information and will be considered a mere drag-chain, an assembly of impotent faultfinders and know-it-alls. In turn, the bureaucracy will then easily appear to parliament and its voters as a caste of careerists and henchmen who subject the people to their annoying and largely superfluous activities.

Things are different when parliament has accomplished the following: Either, that the administrative heads must be recruited from its midst . . . or that they need the express confidence of its majority for holding office or must at least resign upon losing its confidence—the *parliamentary* selection of the leaders; that they must account for their actions exhaustively to parliament, subject to verification by that body or its committees—parliamentary accountability of the leaders; further, that they must run the administration according to the guidelines approved by parliament—*parliamentary* control of the administration . . .

Nowhere in the world . . . can the parliamentary body as such govern and determine policies. The broad mass of deputies functions only as a following for the leader or the few leaders who form the government, and it blindly follows them *as long as* they are successful. *This is the way it should be.* Political action is always determined by the "principle of small numbers," that means, the superior political maneuverability of small leading groups. In mass states, this caesarist element is ineradicable. However, this element alone guarantees that *responsibility* toward the public, which would evaporate within an assembly governing at large, rests upon clearly identifiable persons. This is especially true of a democracy proper . . .

Only a working, not a merely speech-making parliament can provide the ground for the growth and selective ascent of genuine leaders, not merely demagogic talents. A working parliament, however, is one which supervises the administration by continuously sharing its work . . . Officialdom has been brilliant wherever it had to prove its sense of duty, its impartiality and mastery of organizational problems in the face of official, clearly formulated tasks of a specialized nature . . . But here we are concerned with political, not bureaucratic achievements, and the facts themselves provoke the recognition which nobody can truthfully deny: That bureaucracy failed *completely* whenever it was expected to deal with *political* problems.

This is no accident; rather, it would be astonishing if capabilities inherently so alien to one another would emerge within the same political structure . . . But the heads of the bureaucracy must continuously solve political problems . . . Parliament's first task is the supervision of these policy-makers. However, not only the tasks assigned to the top ranks of the bureaucracy but also every single technicality on the lower administrative levels may become politically important and its solution may depend on political criteria. *Politicians must be the countervailing force against bureaucratic domination* [italics supplied]. This, however, is resisted by the power interests of the administrative policy-makers, who want to have maximum freedom from supervision and to establish a monopoly on cabinet posts . . .

Effective supervision over the officialdom depends upon certain preconditions. Apart from being rooted in the administrative division of labor, the power of all bureaucrats rests upon *knowledge* of two kinds: First, technical know-how in the widest sense of the word, acquired through specialized training. Whether this kind of knowledge is also represented in parliament or whether deputies can privately consult specialists in a given case, is incidental and a private matter. There is no substitute for the systematic cross-examination (under oath) of experts before a parliamentary commission in the presence of the respective departmental officials. This alone guarantees public supervision and a thorough inquiry . . .

However, expertise alone does not explain the power of the bureaucracy. In addition, the bureaucrat has *official information,* which is only available through administrative channels and which provides him with the facts on which he can base his actions. Only he who can get access to these facts independently of the officials' good will can effectively supervise the administration. According to the circumstances, the appropriate means are the inspection of documents, on-the-spot inquiry, and, in extreme cases, the official's cross-examination under oath before a parliamentary commission . . . The parliamentary right of inquiry should be an auxiliary means and, for the rest, a whip, the mere existence of which will force the administrative chiefs to account for their actions in such a way as to make its use unnecessary.

The best accomplishments of the British parliament have been due to the judicious use of this right. The integrity of British officialdom and the public's high level of political sophistication are largely founded on it; it has often been emphasized that the best indicator for political maturity lies in the manner in which the committee proceedings are followed by the British press and its readers. This maturity is reflected not in votes of no-confidence, indictments of ministers and similar spectacles of French-Italian *unorganized* parliamentarism, but in the fact that the nation keeps itself informed about the conduct of its affairs by the bureaucracy, and continuously supervises it. Only the committees of a powerful parliament can be the vehicle for exercising this wholesome pedagogic influence . . .

[Mass Leaders/Demagogues and the Countervailing Power of Parliament]

We are concerned here not with the issue of democratization in the social sphere, but only with that of democratic—that is, equal—suffrage in its relation to parliamentarism . . . Parliamentarization and democratization are not necessarily interdependent, but often opposed to one another . . . In England the old parliamentarism was indeed, as befits its feudal origin, not really "democratic" in the Continental sense, even after the Reform Bill and up until the [First

World] War . . . But the existence and formal power position of the parliaments are not threatened by democratic suffrage. This is demonstrated by France and other countries with equal suffrage, where the governments are ordinarily recruited from parliament and rely on parliamentary majorities . . .

The political question is: What are the consequences of progressive democratization of the means and organizational forms of political combat for the structure of the political enterprise inside and outside of parliament? . . . The decisive point is that for the tasks of national leadership only such men are prepared who have been selected in the course of the political struggle, since the essence of all politics is struggle. It simply happens to be a fact that such preparation is, on the average, accomplished better by the much-maligned "craft of demagoguery" than by the clerk's office, which in turn provides an infinitely superior training for efficient administration . . . Democratization and demagogy belong together . . . insofar as the masses can no longer be treated as purely passive objects of administration, that is, insofar as their attitudes have some active import . . .

Active mass democratization means that the political leader is no longer proclaimed a candidate because he has proved himself in a circle of *honoratiores*, then becoming a leader because of his parliamentary accomplishments, but that he gains the trust and the faith of the masses in him and his power with the means of mass demagogy. In substance, this means a shift toward the *caesarist* mode of selection. Indeed, every democracy tends in this direction. After all, the specifically caesarist technique is the plebiscite. It is not an ordinary vote or election, but a profession of faith in the calling of him who demands these acclamations . . .

The contrast between the plebiscitary and the parliamentary selection of leaders is quite real. However, the *existence* of parliament is not useless for that matter. Vis-à-vis the factually caesarist representative of the masses it safeguards in England (1) the continuity and (2) the supervision of his power position, (3) the preservation of civil rights, (4) a suitable political proving ground of the politicians wooing the confidence of the masses, and (5) the peaceful elimination of the caesarist dictator once he has lost the trust of the masses.

However, since the great political decisions, even and especially in a democracy, are unavoidably made by few men, mass democracy has bought its successes since Pericles' times with major concessions to the caesarist principle of selecting leaders. In the large American municipalities, for example, corruption has been checked only by plebiscitary municipal dictators, whom the trust of the masses gave the right of establishing their own administrative agencies. And wherever democratic mass parties found themselves confronted with great tasks, they were obliged to submit more or less unconditionally to leaders who held the confidence of the masses . . .

The Power Elite

C. Wright Mills

The Higher Circles

The powers of ordinary men are circumscribed by the everyday worlds in which they live, yet even in these rounds of job, family, and neighborhood they often seem driven by forces they can neither understand nor govern. "Great changes" are beyond their control, but affect their conduct and outlook none the less. The very framework of modern society confines them to projects not their own, but from every side, such changes now press upon the men and women of the mass society, who accordingly feel that they are without purpose in an epoch in which they are without power.

But not all men are in this sense ordinary. As the means of information and of power are centralized, some men come to occupy positions in American society from which they can look down upon, so to speak, and by their decisions mightily affect, the everyday worlds of ordinary men and women. They are not made by their jobs; they set up and break down jobs for thousands of others; they are not confined by simple family responsibilities; they can escape. They may live in many hotels and houses, but they are bound by no one community. They need not merely "meet the demands of the day and hour"; in some part, they create these demands, and cause others to meet them. Whether or not they profess their power, their technical and political experience of it far transcends that of the underlying population. What Jacob Burckhardt said of "great men," most Americans might well say of their elite: "They are all that we are not."[1]

Excerpted from *The Power Elite* by C. Wright Mills (New York, 1956), 3–4, 7–9, 298–300, 323–324. Copyright © 1956 by Oxford University Press, Inc.; renewed 1984 by Yaraslava Mills. Reprinted by permission of the publisher.

The power elite is composed of men whose positions enable them to transcend the ordinary environments of ordinary men and women; they are in positions to make decisions having major consequences. Whether they do or do not make such decisions is less important than the fact that they do occupy such pivotal positions: their failure to act, their failure to make decisions, is itself an act that is often of greater consequence than the decisions they do make. For they are in command of the major hierarchies and organizations of modern society. They rule the big corporations. They run the machinery of the state and claim its prerogatives. They direct the military establishment. They occupy the strategic command posts of the social structure, in which are now centered the effective means of the power and the wealth and the celebrity which they enjoy.

The power elite are not solitary rulers. Advisers and consultants, spokesmen and opinion-makers are often the captains of their higher thought and decision. Immediately below the elite are the professional politicians of the middle levels of power, in the Congress and in the pressure groups, as well as among the new and old upper classes of town and city and region. Mingling with them in curious ways which we shall explore, are those professional celebrities who live by being continuously displayed but are never, so long as they remain celebrities, displayed enough. If such celebrities are not at the head of any dominating hierarchy, they do often have the power to distract the attention of the public or afford sensations to the masses, or, more directly, to gain the ear of those who do occupy positions of direct power. More or less unattached, as critics of morality and technicians of power, as spokesmen of God and creators of mass sensibility, such celebrities and consultants are part of the immediate scene in which the drama of the elite is enacted. But that drama itself is centered in the command posts of the major institutional hierarchies . . .

Within each of the big three, the typical institutional unit has become enlarged, has become administrative, and, in the power of its decisions, has become centralized. Behind these developments there is a fabulous technology, for as institutions, they have incorporated this technology and guide it, even as it shapes and paces their developments.

The economy—once a great scatter of small productive units in autonomous balance—has become dominated by two or three hundred giant corporations, administratively and politically interrelated, which together hold the keys to economic decisions.

The political order, once a decentralized set of several dozen states with a weak spinal cord, has become a centralized, executive establishment which has taken up into itself many powers previously scattered, and now enters into each and every cranny of the social structure.

The military order, once a slim establishment in a context of distrust fed by state militia, has become the largest and most expensive feature of government, and, although well versed in smiling public relations, now has all the grim and clumsy efficiency of a sprawling bureaucratic domain.

In each of these institutional areas, the means of power at the disposal of decision makers have increased enormously; their central executive powers have been enhanced; within each of them modern administrative routines have been elaborated and tightened up.

As each of these domains becomes enlarged and centralized, the consequences of its activities become greater, and its traffic with the others increases. The decisions of a handful of corporations bear upon military and political as well as upon economic developments around the world. The decisions of the military establishment rest upon and grievously affect political life as well as the very level of economic activity. The decisions made within the political domain determine economic activities and military programs. There is no longer, on the one hand, an economy, and, on the other hand, a political order containing a military establishment unimportant to politics and to money-making. There is a political economy linked, in a thousand ways, with military institutions and decisions. On each side of the world-split running through central Europe and around the Asiatic rimlands, there is an ever-increasing interlocking of economic, military, and political structures. If there is government intervention in the corporate economy, so is there corporate intervention in the governmental process. In the structural sense, this triangle of power is the source of the interlocking directorate that is most important for the historical structure of the present.

The fact of the interlocking is clearly revealed at each of the points of crisis of modern capitalist society—slump, war, and boom. In each, men of decision are led to an awareness of the interdependence of the major institutional orders. In the nineteenth century, when the scale of all institutions was smaller, their liberal integration was achieved in the automatic economy, by an autonomous play of market forces, and in the automatic political domain, by the bargain and the vote. It was then assumed that out of the imbalance and friction that followed the limited decisions then possible a new equilibrium would in due course emerge. That can no longer be assumed, and it is not assumed by the men at the top of each of the three dominant hierarchies.

For given the scope of their consequences, decisions—and indecisions—in any one of these ramify into the others and hence top decisions tend either to become co-ordinated or to lead to a commanding indecision. It has not always been like this. When numerous small entrepreneurs made up the economy, for example, many of them could fail and the consequences still remain local; political and military authorities did not intervene. But now, given political expectations and military commitments, can they afford to allow key units of the private corporate economy to break down in slump? Increasingly they do intervene in economic affairs, and as they do so, the controlling decisions in each order are inspected by agents of the other two, and economic, military, and political structures are interlocked.

At the pinnacle of each of the three enlarged and centralized domains, there have arisen those higher circles which make up the economic, the political, and the military elites. At the top of the economy, among the corporate rich, there are the chief executives; at the top of the political order, the members of the political directorate; at the top of the military establishment, the elite of soldier-statesmen clustered in and around the Joint Chiefs of Staff and the upper echelon. As each of these domains has coincided with the others, as decisions tend to become total in their consequence, the leading men in each of the three domains of power—the warlords, the corporation chieftains, the political directorate—tend to come together, to form the power elite of America . . .

The Mass Society

In the standard image of power and decision, no force is held to be as important as The Great American Public. More than merely another check and balance, this public is thought to be the seat of all legitimate power. In official life as in popular folklore, it is held to be the very balance wheel of democratic power. In the end, all liberal theorists rest their notions of the power system upon the political role of this public; all official decisions, as well as private decisions of consequence, are justified as in the public's welfare; all formal proclamations are in its name.

Let us therefore consider the classic public of democratic theory in the generous spirit in which Rousseau once cried, "Opinion, Queen of the World, is not subject to the power of kings; they are themselves its first slaves."

The most important feature of the public of public opinion, which the rise of the democratic middle class initiates, is the free ebb and flow of discussion. The possibilities of answering back, of organizing autonomous organs of public opinion, of realizing opinion in action, are held to be established by democratic institutions. The opinion that results from public discussion is understood to be a resolution that is then carried out by public action; it is, in one version, the "general will" of the people, which the legislative organ enacts into law, thus lending to it legal force. Congress, or Parliament, as an institution, crowns all the scattered publics; it is the archetype for each of the little circles of face-to-face citizens discussing their public business.

This eighteenth-century idea of the public of public opinion parallels the economic idea of the market of the free economy. Here is the market composed of freely competing entrepreneurs; there is the public composed of discussion circles of opinion peers. As price is the result of anonymous, equally weighted, bargaining individuals, so public opinion is the result of each man's having thought things out for himself and contributing his voice to the great chorus. To be sure, some might have more influence on the state of opinion than others, but no one group monopolizes the discussion, or by itself determines the opinions that prevail.

Innumerable discussion circles are knit together by mobile people who carry opinions from one to another, and struggle for the power of larger command. The public is thus organized into associations and parties, each representing a set of viewpoints, each trying to acquire a place in the Congress, where the discussion continues. Out of the little circles of people talking with one another, the larger forces of social movements and political parties develop; and the discussion of opinion is the important phase in a total act by which public affairs are conducted.

The autonomy of these discussions is an important element in the idea of public opinion as democratic legitimation. The opinions formed are actively realized within the prevailing institutions of power; all authoritative agents are made or broken by the prevailing opinions of these publics. And, insofar as the public is frustrated in realizing its demand, its members may go beyond criticism of specific policies; they may question the very legitimations of legal authority. That is one meaning of Jefferson's comment on the need for an occasional "revolution."

The public, so conceived, is the loom of classic, eighteenth-century democracy; discussion is at once the threads and the shuttle tying the discussion circles together. It lies at the root of the conception of authority by discussion, and it is based upon the hope that truth and justice will somehow come out of society as a great apparatus of free discussion. The people are presented with problems. They discuss them. They decide on them. They formulate viewpoints. These viewpoints are organized, and they compete. One viewpoint "wins out." Then the people act out this view, or their representatives are instructed to act it out, and this they promptly do.

Such are the images of the public of classic democracy which are still used as the working justifications of power in American society. But now we must recognize this description as a set of images out of a fairy tale: they are not adequate even as an approximate model of how the American system of power works. The issues that now shape man's fate are neither raised nor decided by the public at large. The idea of the community of publics is not a description of fact, but an assertion of an ideal, an assertion of a legitimation masquerading—as legitimations are now apt to do—as fact. For now the public of public opinion is recognized by all those who have considered it carefully as something less than it once was.

These doubts are asserted positively in the statement that the classic community of publics is being transformed into a society of masses. This transformation, in fact, is one of the keys to the social and psychological meaning of modern life in America . . .

The idea of a mass society suggests the idea of an elite of power. The idea of the public, in contrast, suggests the liberal tradition of a society without any power elite, or at any rate with shifting elites of no sovereign consequence. For, if a genuine public is sovereign, it needs no master; but the masses, in their full development, are sovereign only in some plebiscitarian moment of adulation to an elite as authoritative celebrity. The political structure of a democratic state requires the public; and, the democratic man, in his rhetoric, must assert that this public is the very seat of sovereignty.

But now, given all those forces that have enlarged and centralized the political order and made modern societies less political and more administrative; given the transformation of the old middle classes into something which perhaps should not even be called middle class; given all the mass communications that do not truly communicate; given all the metropolitan segregation that is not community; given the absence of voluntary associations that really connect the public at large with the centers of power—what is happening is the decline of a set of publics that is sovereign only in the most formal and rhetorical sense. Moreover, in many countries the remnants of such publics as remain are now being frightened out of existence. They lose their will for rationally considered decision and action because they do not possess the instruments for such decision and action; they lose their sense of political belonging because they do not belong; they lose their political will because they see no way to realize it.

The top of modern American society is increasingly unified, and often seems willfully co-ordinated: at the top there has emerged an elite of power. The middle levels are a drifting set of stalemated, balancing forces: the middle does not link the bottom with the top. The bottom of this society is politically fragmented, and even as a passive fact, increasingly powerless: at the bottom there is emerging a mass society.

Note from the Editor

1.   Jacob Burckhardt, *Force and Freedom* (New York: Pantheon Books, 1943), 303 ff.

An Elite Theory of Democracy

*Selections from the Work of
Joseph A. Schumpeter*

I think that most students of politics have by now come to accept
the [following] criticisms leveled at the classical doctrine of democracy.[1] I also think that most of them agree, or will agree before long,
in accepting another theory which is much truer to life and at the
same time salvages much of what sponsors of the democratic method
really mean by this term. Like the classical theory, it may be put into
the nutshell of a definition.

[Another Conception of Democracy]

Our chief troubles about the classical theory center in the proposition that "the people" hold a definite and rational opinion about
every individual question and that they give effect to this opinion—
in a democracy—by choosing "representatives" who will see to it
that opinion is carried out. Thus the selection of the representatives
is made secondary to the primary purpose of the democratic arrangement which is to vest the power of deciding political issues in
the electorate.

Suppose we reverse the roles of these two elements and make
the deciding of issues by the electorate secondary to the election of
the men who are to do the deciding. To put it differently, we now
take the view that the role of the people is to produce a government,
or else an intermediate body which in turn will produce a national
executive or government. And we define: the democratic method is
that institutional arrangement for arriving at political decisions in

Excerpts from Joseph A. Schumpeter, *Capitalism, Socialism and Democracy* (London:
Routledge [Unwin], 1954), 268–297. Reprinted by permission of Routledge. Bracketed
headings have been created by the editor of this volume.

which individuals acquire the power to decide by means of a competitive struggle for the people's vote.

Defense and explanation of this idea will speedily show that, as to both plausibility of assumptions and tenability of propositions, it greatly improves the theory of the democratic process. First of all, we are provided with a reasonably efficient criterion by which to distinguish democratic governments from others. The classical theory meets with difficulties on that score because both the will and the good of the people may be, and in many historical instances have been, served just as well or better by governments that cannot be described as democratic according to any accepted usage of the term. Now we are in a somewhat better position, partly because we are resolved to stress a *modus procedendi* the presence or absence of which it is in most cases easy to verify . . .

Second, the theory embodied in this definition leaves all the room we may wish to have for a proper recognition of the vital fact of leadership. The classical theory did not do this but, as we have seen, attributed to the electorate an altogether unrealistic degree of initiative which practically amounted to ignoring leadership. But collectives act almost exclusively by accepting leadership—this is the dominant mechanism of practically any collective action which is more than a reflex. Propositions about the working and the results of the democratic method that take account of this are bound to be infinitely more realistic than propositions which do not. They will not stop at the execution of a *volonté générale* but will go some way toward showing how it emerges or how it is substituted or faked. What [may be] termed Manufactured Will is no longer outside the theory, an aberration for the absence of which we piously pray; it enters on the ground floor as it should.

Third, however, so far as there are genuine group-wise volitions at all—for instance the will of the unemployed to receive unemployment benefit or the will of other groups to help—our theory does not neglect them. On the contrary we are now able to insert them in exactly the role they actually play. Such volitions do not as a rule assert themselves directly. Even if strong and definite they remain latent, often for decades, until they are called to life by some political leader who turns them into political factors. This he does, or else his agents do it for him, by organizing these volitions, by working them up and by including eventually appropriate items in his competitive offering. The interaction between sectional interests and public opinion and the way in which they produce the pattern we call the political situation appear from this angle in a new and much clearer light.

Fourth, our theory is of course no more definite than is the concept of competition for leadership. This concept presents similar difficulties as the concept of competition in the economic sphere, with which it may be usefully compared. In economic life competition is never completely lacking, but hardly ever is it perfect. Similarly, in political life there is always some competition, though perhaps only a potential one, for the allegiance of the people. To simplify matters we have restricted the kind of competition for leadership which is to define democracy, to free competition for a free vote. The justification for this is that democracy seems to imply a recognized method by which to conduct the competitive struggle, and that the electoral method is practically the only one available for communities of any size.

But though this excludes many ways of securing leadership which should be excluded, such as competition by military insurrection, it does not exclude the cases that are strikingly analogous to the economic phenomena we label "unfair" or "fraudulent" competition or restraint of competition. And we cannot exclude them because if we did we should be left with a completely unrealistic ideal. Between this ideal case which does not exist and the cases in which all competition with the established leader is prevented by force, there is a continuous range of variation within which the democratic method of government shades off into the autocratic one by imperceptible steps. But if we wish to understand and not to philosophize, this is as it should be. The value of our criterion is not seriously impaired thereby.

Fifth, our theory seems to clarify the relation that subsists between democracy and individual freedom. If by the latter we mean the existence of a sphere of individual self-government the boundaries of which are historically variable . . . *no* society reduces that sphere to zero—the question clearly becomes a matter of degree. We have seen that the democratic method does not necessarily guarantee a greater amount of individual freedom than another political method would permit in similar circumstances. It may well be the other way round. But there is still a relation between the two. If, on principle at least, everyone is free to compete for political leadership by presenting himself to the electorate, this will in most cases though not in all mean a considerable amount of freedom of discussion *for all*. In particular it will normally mean a considerable amount of freedom of the press. This relation between democracy and freedom is not absolutely stringent and can be tampered with. But, from the standpoint of the intellectual, it is nevertheless very important. At the same time, it is all there is to that relation.

Sixth, it should be observed that in making it the primary function of the electorate to produce a government (directly or through an intermediate body) I intended to include in this phrase also the function of evicting it. The one means simply the acceptance of a leader or a group of leaders, the other means simply the withdrawal of this acceptance. This takes care of an element the reader may have missed. He may have thought that the electorate controls as well as installs. But since electorates normally do not control their political leaders in any way except by refusing to re-elect them or the parliamentary majorities that support them, it seems well to reduce our ideas about this control in the way indicated by our definition. Occasionally, spontaneous revulsions occur which upset a government or an individual minister directly or else enforce a certain course of action. But they are not only exceptional, they are, as we shall see, contrary to the spirit of the democratic method . . .

According to the view we have taken, democracy does not mean and cannot mean that the people actually rule in any obvious sense of the term "people" and "rule." Democracy means only that the people have the opportunity of accepting or refusing the men who are to rule them. But since they might decide this also in entirely undemocratic ways, we have had to narrow our definition by adding a further criterion identifying the democratic method, viz., free competition among would-be leaders for the vote of the electorate . . .

The conditions which I hold must be fulfilled for the democratic method to be a success—in societies in which it is possible for it to work at all—I shall group under four headings; and I shall confine myself to the great industrial nations of the modern type.

[The Requirement for a High-Quality Leadership]

The first condition is that the human material of politics—the people who man the party machines, are elected to serve in parliament, rise to cabinet office— should be of sufficiently high quality . . . There may be many ways in which politicians of sufficiently good quality can be secured. Thus far, however, experience seems to suggest that the only effective guarantee is in the existence of a social stratum, itself a product of a severely selective process, that takes to politics as a matter of course.

If such a stratum be neither too exclusive nor too easily accessible for the outsider and if it be strong enough to assimilate most of the elements it currently absorbs, it not only will present for the political career products of stocks that have successfully passed many tests in other fields—served, as it were, an apprenticeship in private affairs—but it will also increase their fitness by endowing them with traditions that embody experience, with a professional code and with a common fund of views. It is hardly mere coincidence that England, which is the only country to fulfill our condition completely, is also the only country to have a political society in this sense . . .

[The Requirement for the Autonomy of Elites]

The second condition for the success of democracy is that the effective range of political decision should not be extended too far. How far it can be extended depends not only on the general limitations of the democratic method which follow from the analysis presented in the preceding section but also on the particular circumstances of each individual case . . .

Of course there cannot be any legal limits to what a parliament, led by the prime minister, might subject to its decision, if need be, by means of a constitutional amendment. But, so Edmund Burke argued in discussing the behavior of the English government and Parliament with respect to the American colonies, in order to function properly that all-powerful parliament must impose limits upon itself. Similarly we may argue that, even within the range of matters that have to be submitted to parliamentary vote, it is often necessary for government and parliament to pass measures on which their decision is purely formal or, at most, of a purely supervisory nature . . .

Democracy does not require that every function of the state be subject to its political method. For instance, in most democratic countries a large measure of independence from political agencies is granted to the judges. Another instance is the position held by the Bank of England until 1914. Some of its functions were in fact of a public nature. Nevertheless these functions were vested with what legally was just a business corporation that was sufficiently independent of the political sector to have a policy of its own. Certain federal agencies in this country are other cases in point. The Interstate Commerce Commission embodies an attempt to extend the sphere of public authority without extending the sphere of political decision. Or, to present still another example, certain of our states finance state universities "without any strings," that is to say, without interfering with what in some cases amounts to practically complete autonomy . . .

[The Requirement for an Independent Bureaucracy]

As a third condition, democratic government in modern industrial society must be able to command, for all purposes the sphere of public activity is to include—no matter whether this be much or little—the services of a well-trained bureaucracy of good standing and tradition, endowed with a strong sense of duty and a no less strong *esprit de corps*. Such a bureaucracy is the main . . . answer to the question about how our second condition can be fulfilled whenever the sphere of public control is wide.

It is not enough that the bureaucracy should be efficient in current administration and competent to give advice. It must also be strong enough to guide and, if need be, to instruct the politicians who head the ministries. In order to be able to do this it must be in a position to evolve principles of its own and sufficiently independent to assert them. It must be a power in its own right. This amounts to saying that in fact though not in form appointment, tenure and promotion must depend largely—within civil service rules that politicians hesitate to violate—on its own corporate opinion in spite of all the clamor that is sure to arise whenever politicians or the public find themselves crossed by it as they frequently must . . .

[The Requirement for Self-Restraint by the Opposition and the Public]

The fourth set of conditions may be summed up in the phrase Democratic Self-control. Everybody will of course agree that the democratic method cannot work smoothly unless all the groups that count in a nation are willing to accept any legislative measure as long as it is on the statute book and all executive orders issued by legally competent authorities. But democratic self-control implies much more than this . . . In particular, politicians in parliament must resist the temptation to upset or embarrass the government each time they could do so. No successful policy is possible if they do this. This means that the supporters of the government must accept its lead and allow it to frame and act upon a program and that the opposition should accept the lead of the "shadow cabinet" as its head and allow it to keep political warfare within certain rules . . .

The voters outside of parliament must respect the division of labor between themselves and the politicians they elect. They must not withdraw confidence too easily between elections and they must understand that, once they have elected an individual, political action is his business and not theirs. This means that they must refrain from instructing him about what he is to do . . . If [this] principle be accepted, not only instructions as formal as those French *cahiers* but also less formal attempts at restricting the freedom of action of members of parliament—the practice of bombarding them with letters and telegrams for instance—ought to come under the same ban.

We cannot enter into the various delicate problems which this raises concerning the true nature of democracy as defined by us. All that matters here is that successful democratic practice in great and complicated societies has invariably been hostile to political backseat driving—to the point of resorting to secret diplomacy and lying about intentions and commitments—and that it takes a lot of self-control on the part of the citizen to refrain from it.

[The Requirement for Tolerance and Compromise]

Finally, effective competition for leadership requires a large measure of tolerance for difference of opinion. It has been pointed out before that this tolerance never is and never can be absolute. But it must be possible for every would-be leader who is not lawfully excluded to present his case without producing disorder. And this may imply that people stand by patiently while somebody is attacking their most vital interests or offending their most cherished ideals—or as an alternative, that the would-be leader who holds such views restrains himself correspondingly. Neither is possible without genuine respect for the opinions of one's fellow citizens amounting to a willingness to subordinate one's own opinions.

Every system can stand deviating practice to a certain extent . . . And nowhere will that self-control stand tests beyond a varying degree of severity. In fact the reader need only review our conditions in order to satisfy himself that democratic government will work to full advantage only if all the interests that matter are practically unanimous not only in their allegiance to the country but also in their allegiance to the structural principles of the existing society. Whenever these principles are called in question and issues arise that rend a nation into two hostile camps, democracy works at a disadvantage. And it may cease to work at all as soon as interests and ideals are involved on which people refuse to compromise . . .

Note from the Editor

1. The democratic theory that came into being in the eighteenth and nineteenth centuries, such as that by J. J. Rousseau and J. S. Mill.

The Ruling Minorities
in Western Societies

*Selections from the Work of
Raymond Aron*

Government today must, as it always has, manage the external affairs of the collectivity, arbitrate conflicts between interest groups,
establish rules according to which individuals may compete, maintain public order, and safeguard the interest of the nation. Those
who govern make decisions affecting the lives of everyone (peace or
war); a few make these decisions in *the name of all.* Every society
develops a system which determines the method by which these few
are chosen, and the way in which they exercise power.

[The Dissociation of the Ruling Minorities]

The originality of industrial societies does not reside in the perma-
nence of a political subsystem, but in the differentiation of the ruling hierarchies. In Western societies the same men do not control
public administration and private enterprise; legislators and public
officials are for the most part professional politicians. Scholars, artists, writers, professors are all christened intellectuals and consider
themselves dependent in their own activities solely upon the judgment of their peers; officials of trade unions do not obey the captains of industry; priests neither command nor obey the scholars or
the political rulers. In short, the apparently characteristic order of
Western industrial society consists of a dissociation of powers. Temporal authority is shared by business leaders, politicians, popular leaders, and military commanders; spiritual authority by theologians,

intellectuals, and ideologues. The primary datum, then, is the plurality of ruling minorities, a plurality that permits objective comparisons of the various regimes.

There are certain leading roles to be performed in any industrial society, and consequently the same kinds of men appear to perform them. According to Saint-Simonian doctrine, productive labour is the primordial activity; organized within the framework of an enterprise, it requires competent leaders from foreman to general manager and continuing through the various echelons of the technical or administrative bureaucracy. At the higher level of the state, regulations must be promulgated or decisions made from day to day, no matter how much weight is given to planning or to operation of the free market. In the Soviet Union, managers of enterprises and political administrators constitute a single corps. In the West, where most businesses are not the property of the state, business and government administrators are selected in a different manner and do not go through the same mill, although movement back and forth from private to public life is becoming more common even in countries still regarded as capitalistic . . .

Both the Communist single party and the multiple parties of the West are indispensable organs of what sociologists call the political subsystem. Government personnel are chosen and replaced by means of this subsystem. The single party is essential to the formula of Soviet legitimacy . . . [In the West], multiple parties are engaged in peaceful competition for power in accordance with the formula of democratic legitimacy based on the process of free elections. Western parties—at least those which abide by the rules of the democratic game—are not "total" organizations. Their activity is limited and secondary, except at election time. In no case do they constitute a hierarchy paralleling that of the official administration; they have no formal representatives in business, in most regional and municipal administrative bureaucracies, or in the armed forces; they do not dominate the labour unions.

A multiple-party state limits the influence of the political on the social order; the one-party state (where the state and single party are practically one) places the stamp of the political upon the entire social order. It does not suppress the political or governmental function but rather tends to confuse it with the administrative function

by suppressing the neutrality of the latter . . . Thus the Western social order, characterized by dissociation of the ruling minorities, stands
in contrast to the social order in the Soviet Union, China, and the
people's democracies, where all such groups are unified in the single-
party system . . .

One line of attack on the West attempts to demonstrate that
the pluralism of the strategic minorities is but an illusion and one
minority is really behind the curtain, the master of the game . . . How
much truth resides in the Marxist and the neo-Machiavellian charges[1]
against Western pluralism? . . .

The Distribution of Power

Let us now go over the evidence again. Power is unequally distributed among individuals in all collectivities, partial or global. Even
when they freely elect their representatives, most individuals do not
feel that they have real influence over the course of events or the
conduct of diplomacy. In a complex society no regime can promise
all its members effective participation in ultimate decision-making
and rarely do they give any assurances of such participation. It is
probably not misleading to assert that even in the United States only
a few thousand people have any *direct* influence on the conduct of
foreign affairs.

The issue raised by both Marxists and neo-Machiavellian po-
lemics can be summed up in these questions: Is the dissociation of
ruling minorities genuine? Does a minority overtly or clandestinely
dominate all other minorities so that pluralism is only fiction, as is
true competition between parties? Marxist-Leninist propaganda denounces political monopolists; C. Wright Mills equated this with a
power elite; the disciples of Mosca and Pareto discerned the persistence of a ruling class behind the veil of democracy. Attacks of this
kind are difficult to refute because they oscillate between banality
and paradox, advance facts that are accurate but draw false conclusions from them.

Regimes of the Western type become stable when the representatives of the different minorities accept almost unanimously the
regime itself and agree upon the rules of the game. If we presume
that a portion of the ruling minorities, the leaders of the masses in
unions or political parties, say, and the intellectuals or ideologists

are hostile to the regime, its defenders will tend toward solidarity in the face of common danger and unite against those who, once in power, would set up a radically different system and thereby remove the heads of the erstwhile regime. (Historical experience, of course, proves that privileged groups have not always been able to unite against an absolute enemy.)

When the ruling minorities all rally to the existing order, and refuse to cooperate with those who are not of their group, Marxists and neo-Machiavellians would find it easy to demonstrate that the categories really constitute a single group with a single purpose. As soon as "the essential" is at issue, it is enough for the demonstration to give an appropriate definition of "the essential." For example, the Marxist will say that only the complete nationalization of the means of production is essential. From that he will deduce that all ruling categories are in agreement when the essential is at stake and that pluralism is a fiction . . . However, there are many tests to demonstrate that dissociation of groups within the power structure is not an empty fiction. Empirical studies show that while business leaders do have effective influence in Western democracies they are merely one of many pressure groups shaping government policy. Depending on which capitalist country one is talking about, and on the policy at issue, this influence varies in importance . . .

Speaking more generally, the sources of power appear to be separated rather than joined at all levels, in small cities as well as in central governments. The same men do not have all the prestige simultaneously nor do they exert influence simultaneously in all domains. This does not mean that the notables of the community, the leaders of the nation—high officials, legislators, business leaders, journalists, presidential advisers—pay no attention to one another. They have to know each other, and they have to cooperate. But the hierarchy that characterizes each segment of social activity is not so clearcut in the so-called Establishment created by all the leaders of the various categories when they are taken together. In their relationships they come together more or less as equals, and the prevailing mode of intercourse is one of discussion and dialogue.

Is it proper, then, to lump together as the ruling class all the leaders of the various groups, clustering around the politicians who are directly linked with the principle of legitimacy? This is a matter of semantics. What matters is not to ascribe to this ruling class a coherence and a continuity handed down from generation to generation which it does not possess. It is in fact a wide-open class, in accordance with the basic principles of today's democratic order. No one occupies a definitive place in it permanently. The electoral process exposes today's victor to the inconstancy of fortune and offers the vanquished an opportunity for revenge. Aside from politics, many are given the chance to climb to an establishment into which they were not born—by the trade unions, the business community, the universities, the military, the church, the intellectual community, and the research laboratories.

Actually, the agencies through which individuals join the Western social order are more often threatened by the absence of *one* ruling class than by the existence of any approximation of absolute power; it is more threatened by the division of parties and the conflict of ideas than by the conspiracies of monopolists. The early theoreticians of industrial society feared the consequences of lost spiritual unity; what could be the basis of any *consensus* if, as a consequence of the weakening of the religions of salvation, the members of society no longer believed in the same God and no longer acknowledged the sovereignty of the same modes of thought? The industrial societies of today are even further removed from spiritual unity than they were a century ago when these fears were first voiced. They have not split up, but during the period between the two world wars the danger of such a disintegration at times appeared imminent.

In any case, as the example of the new countries often demonstrates, what renders the order of pluralistic societies precarious, when the old oligarchies are broken up by industrialization, is not the fact of oligarchy, nor the inadequacy of democracy, but the dissociation of the ruling minorities and their quarrels. The process of modernization must create an order acceptable to the majority as well as to the privileged few; this requires a continuous dialogue among interest groups, political parties, and ideologies to further the establishment of an effective authority based on a common purpose . . .

[The Dissociation of the Ruling Minorities and the Public]

It is easy to point up the originality of the Western regimes. To be sure, the electoral process does not always or in every circumstance guarantee that the people, the "common man," will have an effective influence . . . Even the introduction of universal suffrage does not guarantee that the governed will effectively influence the rulers. When land owners and factory owners, the present day "feudal lords," control locally all the reins of power, representative institutions serve as an instrument of social conservatism . . .

[Yet] with increasing diversity of the roles to be played, accompanied by impersonality of individual relationships, the electoral process no longer furthers the manipulation of the masses by those in power; rather, it becomes a challenge of sorts launched against the powerful, who themselves are divided into groups, each of which hopes to maintain the existing order. The way these groups triumph over their rivals is to obtain the most votes, which requires some response to the needs and demands of the voters.

As society becomes more and more modernized, the dissociation of the ruling minorities results in the increasing effectiveness of the electoral process. Pressure groups, intellectuals, and ideologists represent numbers, ideas, diverse levels of society, and contradictory claims. They exert a direct or indirect influence on the politicians and the rulers. The leaders of some categories at least are themselves obliged to heed the complaints and the demands of those whom they represent. Indirectly, by means of social pluralism and competing political parties, industrial society is nearing the democratic ideal. This is not to say that the people govern or that they have a "general will" of their own apart from the incessant exchanges between individuals and groups; but free discussion between the controlling majority and its opposition, between labour unions and pressure groups, between intellectuals and those in power—despite the iron law of oligarchy—assures the ruled those guarantees which they may reasonably expect and gives the rulers little opportunity to misunderstand the profound desires of the masses . . .

Note from the Editor

1. Here Aron refers to the critiques of Western democracy by the mainstream elite theorists, such as Pareto, Mosca, and Mills (see the contributions by these theorists in this volume).

Part III

Classes in Democracy and Democratization— New Analyses

Introduction

As we move from the past to the present, we confront a number of intriguing questions. Foremost is the question of whether the classical thinkers have been able to perpetuate their ideas into the present by giving birth to a new generation of scholars in their own image; whether—to use a Marxist expression—they have succeeded in reproducing themselves. Further, we must ask whether, if such new scholars have appeared upon the scene, they have succeeded in invigorating their predecessors' theories with truly new ideas; and if so, whether these are of help to us as we confront the complex scene of democracy and democratization today.

Turning, first, to the new class analyses of democracy in Western, capitalist regimes, we encounter some writers, including Poulantzas, Foucault, Bowles, Gintis, as well as Manley, whose ideas are not merely new and forceful, but already are so central to the intellectual scene that they hold out a fair promise of shortly becoming classics in their own right. Their numbers—it must be admitted—are not large. And they, too, of course, have been criticized (how tedious the intellectual scene would be if this were not the case). But the more they are being criticized, the more resilient they seem to become.

Working within an orthodox Marxist tradition, Poulantzas accepts Marx's presumption that the capitalist state promotes the interests of the bourgeoisie, the ruling class. To this he adds his own contribution which is, that the capitalist state—whose legitimacy derives from the institutions of political democracy—possesses a relative autonomy vis-à-vis the ruling class. This itself, however, works in favor of that class, since the state can only promote the common purpose of that class, and organize its rule, insofar as it is not overly committed to any of its diverse and frequently warring fractions.

This argument has raised the query of whether the state indeed merely serves as a lackey of the "ruling class," and, moreover, if so, from where its relative autonomy from that same class derives. Not only Marx's own pertinent ideas, but their further elaboration by Poulantzas, have thus elicited the critique that they depict reality as overly simple, failing to come to terms with the complexities of power in a democracy.

A greater departure from orthodox Marxism, which yet implies acceptance of the idea of the bourgeoisie as the dominant class in Western democracy, may be found in the widely acclaimed piece by Foucault. In it Foucault contrasts the principles of the sovereignty of the people—creating a semblance of democracy—with the hidden micromechanisms of power—creating a reality of coercive domination. He sees these brutal mechanisms of subjugation, which the principles of the people's sovereignty serve to conceal and to promote at one and the same time, as being embedded in the discourse of truth and knowledge, as being diffused throughout society, and yet as working in the interest of the bourgeoisie.

Whether or not the micromechanisms of power which Foucault brings into relief are indeed as vicious as he makes them out to be, and whether or not they do indeed work in the interest of the bourgeoisie, one thing at least is clear. Foucault's ideas are unquestionably among the most widely revered (and disputed) ideas in the social sciences and the humanities today. Whether they are merely trendy today and doomed to be forgotten tomorrow, or whether they will remain a focus of controversy for years to come, is another question, to which, however, it is neither possible nor necessary to supply the answer today.

Adhering to Marxism by stressing the incompatibility between the economic class inequalities of capitalism and the rights and liberties of democracy, yet also opening new pathways, are the selection from Bowles and Gintis and the new contribution by Manley. Bowles and Gintis specify various institutional accommodations by means of which the advanced capitalist societies have tried to cope with this incompatibility, all of which worked for a time but then broke down. The most recent of these is the Keynesian model of capitalist ownership and profit, coupled with concessions to the working class. Like its predecessors, this accommodation served capitalism well for some time, but eventually it faltered, and this is the source of the instability experienced by advanced capitalist countries in recent years.

Focusing on the United States, Manley points to a special type of contradiction between capitalism and democracy. This is the contradiction between the American dream of advancement for the few, which implies economic class inequalities, and the democratic dream, which—according to Manley—is also an economically egalitarian dream. This democratic dream (though overshadowed by the American dream), also recurs throughout American history. Manley traces this dream in the writings of various thinkers, most notably Jefferson, and concludes by forcefully making the case for its relevance today. Thereby he, like Bowles and Gintis, lays himself open to the charge that his ideas, however forceful, also contain some wishful thinking. In the case of Bowles and Gintis such wishful thinking is expressed in the notion on the recent instability of capitalism; in the case of Manley it is expressed in the (complementary) notion on the feasibility of a nineteenth-century democratic/egalitarian dream—at the close of the twentieth.

The classical and new class analyses mentioned so far are focused almost exclusively on Western/capitalist democracy. Further, they either do not assign a central role to the working class in their analyses, or else regard it as merely the victim of capitalist inequality and exploitation. There are other class analyses, however, that are concerned with democratization in both the West and other parts of the world. These are analyses that (in contradistinction to the traditional Marxist view) see democracy (even in capitalist regimes) as working at least to some extent in the interest of the working class. And most of them assign a prominent role to this class in the promotion and preservation of this regime.

In this context, Przeworski views democratization as the implementation of a class compromise between the capitalist and the working class, which—though based on institutionalized uncertainty—cannot lead to the violation of either capitalist or working class interests beyond specific limits. While Przeworski sees the working class as one major partner in a democratic class compromise, Therborn (in his analysis of the advent of mainly Western democracy), as well as Huber, Rueschemeyer, and Stephens (in their analysis of the advent of democracy in both Europe and Latin America) regard the working class as a (if not *the*) major force in the promotion of democracy.

In similarity to Moore and to Lipset (in Part I of the volume) they emphasize that economic, capitalist development fosters democracy. But for them it does so because it leads to the empowerment of the working class, through its numerical growth and its organization in unions and parties. These then articulate this class's interests, while also taking up the struggle for democracy. The working class needs the bourgeoisie, fractions thereof, or the middle class, as allies; but once these have attained constitutional government and the franchise for themselves, it is only the working class which may gain from the further development of democracy; hence it is this class which struggles most consistently for its implementation.

Although the claim that the working class is central to the promotion of democracy can hardly be refuted, the question that almost automatically arises is whether this class on its own (or even with other class allies), may accomplish this feat. And if so, how it comes about that there have been and still are industrial societies, which necessarily spawn large working classes (such as the Soviet Union up until recently and China today), that have not produced democracy. Quite evidently, there must be other important factors which come into play as well; not least among them are the elites, whose role in either blocking, promoting, or sustaining democracy is brought into relief in the following part of the volume.

The Relative Autonomy of the Capitalist State, Democracy, and Dominant Class Hegemony

Selections from the Work of
Nicos Poulantzas

The specific unity and relative autonomy of the capitalist type of state vis-à-vis the dominant classes and fractions depends on the position of this state in the structures of the capitalist mode of production and on its particular relation to the field of the class struggle in this mode . . . Capitalist relations of production (i.e., the separation of the direct producer from his means of production in the framework of the relation of real appropriation) assign to the state's juridico-political superstructure a specific autonomy vis-à-vis the relations of production . . .

On the level of the relations of the state to the political struggle, this leads to a result which seems *paradoxical*, but which in fact constitutes the "secret" of this national-popular-class-state: the institutionalized power of the capitalist class state presents *its own class unity*, precisely insofar as it can pose as a national-popular state, i.e., as a state which does not represent the power of one or several determinate classes, but which represents the power of the political unity of private agents, given over to economic antagonisms which the state claims to have the function of surmounting by unifying these agents within a "popular-national" body.

[Political Democracy as Legitimizing the Capitalist State]

This characteristic of the capitalist state is related to a precise *ideological function*: given the specific efficacy of the ideological, and its

The extracts from *Political Power and Social Classes* (1978) by Nicos Poulantzas as reproduced by kind permission of the publishers, Verso, from pp. 275–279, 284–289, 296–303. Bracketed headings have been created by the editor of this volume.

role in the framework of the capitalist state, it would be wrong to underestimate the importance of this function, which in fact concerns the complex problem of the *legitimacy* of this state . . . In effect, this state is supposed to represent the general interest, the general will and the political unity of the people and the nation. In the characteristic forms of the principle of representation, the general interest, public opinion, universal suffrage, public liberties, it presents the normative institutional ensemble of *political democracy.* However, in order to examine the problem of the state's unity, I shall refer in particular to the concept of popular sovereignty and to the formation of the concept of the people.

In political theory, this concept of popular sovereignty, which covers that of the capitalist state, is linked to the problem of the *unity peculiar* to institutionalized political power. The problem of sovereignty had already been forged in connection with the absolutist state, where it indicated (still in a fairly confused way) the unitary structure of political power which had gained autonomy from the economic. In the sense of popular sovereignty, it designates an ensemble of citizens, of formally and abstractly free and equal individuals set up as political persons, as a source of the state's legitimacy. This ensemble is conceived as the body politic of society, as the people. However it is more important for us to note here that *the state's sovereignty and popular sovereignty are identical.*

This people, composed of citizens, is supposed to acquire its existence as the body politic, as the source of legitimacy, only in so far as it takes on a unity directly embodied in the unity of state power . . . This unitary institutional framework, coupled with the ideological function peculiar to this state, allows the state to function, in its relation to the class struggle, as the *unambiguous* political power *of the dominant classes or fractions,* and also to show in what precise sense the unambiguous functioning of this state implies its relative autonomy from these classes and fractions . . .

[The State's Relative Autonomy and Its Role as Organizer of Dominant Class Hegemony]

What then is the role of the capitalist class state in this context? It can be stated as follows: it takes charge, as it were, of the bourgeoisie's political interests and realizes the function of political hegemony which the bourgeoisie is unable to achieve. But *in order to do this, the capitalist state assumes a relative autonomy with regard to the bourgeoisie* . . . This relative autonomy allows the state to intervene not only in order to arrange compromises vis-à-vis the dominated classes, which, in the long run, are useful for the actual economic interests of the dominant classes or fractions; but also (depending on the concrete conjuncture) to intervene against the long-term economic interests of *one or other* fraction of the dominant class: for such compromises and sacrifices are sometimes necessary for the realization of their political class interests.

A good example are the state's so called "social functions" which have nowadays assumed an increased importance. While it is true that these social functions at the moment conform to the policies of state investment (i.e., they are intended to absorb the surplus of monopoly production) and so conform to the economic interests of the monopolies, it is equally true that they have been *imposed* on the dominant classes by the state, through the pressure of the dominated classes: this is often revealed by a hostility between the state and the dominant classes. Such functions have even sometimes been imposed by *social democratic* governments; but, strictly speaking, this does not alter the situation. These governments used the state and its relative autonomy to function as the political organizers of the dominant classes.

However, in order concretely to take on this relative autonomy which, inscribed in the play of its institutions, is what is precisely necessary for hegemonic class domination, the state *is supported by* certain dominated classes of the society, in that it presents itself, through a complex ideological process, as their representative: it encourages them in various ways, to work against the dominant class or classes, but to the political advantage of these latter. In this way it succeeds precisely in *making* the dominated classes *accept* a whole series of compromises which appear to be to *their* political interest . . .

For example, the state may function as the *factor of the political organization* of these classes, a function which manifests itself in the complex relation of the state to the parties of these classes. In this case, the state's relative autonomy is to be deciphered in its relation to these parties, which continue to take on their own organizational function. Or else the state may *substitute* itself for these parties by continuing to function as the factor of hegemonic organization of these classes. Or again in certain situations it may even *take total control of the political interests of these classes* . . . In this last case, the relative autonomy of the state is such that the dominant classes or fractions appear to renounce their political power . . .

The *paradoxical* character of this relation lies in the fact that this state assumes a relative autonomy with regard to these classes, precisely in so far as it constitutes their *unambiguous* and *exclusive* political power. In other words, this autonomy vis-à-vis the politically dominant classes, inscribed in the institutional play of the capitalist state, neither authorizes the dominated classes *effectively to participate* in political power nor cedes "parcels" of institutionalized power to them . . . [The state's] relative autonomy, which is a function of its unifying feature as a national-popular-state is, in the last analysis, only that autonomy necessary for the hegemonic organization of the dominant classes: i.e., it is only that relative autonomy which is indispensable for the unambiguous power of these classes . . .

[The State's Relative Autonomy and Its Role as Organizer of the Dominant Class Fractions]

Up to now, we have examined the unity and relative autonomy of the capitalist type of state from the particular viewpoint of their relation to the general field of the class struggle; we must now also examine them from the viewpoint of their specific function in the *relation between the dominant classes and fractions* within a capitalist formation . . .

Along with the coexistence on the terrain of political domination of the several classes and fractions which make up the power bloc, we find their characteristic incapacity to raise themselves to political unity under the protection of the hegemonic class or fraction. In other words, we find that the bourgeois class or fractions of that class are incapable of raising themselves to the hegemonic level through their own parties on the political scene. They are incapable (*through their own organizational means*) of transforming their specific interest into the political interest which would polarize the interests of the other classes and fractions of the power bloc. Thus, they cannot provide the unity of the classes and fractions of this bloc. This is principally due to the profound division of the bourgeois class into antagonistic fractions, a division which starts from the level of the actual relations of production . . .

Left to themselves the classes and fractions at the level of political domination are not only exhausted by internal conflicts but, more often than not, founder in contradictions which make them incapable of governing politically . . . What is the role of the state in this case? In fact, it is *the factor of the political unity of the power bloc under the protection of the hegemonic class or fraction. In other words, it is the factor of hegemonic organization of this class or fraction* . . .

With regard to the dominant classes and fractions, the capitalist state *presents an intrinsic unity*, combined with its relative autonomy, not because it is a tool of an already politically unified class, but precisely because it is the *unifying factor* of the power bloc. Social forces, therefore, do not *share* institutionalized power; what we have here is a case of several classes and fractions present on the terrain of political domination, which are able to assure this domination only to the extent that they are politically unified. The state derives its own unity from this plurality of dominant classes and fractions, in so far as their relation is incapable of functioning by means of a share-out of power and needs the state as the organizational factor of their strictly political unity. This unity is realized under the protection of the hegemonic class or fraction . . . In this sense the unity of state power is, in the last analysis, to be found in the state's particular relation to the hegemonic class or fraction, i.e., in the fact of the *univocal correspondence of the state to the specific interests of that class or fraction* . . .

Moreover, this function of the capitalist state also determines its *relative autonomy* vis-à-vis the power bloc and the hegemonic class or fraction, an autonomy which may take on several concrete forms. The state may, for example, present itself as the political guarantor of the interests of various classes and fractions of the power bloc against the interests of the hegemonic class or fraction, and it may sometimes play off those fractions and classes against the latter. But it does this in its function of political organizer of the hegemonic class or fraction and forces it to admit the sacrifices necessary for its hegemony . . .

This relative autonomy of the state from the power bloc and the hegemonic class or fraction does not depend on an equilibrium of

the forces *of the dominant classes and fractions,* amongst which institutionalized power operates as arbitrator. In fact, as a general rule, it
is precisely that hegemonic class or fraction whose political organization is constituted by the state, which is preponderant amongst the
other forces of the power bloc: but this privileged position which it
occupies does not prevent the relative autonomy of the state from
it . . .

Democratic Sovereignty, the Bourgeoisie's Dominance, and Disciplinary Power in the West

Selections from the Work of
Michel Foucault

[Truth, Right, and Power]

The course of study that I have been following . . . has been concerned with the *how* of power. I have tried, that is, to relate its mechanisms to two points of reference, two limits: on the one hand, to the rules of right that provide a formal delimitation of power; on the other, to the effects of truth that this power produces and transmits, and which in their turn reproduce this power. Hence we have a triangle: power, right, truth . . . In any society, there are manifold relations of power which permeate, characterise and constitute the social body, and these relations of power cannot themselves be established, consolidated nor implemented without the production, accumulation, circulation and functioning of a discourse. There can be no possible exercise of power without a certain economy of discourses of truth which operates through and on the basis of this association. We are subjected to the production of truth through power and we cannot exercise power except through the production of truth.

This is the case for every society, but I believe that in ours the relationship between power, right and truth is organised in a highly specific fashion. . . . We are forced to produce the truth of power that our society demands, of which it has need, in order to function: we *must* speak the truth; we are constrained or condemned to confess or to discover the truth. Power never ceases its interrogation, its inquisition, its registration of truth: it institutionalises, profession-

Excerpts from Michel Foucault, *Power/Knowledge*, ed. C. Gordon; trans. C. Gordon, L. Marshall, J. Mepham, and Kate Soper (New York: Pantheon Books, 1980), 92–108. Reprinted by permission of Prentice-Hall. Bracketed headings have been created by the editor of this volume.

alises, and rewards its pursuit. . . . In the end, we are judged, condemned, classified, determined in our undertakings, destined to a certain mode of living or dying, as a function of the true discourses which are the bearers of the specific effects of power . . .

[The Theory of Right and Power in the West]

As regards the general principle involved in a study of the relations between right and power, it seems to me that in Western societies since Medieval times it has been royal power that has provided the essential focus around which legal thought has been elaborated . . . When it comes to the general organisation of the legal system in the West, it is essentially with the King, his rights, his power and its eventual limitations that one is dealing . . . It is of royal power that we are speaking in every case when we speak of those grandiose edifices of legal thought and knowledge.

There are two ways in which we do so speak. Either we do so in order to show the nature of the juridical armory that invested royal power, to reveal the monarch as the effective embodiment of sovereignty, to demonstrate that his power, for all that it was absolute, was exactly that which befitted his fundamental right. Or, by contrast, we do so in order to show the necessity of imposing limits upon this sovereign power, of submitting it to certain rules of right, within whose confines it had to be exercised in order for it to remain legitimate. The essential role of the theory of right, from medieval times onwards, was to fix the legitimacy of power; that is the major problem around which the whole theory of right and sovereignty is organised.

When we say that sovereignty is the central problem of right in Western societies, what we mean basically is that the essential function of the discourse and techniques of right has been to efface the domination intrinsic to power . . . My general project over the past few years has been . . . to reverse [this] mode of analysis . . . to give due weight, that is, to the fact of domination, to expose both its latent nature and its brutality. I then wanted to show not only how right is, in a general way, the instrument of this domination—which scarcely needs saying—but also to show the extent to which, and the forms in which, right (not simply the laws but the whole complex of apparatuses, institutions and regulations responsible for their application) transmits and puts in motion relations that are not relations of sovereignty but of domination.

Moreover, in speaking of domination I do not have in mind that solid and global kind of domination that one person exercises over others, or one group over another, but the manifold forms of domination that can be exercised within society. Not the domination of the King in his central position, therefore, but that of his subjects in their mutual relations: not the uniform edifice of sovereignty, but the multiple forms of subjugation that have a place and function within the social organism . . .

[Dominance of the Bourgeoisie and Disciplinary Power]

[A] descending type of analysis, the one of which I believe one ought to be wary, will say that the bourgeoisie has, since the sixteenth or seventeenth century, been the dominant class; from this premise, it will then set out to deduce the internment of the insane. One can always make this deduction, it is always easily done and that is precisely what I would hold against it. It is in fact a simple matter to show that since lunatics are precisely those persons who are useless to industrial production, one is obliged to dispense with them. One could argue similarly in regard to infantile sexuality . . . Given the domination of the bourgeois class, how can one understand the repression of infantile sexuality? Well, very simply—given that the human body had become essentially a force of production from the time of the seventeenth and eighteenth century, all the forms of its expenditure which did not lend themselves to the constitution of productive forces—and were therefore exposed as redundant—were banned, excluded and repressed.

These kinds of deduction are always possible. They are simultaneously correct and false. Above all they are too glib, because one can always do exactly the opposite and show, precisely by appeal to the principle of the dominance of the bourgeois class, that the forms of control of infantile sexuality could in no way have been predicted . . . I believe that anything can be deduced from the general phenomenon of the domination of the bourgeois class. What needs to be done is something quite different. One needs to investigate historically, and beginning from the lowest level, how mechanisms of power have been able to function. In regard to the confinement of the insane, for example, or the repression and interdiction of sexuality, we need to see the manner in which, at the effective level of the family, of the immediate environment, of the cells and most basic units of society, these phenomena of repression or exclusion possessed their instruments and their logic, in response to a certain number of needs.

We need to identify the agents responsible for them, their real agents (those which constituted the immediate social *entourage:* the family, parents, doctors, etc.), and not be content to lump them under the formula of a generalised bourgeoisie. We need to see how these mechanisms of power, at a given moment, in a precise conjuncture and by means of a certain number of transformations, have begun to become economically advantageous and politically useful. I think that in this way one could easily manage to demonstrate that what the bourgeoisie needed, or that in which its system discovered its real interests, was not the exclusion of the mad . . . but rather the techniques and procedures themselves of such an exclusion. It is the mechanisms of that exclusion that are necessary, the apparatuses of surveillance, the medicalisation of sexuality, of madness, of delinquency, all the micro-mechanisms of power, that came, from a certain moment in time, to represent the interests of the bourgeoisie . . .

To put this somewhat differently: the bourgeoisie has never had any use for the insane; but the procedures it has employed to exclude them have revealed and realised—from the nineteenth century onwards, and again on the basis of certain transformations—a political advantage, on occasion even a certain economic utility, which have consolidated the system and contributed to its overall functioning. The bourgeoisie is interested in power, not in madness, in the system of control of infantile sexuality, not in that phenomenon itself. The bourgeoisie could not care less about delinquents, about their punishment and rehabilitation, which economically have little importance, but it is concerned about the complex mechanisms with which delinquency is controlled, pursued, punished and reformed, etc.

[Democratisation of Sovereignty and Disciplinary Power]

I would say that we should direct our researches on the nature of power not toward the juridical edifice of sovereignty, the State apparatuses and the ideologies which accompany them, but towards . . . forms of subjection and the inflections and utilisations of their localised systems . . . I believe that what then comes into view is a solid body of historical fact, which will ultimately bring us into confrontation with the problems of which I want to speak this year. This solid, historical body of fact is the juridical-political theory of sovereignty of which I spoke a moment ago, a theory which has had four roles to play. In the first place it has been used to refer to a mechanism of power that was effective under the feudal monarchy. In the second place, it has served as an instrument and even as justification for the construction of the large scale administrative monarchies. Again, from the time of the sixteenth century and more than ever from the seventeenth century onwards, but already at the time of the wars of religion, the theory of sovereignty has been a weapon which has circulated from one camp to another, which has been utilised in one sense or another, either to limit or else to re-inforce royal power.

We find it among Catholic monarchists and Protestant antimonarchists, among Protestant and more or less liberal monarchists, but also among Catholic partisans of regicide or dynastic transformation. It functions both in the hands of aristocrats and in the hands of parliamentarians. It is found among the representatives of royal power and among the last feudatories. In short, it was the major instrument of political and theoretical struggle around systems of power of the sixteenth and the seventeenth centuries. Finally, in the eighteenth century, it is again this same theory of sovereignty, reactivated through the doctrine of Roman law, that we find in its essentials in Rousseau and his contemporaries, but now with a fourth role to play: now it is concerned with the construction, in opposition to the administrative, authoritarian and absolutist monarchies, of an alternative model, that of parliamentary democracy. And it is still this role that it plays at the moment of the revolution . . .

As long as a feudal type of society survived, the problems to which the theory of sovereignty was addressed were in effect confined to the general mechanisms of power, to the way in which its forms of existence at the higher level of society influenced its exercise at the lowest levels . . . In effect, the mode in which power was exercised could be defined in its essentials in terms of the relationship sovereign-subject. But in the seventeenth and eighteenth centuries, we have the production of an important phenomenon, the emergence, or rather the invention, of a new mechanism of power possessed of highly specific procedural techniques, completely novel instruments, quite different apparatuses, and which is also, I believe, absolutely incompatible with the relations of sovereignty.

This new mechanism of power is more dependent upon bodies and what they do than upon the Earth and its products. It is a mechanism of power which permits time and labour, rather than wealth and commodities, to be extracted from bodies. It is a type of power which is constantly exercised by means of surveillance rather than in a discontinuous manner by means of a system of levies or obligations distributed over time. It presupposes a tightly knit grid of material coercions rather than the physical existence of a sovereign. It is ultimately dependent upon the principle, which introduces a genuinely new economy of power, that one must be able simultaneously both to increase the subjected forces and to improve the force and efficacy of that which subjects them. This type of power is in every aspect the antithesis of that mechanism of power which the theory of sovereignty described or sought to transcribe . . .

This new power, which can no longer be formulated in terms of sovereignty, is, I believe, one of the great inventions of bourgeois society. It has been a fundamental instrument in the constitution of industrial capitalism and of the type of society that is its accompaniment. This non-sovereign power, which lies outside the form of sovereignty, is disciplinary power. Impossible to describe in the terminology of the theory of sovereignty from which it differs so radically, this disciplinary power ought by rights to have led to the disappearance of the grand juridical edifice created by that theory. But in reality, the theory of sovereignty has continued not only to exist as an ideology of right, but also to provide the organising principle of the legal codes which Europe acquired in the nineteenth century, beginning with the Napoleonic Code.

Why has the theory of sovereignty persisted in this fashion? . . . For two reasons I believe. On the one hand, it has been, in the eighteenth and again in the nineteenth century, a permanent instrument of criticism of the monarchy and of all the obstacles that can thwart the development of disciplinary society. But at the same time, the theory of sovereignty, and the organisation of a legal code centred upon it, have allowed a system of right to be superimposed upon the mechanisms of discipline in such a way as to conceal its actual procedures, the element of domination inherent in its techniques, and to guarantee to everyone, by virtue of the sovereignty of the State, the exercise of his proper sovereign rights. The juridical systems—and this applies both to their codification and to their theorisation—have enabled sovereignty to be *democratised* through the constitution of a public right articulated upon collective sovereignty, while at the same time this *democratisation of sovereignty was fundamentally determined by and grounded in mechanisms of disciplinary coercion* [italics supplied].

To put this in more rigorous terms, one might say that once it became necessary for disciplinary constraints to be exercised through mechanisms of domination and yet at the same time for their effective exercise of power to be disguised, a theory of sovereignty was required to make an appearance at the level of the legal apparatus, and to re-emerge in its codes. Modern society, then from the nineteenth century up to our own day, has been characterised on the one hand, by a legislation, a discourse, an organisation based on public right, whose principle of articulation is the social body and the delegative status of each citizen; and on the other hand, by a closely linked grid of disciplinary coercions whose purpose is in fact to assure the cohesion of this same social body . . . The powers of modern society are exercised through, on the basis of, and by virtue of, this very heterogeneity between a public right of sovereignty and a polymorphous disciplinary mechanism . . . And I believe that in our own times power is exercised simultaneously through this right and these techniques . . .

When today one wants to object in some way to the disciplines and all the effects of power and knowledge that are linked to them, what is it that one does, concretely, in real life . . . if not precisely appeal to this canon of right . . . the right of sovereignty? But I believe that we find ourselves here in a kind of blind alley: it is not through recourse to sovereignty against discipline that the effects of disciplinary power can be limited, because sovereignty and disciplinary mechanisms are two absolutely integral constituents of the general mechanism of power in our society. If one wants to look for a non-disciplinary form of power, or rather, to struggle against disciplines and disciplinary power, it is not towards the ancient right of sovereignty that one should turn, but towards the possibility of a new form of right, one which must indeed be anti-disciplinarian, but at the same time liberated from the principle of sovereignty . . .

Democracy and Capitalism
[Contradiction, Accommodation, and
Instability]

Selections from the Work of
Samuel Bowles and Herbert Gintis

This work is animated by a commitment to the progressive extension of people's capacity to govern their personal lives and social
histories. Making good this commitment, we will argue, requires
establishing a democratic social order and eliminating the central
institutions of the capitalist economy. So stark an opposition between "capitalism" and "democracy," terms widely held jointly to
characterize our society, may appear unwarranted. But we will maintain that no capitalist society today may reasonably be called democratic in the straightforward sense of securing personal liberty and
rendering the exercise of power socially accountable.

"Democratic capitalism" suggests a set of harmonious and mutually supportive institutions, each promoting a kind of freedom in
distinct realms of social life. Yet we will show that capitalism and
democracy are not complementary systems. Rather they are sharply
contrasting rules regulating both the process of human development
and the historical evolution of whole societies: the one is characterized by the preeminence of economic privilege based on property
rights, the other insists on the priority of liberty and democratic
accountability based on the exercise of personal rights . . .

Democratic institutions have often been mere ornaments in the
social life of the advanced capitalist nations: proudly displayed to
visitors, and admired by all, but used sparingly. The places where
things really get done—in such core institutions as families, armies,

factories, and offices—have been anything but democratic. Representative government, civil liberties, and due process have, at best, curbed the more glaring excesses of these realms of unaccountable power while often obscuring and strengthening underlying forms of privilege and domination.

[The Contradiction Between Capitalism and Democracy]

But democracy does not stand still. Where democratic institutions have taken root, they have often expanded and deepened. Where a democratic idiom has become the lingua franca of politics, it has often come to encompass unwonted meanings. In the course of its development, democracy thus may challenge, indiscriminately and irreverently, all forms of privilege. The road from the eighteenth-century Rights of Man, which excluded not only women but most people of color as well, to the late twentieth-century civil rights movements, feminism, and the right to a job has been a tortuous one, but the route was amply prefigured even in the discourse of eighteenth-century liberalism. When democratic sentiments begin to so encroach upon a fundamental social institution as to threaten its ability to function, democratic institutions will find themselves obliged to supplant it or to retreat. This situation precisely captures the present predicament of the liberal democratic capitalist societies of Europe and North America . . .

[Liberal, democratic capitalist societies are characterized by a] tension between property rights and personal rights . . . The clash of rights is elevated to a central dynamic of liberal democratic capitalist societies by two fundamental historical tendencies. The first is the expansionary logic of personal rights, progressively bringing ever-wider spheres of society—the management of the economy and the internal relationships of the family, for example—under at least the formal if not the substantive rubric of liberal democracy. The second tendency concerns the expansionary logic of capitalist production, according to which the capitalist firm's ongoing search for profits progressively encroaches upon all spheres of social activity, leaving few realms of life untouched by the imperatives of accumulation and the market. If we are correct, the present and future trajectories of liberal democratic capitalism will be etched in large measure by the collision of these two expansionary tendencies . . .

Liberal democratic capitalism is a contradictory ensemble of institutions in which distinct rights are as often conflicting as they are mutually reinforcing. Major forms of social change in this contradictory system, however far-reaching and substantive, have been internal transformations of the dominant organization of rights. Not socialism, but the full extension of personal rights has been the fundamental threat facing the capitalist order in the liberal context . . . Social change in liberal capitalism is [best] understood as the product of the interaction of the two systemwide expansionary logics of personal and property rights . . .

[Institutional Accommodations and Their Instability]

But if personal and property rights do not form a harmonious unity, and if each follows an expansionary logic in the course of liberal capitalist development, why do not conflicting forces simply cause the system to fly apart? Why, indeed, . . . do not the many deploy their personal rights against the privileges of property? And equally, why do not the propertied deploy the formidable weapons that wealth may command to overturn the system of personal rights altogether?

We suggest that social stability in the face of the contradictory nature of rights has depended upon a series of historically specific institutional accommodations. In Europe and North America, these accommodations have deployed such diverse mechanisms as what might be termed the Lockean practice of limiting political participation to the propertied, the Jeffersonian vision of distributing property widely among the citizenry, the Madisonian strategy of fostering a sufficient heterogeneity of interests among citizens so as to prevent the emergence of a common political program of the nonpropertied, and the Keynesian model of economic growth through redistribution of income with the resulting communality of interests between the dispossessed and the wealthy.

Each of these accommodations—Lockean, Jeffersonian, Madisonian, and Keynesian—constituted a definition of the range of application of personal rights and property rights capable of muting the explosive potential of the clash of these rights. At the same time, each promoted, or at least was powerless to prevent, the evolution of new tensions. In each case the result was the erosion of the dominant form of accommodation in favor of a novel form or combination of forms.

The period extending from World War II to the 1970s exemplifies the most recent of these accommodations, which we call "Keynesian" in recognition of the role played by egalitarian state redistribution and macroeconomic management in spurring both capital accumulation and social harmony. The faltering of this accommodation, we shall argue, is both cause and effect of the period of economic stagnation and instability experienced by the advanced capitalist countries during the 1970s and 1980s . . .

[The Keynesian Accommodation]

In the closing days of World War II, few could have suspected that Europe and America were on the eve of an unprecedented era of political calm and economic boom. The tumult and stagnation of the years between the two world wars seemed a more likely trajectory. The precarious modus vivendi of liberal democracy and capitalism appeared if anything to have been weakened, for the interwar years had brought not only universal adult suffrage, but a growing commitment—even on the part of business—to an economically interventionist state. The collision of property rights and personal rights could no longer be averted by the liberal walls that separated a private economy from a quarantined public state. But paradoxically, if a case may be made on historical grounds for the enduring compatibility of capitalism and liberal democracy, it would have to draw heavily on the experience of precisely this apparently ill-starred post-World War II period . . .

After World War II a group of some two dozen liberal democratic states emerged, the number and internal stability of which were historically without precedent. Equally important, these countries enjoyed a period of unusually rapid and stable economic growth: even setting aside the disastrous economic record of the Great Depression and the war years, per capita product in Germany, France, the United Kingdom, and the United States grew well over twice as fast during the two decades after 1950 than during the sixty years before 1929. The pessimism of the immediate post-World War II years rapidly gave way to an optimistic conception of the enduring affinity of capitalist property and democratic citizenship . . .

The optimism of the early 1960s could not be sustained, however . . . Economic performance in the advanced capitalist nations began to falter in the mid–1960s to early 1970s. The trajectory of two sure indicators of the health of the capitalist economy attests to the end of the post-World War II economic miracle. First, the business net rate of profit fell in virtually all of the major capitalist nations; the average profit rate in the seven leading nations fell from 18 percent in the mid–1960s to 11 percent in the early 1980s. Second, and partly as a result, the accumulation process slowed: in most countries investment as a fraction of total output peaked during the late 1960s or early 1970s, and has declined since.

The coexistence of rapid economic development and democratic stability in the advanced nations during the two decades or so after World War II now appears to have been . . . the expression not of an intrinsic harmony but rather of a novel, if short-lived, alliance of democracy and capitalism which we call the *Keynesian accommodation*. Whereas the Lockean accommodation politically *excluded* nonpropertied producers, the Jeffersonian promised *property* to the producers, and the Madisonian *divided* them, the Keynesian accommodation *assimilated* the now-powerful class of wage and salary workers. Why do not the economically dispossessed use their civil powers to dispossess the propertied? Keynes's answer to the age-worn question was that egalitarian economic policy and the expansion of state economic activity serves the interest of both capital and labor.

As in the case of the other accommodations, the Keynesian accommodations in Europe and North America differed considerably among countries. Some occurred only partially, others solidified quite late in the period. But all involved a series of mutual concessions. Capital agreed to accept the integration of trade unions into the political and economic process, as well as to the guarantee of minimum living standards, relatively full employment and granting workers a share of productivity gains. Labor accepted capitalist control over production and investment, and acknowledged the criterion of profitability as the fundamental guide to resource allocation—and relatively unencumbered capital mobility and international trade.

The political economy shaped by these accords departed in four critical ways from its predecessors. First, Keynesian regulation involved the management of aggregate demand through a large and growing state sector. Partly as a result, unemployment levels were low and the business cycle considerably tamed compared to the pre-

World War II years. Second, the established political presence of the working class led to a vast extension of the welfare state, with a resultant considerable reduction in the dependence of the working people on the labor market for material security. Among the major capitalist nations, the average fraction of the total product devoted to publicly financed consumption doubled between the early 1950s and the early 1980s. An increasing share of workers' living standards took the form of what some have termed the social wage, referring to the workers' access to goods and services secured simply by dint of citizenship rather than through the sale of labor time. The growth of the social wage represented a major extension of personal rights and, as we shall see, an impingement on the hegemony of property rights in the economy.

Third, workers in general ceased disputing the right of employers to control the workplace, which allowed the consolidation of property rights in the sphere of production. Finally, the general commitment to relatively unimpeded capital mobility and an open international economy strengthened capitalist control of investment and growth, bringing to new heights the capacity of the threat of capital flight to serve as a check upon state policy deemed unfavorable to capitalist profits. Workers and citizens now had the formal power to impinge on capitalist prerogatives and the accumulation process by virtue of their increased presence in an increasingly interventionist state. On the other hand, capitalist control of production and investment and the mobility of capital posed an effective counterweight to this popular power. The Keynesian accommodation thus promoted a strong tendency for capitalist property relations to deepen and consolidate its control of production and investment within the economy, while democratic rights were deepened and consolidated in the spheres of political life and economic policy.

Regulating this tenuous balance in the conflict of rights during the Keynesian accommodation was a distinct structure of economic growth which muted distributional conflicts between capital and labor. [Certain] aspects of this new structure are of critical importance. First, the Keynesian logic of *demand constrained growth* led to a distributional symbiosis: working-class living standards and profits became complementary rather than competitive objectives. This counterintuitive logic resulted because egalitarian redistributions supported an expanding level of total demand for goods and services, and because high levels of demand contributed to the relatively full utilization of productive capacity. This in turn supported a high level of profits, giving rise to a positive relationship among wage growth, the egalitarian redistributions of the welfare state, and corporate profitability.

Second, the consequent rapid growth in the demand for labor brought about shortages of trained labor and increased social and private returns to education and other forms of human resource development. The expansion of educational opportunity thus afforded another reciprocal relationship between egalitarian social policy and profitability. In addition, the rapid development of nonmanual and service-related jobs in the postwar economy favored the substitution of upward individual social mobility for changes in the rules of the game as the focus of group conflict. With a rapidly expanding pie, it became less critical to dispute the inegalitarian character of its distribution . . .

One political consequence of the Keynesian accords was a narrowing of the political spectrum: the deradicalization of labor in Europe and North America alike, and the parallel defeat of right-wing capital. This development was no doubt favored by the rapid rate of growth of living standards. Those who favored alternatives of either the Right or the Left were up against the most sustained period of prosperity in living memory. A second and parallel consequence was the depoliticization of capital-labor conflict. The late 1940s and early 1950s had witnessed a series of state interventions against the labor movements of many countries, and particularly against its more leftist elements. Such conflict was not abolished, but business organizations had increasingly little need (or capacity) to resort to direct governmental intervention against workers to secure the conditions for profitable production and investment. Labor discipline was secured not through state intervention but by the force of macroeconomic conditions—the prospect of capital flight and unemployment being paramount.

[The Instability and Demise of the Keynesian Accommodation]

The Keynesian accommodation, however, led cumulatively to serious economic difficulties, which came to a head in the period be-

tween 1965 and 1974 . . . It was at least in part the very success of
the Keynesian model that spelled its demise. The effectiveness of the
international and domestic aspects of the policies adopted under the
Keynesian accommodation, we believe, are directly implicated in
the extinction of both the distributional symbiosis and the favorable
conditions of profitability, both of which had been essential to its
ability to contain the explosive potential of the clash of rights.

Profits were squeezed by a pincer that was in part the creation
of the postwar accommodation itself—namely, cost pressures from
labor that could not be passed on to consumers because of the increasingly competitive and open world economy. The combined effect of the growth of the social wage and the generally low levels of
unemployment greatly enhanced labor's bargaining power by taking
some of the bite out of the employer's threat of job termination.
Labor's new bargaining power could not be easily accommodated,
however, for price increases by employers were met with losses in
market shares due in part to the burgeoning of international competition, especially in the years since the late 1960s. The profit squeeze
was considerably tightened in the mid–1970s, because in most countries labor was strong enough to resist paying in full the cost of the
increasingly adverse international terms of trade and the rising price
of oil in particular. The result was a rise in labor's share of the national income in virtually every major capitalist country extending
from the early 1950s through the mid–1970s.

The conditions of labor scarcity underlying the profit squeeze
point to a second development tending to erode the Keynesian accommodation. As the economies of Europe and North America more
nearly approached full capacity production in the 1960s and early
1970s, the Keynesian expansion of total demand through egalitarian redistribution no longer supported higher profits. Rather it tended
to step up the demand for labor, thereby further strengthening labor's
bargaining position. As the advanced capitalist economies moved from
a demand-constrained growth logic into a situation of both demand-
and supply-constrained economic growth, the fortuitous distributional
symbiosis of the Keynesian accommodation evaporated. The capitalist economy increasingly resembled a zero-sum game.

This erosion of the conditions for both capitalist profitability
and the hegemony of an egalitarian public ideology under the

Keynesian accommodation is the background to the monetarist resurgence in the 1970s. But the monetarist strategy—of restoring the power of capital by escalating the scarcity of jobs and halting or reversing the growth of the social wage—has itself proved remarkably costly. In part as a result of the social policies of the Keynesian accommodation, the neutral rate of unemployment—the unemployment rate at which the share of labor wages as a claim on net output neither rises nor falls—has drifted upward. Ever more unemployment is needed to maintain a given level of power of capital over labor. The result has been a sharply rising cost of using labor market slack to control labor. And under these new conditions, only *very* high unemployment rates over prolonged periods appear to be able to shift the distributional advantage toward capital. And high levels of unemployment generally are associated with slack demand for output, resulting in high levels of unutilized capital stock and lagging rates of technological innovation—hardly a prescription for buoyant profits.

The monetarist revival of the 1970s was an attempt to deploy the logic of the market against labor's rising power, to reverse labor's encroachments on capital without substantial direct state intervention. The sluggish economic growth of the 1970s, and the (even to monetarists) surprisingly long period of recession required to turn the tide against labor in Britain and the United States since 1979, testifies to the monumental costs (to capital as well as to labor) of this attempt at a market-based system of labor discipline.

[Conclusion]

The Keynesian accommodation, in the end, offered only a temporary respite in the clash of rights. Like the Lockean, Jeffersonian, and Madisonian visions before it, the Keynesian accommodation represented a structure defining the range of applicability of property rights and personal rights. For a time this modus operandi contained the expansionary logics of both. But it did nothing to abolish the underlying contradiction between economic privilege and democratic rights, which has constituted the warp of the rich tapestry of social conflict and solidarity extending over the past two centuries in the now-liberal democratic capitalist nations . . .

Rediscovering the American Democratic Dream

John F. Manley

Three dreams run through American history: the elitist dream, the American dream, and the democratic dream. The elitist dream envisions an America of the superior few and inferior many. It denies that America stands for mass equality, independence, freedom, and emancipation from the curse of poverty. Such rewards go disproportionately to the winners of a competition in which all (allegedly) have an equal opportunity to compete, and losers have no fair complaint against winners. Elitist beliefs have either accommodated or supported slavery, subjugated women, justified displacement and even annihilation of Native Americans, and legitimated capitalism.

The American dream is a compromise of the elitist and democratic dreams. On economic equality, the American dream is elitist: the United States promises equal opportunity to become unequal, not social and economic equality. What purportedly saves the American dream's claim to be democratic is support for legal and political equality; independence, freedom, and real equality are reserved for the successful. For most people, the American dream means marginal economic improvement; democracy, in all but the formal or legalistic sense, is essentially dropped from the promise of American life.

The democratic dream, which is far less well-known than the other two, does not say all people are equal in abilities or talents; it says that no society sharply divided between rich and poor, privileged elite and mass, can be democratic because, in a society where virtually everything has a price, equality is a necessary condition of independence and freedom. Democracy respects the will of the majority, and some economic inequality may be tolerated, but the general social objective is a dominant middle class. This saves the democratic dream from the charge of mindless leveling, while putting popular limits on the degree of inequality thought compatible with democratic society.

Neither conservatism nor liberalism, the two poles between which American politics normally swings, can be expected to advance democracy in America. The conservative elitist dream makes no pretense of concern for social democracy, and the liberal American dream offers at best a less oppressive social order than that envisioned in the conservative dream. For true democracy, an earlier dream of America — the radical democratic dream envisioned by Thomas Jefferson—must be rediscovered and adapted to contemporary American life.

The American Dream

America has long seen itself as a haven for the world's poor and oppressed. America's enduring self-image is that of "The New Colossus," the title of Emma Lazarus' poem engraved on the base of the Statue of Liberty:

> *Give me your tired, your poor,*
> *Your huddled masses yearning to breathe free,*
> *The wretched refuse of your teeming shore.*
> *Send these, the homeless, tempest-tost to me,*
> *I lift my lamp beside the golden door.*

At the beginning of time, the myth of America says, all the world was America, the virgin land, New Canaan, the Garden, Arcadia; at the end of history, if Fukuyama (1993) is right, all the world will be America, capitalist America.

The problem with the exalted American dream is not merely the specter of the homeless wandering America's streets, the stain of slavery and racism and sexism, the persistence of poverty, the terror of everyday violence, environmental destruction, and wars waged on people whose ancestors pursued the American dream thousands of years before America's "discovery" by Europeans. The problem is that the dominant dream of America is an elitist dream which for millions of people undermines the American promise. Culturally, the American dream reinforces capitalism and liberal democracy;

together, all three push classical democratic values aside. According to the elitist American dream, people of talent who work hard can rise as high or low as their abilities take them. The myth of Horatio Alger and the reality of Andrew Carnegie personify the dominant American dream.

The Democratic Dream According to Crèvecoeur and Franklin

Although it is overwhelmed by the American dream, another dream of America, the democratic dream, recurs throughout American history. The pulse of the democratic dream is faint now, but it has never been completely stilled. This dream is as old as the lost history of those who discovered America. It offers a far different vision of America and of a model for the world than the dominant dream; much depends on which dream prevails.

It was not a capitalist vision of America that Crèvecoeur presented when he identified the key difference with Europe as the absence of elites who rob the people of the fruits of their labor. "Here the rewards of his industry follow with equal steps the progress of his labour . . . ," he wrote. New citizens lose that "servility of disposition" which poverty teaches.

The new arrival goes to work, and works moderately; instead of being employed by a haughty person, he finds himself with his equal, placed at the substantial table of the farmer, or else at an inferior one as good; his wages are high, his bed is not like that bed of sorrow on which he used to lie . . . He begins to feel the effects of a sort of resurrection; hitherto he has not lived but simply vegetated; he now feels himself a man (Crèvecoeur, n.d., 64–65).

Benjamin Franklin agreed. Although Franklin is taken by Max Weber as the quintessential representative of the capitalist ethic, Franklin abhorred the idea that industrial capitalism would sink its roots in America. Franklin was well aware of industrial capitalism from his travels in Europe. He wrote sarcastically that if any Americans envy the trade of Europe "let them with three-fourths of the people of Ireland live the year round on potatoes and buttermilk, without shirts, then may their merchants export beef, butter, and linen. . . . " (Smyth, 1905, V, 362–63). Manufactures are founded in poverty, Franklin wrote, for only the dependent poor, who are without land, must work for low wages for a master. In an early statement of the safety-value thesis, Franklin rejoiced that as long as there is public land in America, manufacturing will amount to little (Labaree, 1959, IX, 73: McCoy, 1973, 605–28).

The Democratic Dream According to Jefferson and Madison

Jefferson concurred. Today Jefferson is dismissed as a spokesman for yeoman farmers, but cities offended Jefferson because they housed a dependent working class. He came to accept industrial capitalism *if* workers could get a high price for their labor and, if exploited, quit working for others and take up independent production. As late as 1814 he believed the high degree of equality and independence in the United States still offered hope for republican government:

The great mass of our population is of laborers; our rich who can live without labor, either manual or professional, being few, and of moderate wealth. Most of the laboring class possess property, cultivate their own lands, have families, and from the demand for their labor are enabled to extract from the rich and competent such prices as enable them to be fed abundantly, clothed above mere decency, to labor moderately and raise their families . . . (Lipscomb, 1904, XIV, 333).

Jefferson believed that a perfectly equal division of property was impracticable, but in keeping with his advice to crush in its birth the aristocracy of monied corporations, he urged legislators to be inventive in subdividing property, including taxes on property in geometrical progression as it rises.

A fourth writer on the democratic dream was James Madison. This Madison is much less well-known than the more conservative Father of the Constitution, but as Alexander Hamilton's financial policies enriched "stock jobbers," Madison wrote a series of radical articles for Philip Freneau's *National Gazette*. In these articles, Madison attacked "immoderate" accumulation of riches, and endorsed laws which, without violating property rights, would "reduce extreme wealth toward a state of mediocrity, and raise extreme indigence toward a state of comfort" (Hunt, 1906, VI, 86). Throughout his life, Madison worried that capitalism would undermine republican society. Great wealth would concentrate in the hands of the few, he felt, and conflict would arise between "wealthy capitalists and indigent labourers" (Meyers, 1973, 504–05, 517, 527).

America, of course, took the capitalist road. This delighted elitists like Alexander Hamilton, who believed that all societies divide themselves into the few and the many. But for observers like Tocqueville, and other nineteenth-century writers, elitism and capitalism raised grave questions about America.

Democracy in America According to Tocqueville

In the 1830s, when Tocqueville toured America, he was most struck by the country's general equality of condition. Equality of condition, he wrote, was the "fundamental fact from which all others seem to be derived and the central point at which all my observations constantly terminated" (Tocqueville, 1954, I, 4). People in the United States were more equal than in any country or age in history, in his view, which was just as well because democracy depended on equality of condition. He gave three reasons for this: without equality of condition, people lack the love of independence that is essential to democracy; the basic difference between aristocracy and democracy is that in the former the rich govern; and without equality of condition, no one's property is truly safe (Tocqueville, 1954, II, 67, 266, 304).

Tocqueville believed that democracy and capitalism were incompatible. Capitalism encouraged the fast gain of commerce over the slow rewards of agriculture; and commerce depended on a large working class. The manufacturing aristocracy of his days was, he believed, one of the harshest aristocracies in history, but one of the most confined. Still, the friends of democracy should be watchful, for if ever a permanent inequality of condition penetrates the world, this is the gate by which it will enter (Tocqueville, II, 171). Democracy flourished in America, Tocqueville believed, because of unusually favorable economic conditions, which encouraged equality of condition.

The Decline of the Democratic Dream

Long before the 1890 Census found that there was no longer an unbroken frontier line in America, and before Frederick Jackson

Turner assessed the significance of the frontier's close, cheap land was seen by some perceptive observers as a uniquely important outlet for class conflict in America. Hegel, in the 1820s, was one of the first to write about this aspect of the American frontier: "By this means the chief source of discontent is removed, and the continuation of the existing civil condition is guaranteed. . . . Had the woods of Germany been in existence the French Revolution would not have occurred. . . . " (Wrobel, 1993, 7). In 1875, European-born journalist Charles Nordhoff saw the frontier as an option for the "non-capitalist population." Even if only one in a thousand poor laborers took advantage of the public domain, he wrote, "the knowledge that any one may do so makes those who do not more contented with their lot, which they thus feel to be one of choice and not of compulsion" (Wrobel, 1993, 10).

With the displacement of independent production by capitalism, the industrialization of America, and the close of the frontier, came the decline of the democratic dream. The American dream became America's unofficial ideology. Capitalism could not promise general equality of condition and an independent population, but it could and did promise material improvement: a rising tide would lift all boats, not equally, to be sure, but significantly. Most Americans accepted these terms (after considerable resistance), and the state accepted the task of ensuring the new social compact.

When capitalism fails to make good its promise, however, and when unemployment and inequality exceed tolerable limits, elements of the democratic dream reappear. America's commitment to capitalism weakens. At moments of great crisis, such as the 1930s, capitalism itself is at risk. People look for alternatives. To date, the capitalist American dream remains in place. But is its place fixed? Is liberal democratic capitalism the end of American history, and the future of the world?

Back to Jefferson's Democratic Dream

Nothing is less fashionable in contemporary American politics than discussing basic questions of democracy. The consensus limiting democracy to political and legal rights, not economic rights, goes unchallenged while political participation and social harmony decline, and the influence of the affluent ascends. Jefferson reminds us that democracy is impossible without a large measure of social and economic equality, which, in an age of growing inequality, may help explain why he is currently so out of favor.

During the 1930s, liberalism came to mean opening government to disadvantaged groups, and passing federal or federal-state programs to help them. Many programs were welcome assists to people in need, but such "interest group liberalism" was a poor substitute for Jeffersonian democracy. Liberals were vulnerable, as Ronald Reagan showed, to the conservative charge that the New Deal was pork barrel politics on a grand scale, that federal financial resources were insufficient unless the state were willing to impose unacceptably high levels of taxation, and that, even if taxes were raised, merely throwing money and bureaucrats at problems was unlikely to work. Such arguments tapped longstanding American skepticism about the efficacy of central government, as well as latent preferences for Jeffersonian government close enough to the people for popular control. Now that east-west relations are in flux, new opportunities exist for developing a theory of democracy superior to that of liberalism. This will require, in the spirit of Jefferson, a willingness to question the compatibility of capitalism and democracy.

Jefferson should not, of course, be made out as more democratic than he was. For instance, his statement that "All men are created equal" was not meant to apply to women. He doubted that blacks were intellectually equal to whites and, although he opposed slavery, he lived off slave labor and protected his estate by emancipating only a few slaves at his death. He also believed the natural aristocracy of talent was a great gift to society, without reconciling that belief with the view that only an egalitarian society can be democratic.

But the nascent American democratic dream is in Jefferson. He failed personally to live up to the democratic dream, but his statement of its general principles could be invoked authoritatively by others. A famous extension of Jefferson is the 1848 Seneca Falls resolution applying the Declaration of Independence to women. Contemporary seekers of democracy have in Jefferson a defense of social and economic democracy (even though individuals may be unequal in talents and abilities) and an argument for transcending the (capitalist) American dream. Far from being irrelevant today, even a passing attention to social conditions suggests that Jefferson and the radical democratic dream have perhaps never spoken more directly to America's immediate concerns.

References

Crèvecoeur, J. Hector St. John. n.d. *Letters from an American Farmer.* Garden City: Doubleday.

Fukuyama, Francis. 1993. *The End of History and the Last Man.* New York: Avon.

Hunt, Gaillard (ed.). 1906. *The Writings of James Madison.* New York: Putnam's.

Labaree, Leonard W. (ed.). 1959. *The Papers of Benjamin Franklin.* New Haven: Yale University Press.

Lipscomb, Andrew A. (ed.). 1904. *The Writings of Thomas Jefferson.* Washington: Thomas Jefferson Memorial Association.

McCoy, Drew. 1973. "Benjamin Franklin's Vision of a Republican Political Economy for America," *William and Mary Quarterly:* 605–628.

Meyers, Marvin (ed.). 1973. *The Mind of the Founder.* Indianapolis: Bobbs-Merrill.

Smyth, Albert H. (ed.). 1905.*The Writings of Benjamin Franklin.* New York: Macmillan.

Tocqueville, Alexis de. 1954. *Democracy in America.* New York: Vintage.

Wrobel, David W. 1993.*The End of American Exceptionalism.* Lawrence: University of Kansas Press.

Transition to Capitalist Democracy as Class Compromise

*Selections from the Work of
Adam Przeworski*

For a variety of reasons, some of which will be discussed below, it is perhaps useful to think of transition from an authoritarian to a democratic system as consisting of two simultaneous but to some extent autonomous processes: a process of disintegration of the authoritarian regime, which often assumes the form of "liberalization," and a process of emergence of democratic institutions. Though both of these transformations are shaped by the particular features of the old regime, at some point specifically democratic institutions must be established. It is important, therefore, to analyze democracy as the final telos of these transformations.

[Democracy as a Conflict-processing System]

Democracy is a particular system of processing and terminating intergroup conflicts. This system has a number of characteristics that distinguish it from other political arrangements:

1. The existence and the organization in pursuit of conflicting interests are explicitly recognized to be a permanent feature of politics. This norm implies specifically that (a) multiple groups can be organized to promote their interests, (b) these groups have an institutionally guaranteed access to political institutions, and (c) losers who play according to the rules do not forsake their right to keep playing.

From Adam Przeworski, "Some Problems in the Study of the Transition to Democracy," in *Transitions from Authoritarian Rule: Comparative Perspectives*, ed. Guillermo O'Donnell, Philippe C. Schmitter, and Laurence Whitehead. Copyright © 1986 by the Johns Hopkins University Press. Reprinted by permission of the Johns Hopkins University Press. Bracketed headings have been created by the editor of this volume.

2. Conflicts are processed and terminated according to rules that
    are specified a priori, explicit, potentially familiar to all partici-
    pants, and subject to change only according to rules. These rules
    specify (a) the criteria for being admitted as a political partici-
    pant, (b) the courses of action that constitute admissible strate-
    gies, and (c) the criteria by which conflicts are terminated . . .
3. Some courses of action are excluded as admissible strategies, in
    the sense that permanently organized physical force can be le-
    gitimately used if any group resorts to it. Such use of force is
    regulated by rules that specify the contingencies in which they
    can be applied universally and *ex ante*. Yet, since physical force
    is permanently organized in anticipation of such contingencies,
    the element of intimidation as well as the potential threat that
    this force might become autonomous is inherent in a demo-
    cratic system . . .
4. Conflicts are organized in a specific manner and their outcomes
    bear some relation to the particular combination of strategies
    pursued by various actors. Characteristic of a democracy is that
    each group has some choice of strategies and that strategies have
    consequences.
5. Since each participant (individual and collective) has a choice
    of strategies, and all strategies do not lead to the same outcome,
    the results of conflicts in a democracy are to some extent inde-
    terminate with regard to positions that the participants occupy
    in all social relations, including the relations of production.
    Capitalists do not always win conflicts that are processed in a
    democratic manner; indeed they have to struggle continuously
    in pursuit of their interests. In a democracy, no one can win
    once and for all: even if successful at one time, victors immedi-
    ately face the prospect of having to struggle in the future . . .
7. Outcomes of democratic conflicts are not simply indeterminate
    within limits. They are uncertain . . . The distribution of the
    probability of realizing group-specific interests—which is noth-
    ing less than political power—is determined jointly by the dis-
    tribution of resources that participants bring into conflicts and
    by specific institutional arrangements . . . Given a distribution
    of resources, the probability that any group will advance its in-
    terests to a definite degree and in a definite manner depends on

the way in which conflicts are organized. Electoral system, judicial procedures, collective bargaining arrangements, laws regulating the access to mass media or land use all shape the prior probabilities of the realization of group-specific interests. Extensions of the franchise to workers did have consequences for the improvement of their material conditions, as did the right to organize, the legalization of collective bargaining, and several other reforms. Reforms are precisely those modifications of the organization of conflicts that alter the prior probabilities of realizing group interests given their resources.

To summarize this description, let me extract three aspects of democracy that are crucial for the process of transition. First, democracy is a form of institutionalization of continual conflicts. Second, the capacity of particular groups to realize their interests is shaped by the specific institutional arrangements of a given system. Finally, although this capacity is given a priori, outcomes of conflicts are not uniquely determined either by the institutional arrangements or by places occupied by participants within the system of production. Outcomes that are unlikely can and do occur . . .

[Transition to Democracy as Contingent Compromise]
The process of establishing democracy is a process of institutionalizing uncertainty, of subjecting all interests to uncertainty. In an authoritarian regime, some groups, typically the armed forces, have the capacity of intervening whenever the result of a conflict is contrary to their program or their interests. Therefore the situation may be uncertain from the point of view of some groups—those that are excluded from the power bloc and that must consider the intervention of armed forces as an eventuality. But some groups have a high degree of control over the situation in the sense that they are not forced to accept undesirable outcomes. In a democracy, no group is able to intervene when outcomes of conflicts violate their self-perceived interests. Democracy means that all groups must subject their interests to uncertainty. It is this very act of alienation of control over outcomes of conflicts that constitutes the decisive step toward democracy . . .

This brings me to my principal thesis. Democratic compromise cannot be a substantive compromise; it can be only a contingent institutional compromise. It is within the nature of democracy that no one's interests can be guaranteed: in principle, workers endowed with universal franchise can even vote to nationalize the privately owned means of production, to dissolve the armed forces, and so on . . . Under democracy, no substantive compromises can be guaranteed. As Adolfo Suarez put it in a speech during the campaign of elections to the Constituent Assembly, "The future is not written because only the people can write it."[1]

What is possible are institutional agreements, that is, compromises about the institutions that shape prior probabilities of the realization of group-specific interests. If a peaceful transition to democracy is to be possible, the first problem to be solved is how to institutionalize uncertainty without threatening the interests of those who can still reverse the process . . .

Class Compromise and Capitalist Democracy

I would like to examine theoretically some rudimentary conditions of class compromise necessary to establish and maintain capitalist democracy . . . Capitalist democracy constitutes a form of class compromise in the sense that in this system neither the aggregate interests of individual capitalists nor the interests of organized wage-earners can be violated beyond specific limits . . . Profits cannot fall so low as to threaten reproduction of capital, and wages cannot fall so low as to make profits appear as a particularistic interest of capital.

Specifically, in a capitalist democracy, capitalists retain the capacity to withhold a part of societal product because the profits that they appropriate are expected to be saved, invested, transformed into productive capacity, and partly distributed as gains to other groups. Wage earners are persuaded to view capitalism as a system in which they can improve their material conditions; they act as if capitalism was a positive-sum system; they organize as participants and behave as if cooperation was in their interests when they expect to benefit in the future from the fact that a part of societal product is currently withheld from them in the form of profit. For their part, capitalists consent as a class when they expect that they will be able to appropriate profits in the future as a consequence of current investment.

This two-class model of democratic compromise is obviously too schematic to be useful in analyzing concrete historical situations.

Wage earners are never organized as a unitary actor. Capitalists compete with one another, not only in the market but also in trying to push upon one another the costs of reproducing workers' consent. The coalitions that underlie particular democratic compromises rarely comprise capitalists and workers as classes; more often than not, they are based on particular fractions allied against other workers and capitalists. Nevertheless, the very logic of class compromise, necessary to establish and maintain a democratic system elucidates the contents of economic projects that are likely to orient the formation of democratic institutions.

The typical democratizing coalition is likely to adopt a Keynesian economic project. A Keynesian orientation constitutes a perfect combination for guiding a tolerable compromise among several groups. It leaves the ownership of the means of production in private hands, and with it the authority to organize production. At the same time, it treats increases in lower incomes not only as just but also as technically efficient from the economic point of view. Moreover, it assigns an active role to the state in regulating the economy against cyclical crises. This combination of private property, redistribution of income, and a strong state seems like an ideal package for almost everyone.

Yet several experiences, including the second Peronist period in Argentina, demonstrate that the Keynesian project is extremely fragile. As long as private property is preserved, accumulation requires that capitalists appropriate profits and invest them. A redistribution of income, even if it increases consumption, aggregate demand, and supply in the short run, must eventually lead to crises of profitability and hence of investment. Indeed, if the economic structure is highly concentrated, rapid wage increases seem to result simultaneously in unemployment and inflation. And if wage increases are rapidly eroded by price increases and unemployment, the organizations that represent the poorer sectors of the population in the nascent democratic system are likely to lose their popular support. On the other hand, far reaching demands for the nationalization of the means of production are likely to meet with immediate resistance from indigenous and foreign capitalists and the withdrawal of their support for the democratic transformation.

Keynesian projects may thus be more appealing from the point of view of building a democratic coalition than they are auspicious for establishing a stable democratic regime: a good net to catch allies, but one highly vulnerable to anyone with sharp teeth. It seems as if an almost complete docility and patience on the part of organized workers are needed for a democratic transformation to succeed. Here it may be worth noting that the democratic system was solidified in Belgium, Sweden, France, and Great Britain only after organized workers were badly defeated in mass strikes and adopted a docile posture as a result . . . Indeed, a striking feature of the Spanish transition to democracy is that the political system has been transformed without affecting economic relations in any discernible manner . . .

[Conclusion]

We cannot avoid the possibility that a transition to democracy can be made only at the cost of leaving economic relations intact, not only the structure of production but even the distribution of income. Freedom from physical violence is as essential a value as freedom from hunger, but unfortunately authoritarian regimes often produce as a counterreaction the romanticization of a limited model of democracy. Democracy restricted to the political realm has historically coexisted with exploitation and oppression at the workplace, within the schools, within bureaucracies, and within families. Struggle for political power is necessary because without it all attempts to transform the society are vulnerable to brutal repression. Yet what we need, and do not have, is a more comprehensive, integral, ideological project of antiauthoritarianism that would encompass the totality of social life.

Note from the Editor

1. Cited in P. L. Verou, *Critica Juridico-Politica de la Reforma Suarez* (Madrid: Editorial Tecnos, 1976).

The Rule of Capital and the Rise of Democracy

Göran Therborn

[Capitalism and Democracy: Two Paradoxes]

The relationship between advanced capitalism and democracy contains two paradoxes—one Marxist and one bourgeois. Any serious Marxist analysis has to confront the following question: How has it come about that, in the major and most advanced capitalist countries, a tiny majority class—the bourgeoisie—rules by means of democratic forms? The bitter experiences of Fascism and Stalinism, and the enduring legacy of the latter, have taught the firmest revolutionary opponents of capitalism that bourgeois democracy cannot be dismissed as a mere sham. Does contemporary reality then not vitiate Marxist class analysis?

Present-day capitalist democracy is no less paradoxical from a bourgeois point of view. In the nineteenth and early twentieth centuries, as both political practice and constitutional debate clearly demonstrate, prevailing bourgeois opinion held that democracy and capitalism (or private property) were incompatible . . . In modern times, however, since at least the outbreak of the Cold War, bourgeois ideologists have maintained that *only* capitalism is compatible with democracy. What has happened? Is this perhaps just a *post hoc* rationalization of a historical accident? . . .

Although this article presents only a few preliminary reflections [on this], and by no means a definitive account, it will clearly have need of a representative sample of cases . . . One of the least arbitrary ways of choosing a sample is simply to take the members of the

Excerpts from Göran Therborn, "The Rule of Capital and the Rise of Democracy," *New Left Review* 103 (1977): 3–41. Reprinted by permission of the journal. Bracketed headings have been created by the editor of this volume.

OECD, which seems to be the broadest and most significant organization of the core capitalist states . . . The heart of the OECD appears to be the seventeen major capital-exporting states.[1] It is these
seventeen, then, that I shall take as our representative sample . . . In
our sample, the process of attainment of representative government
stretched over a period of two centuries: from the mid-eighteenth century, when a parliamentary cabinet was consolidated in Britain, to
1952, when US occupation of Japan was terminated and the 1947
democratic constitution took effect as the basis of a sovereign state . . .

Capitalism and Democracy: Inherent Tendencies

Bourgeois democracy has been attained by such diverse and tortuous routes that any straightforward derivation from the basic characteristics of capitalism would be impossible, or at best seriously
misleading. Nevertheless, the facts that democracy . . . did not appear anywhere prior to capitalism; that some capitalist countries have
experienced a purely internal development of democracy; and that
all major advanced bourgeois states are today democracies—these
naturally call for some elucidation of the tendencies inherent within
capitalism. These may provisionally be grouped according to their
effect upon two central features of bourgeois democracy: (a) inclusion of the masses in *part* of the political process, (b) under conditions of representative government and electoral competition . . .

Two internal facts seem to have been of the most immediate
strategic importance: the independent strength of the agrarian petty
bourgeois landowners, and divisions within the ruling class. This
statement should at once be qualified by mentioning the enormous
role of the labour movement . . . However, although the labour movement was the only consistent democratic force in the arena, it was
nowhere strong enough to achieve bourgeois democracy on its own,
without the aid of various foreign armies, domestic allies more powerful than itself, or splits in the ranks of the enemy[2] . . .

Bourgeois democracy has always succeeded mass struggles of
varying degrees of violence and protractedness. [An important] inherent tendency, then, will be found in *the conditions favouring popular
struggle.* Legal emancipation of labour and the creation of a free labour
market, industrialization, concentration of capital are all intrinsic
tendencies which simultaneously lay the basis for a working-class

movement of a strength and stability inachievable by the exploited classes of pre-capitalist modes of production. In accordance with Marx's analysis of the growing contradictions of capitalism, the working class is, *ceteris paribus*, strengthened by the advance and development of capitalism. This explains the traditional sociological correlations of democracy with wealth, literacy and urbanization—factors which bear upon the relationship of forces in the class struggle. And, as we have already seen, the labour movement has itself played a vital role in the struggle for democracy.

However, . . . in general the working class has not won a share in the political process in the heat of battle. On the contrary, it has been more common for the bourgeoisie to make concessions after a period of successful resistance to reform. Apparently, working-class participation must in some sense be to the bourgeoisie's advantage. Although in Germany and Austria in 1918 and 1945 (possibly also in Belgium and Sweden in 1918) and in Italy in 1945 the alternative to bourgeois democracy was an attempted socialist revolution, actual defence against proletarian revolution does not seem to have been a directly determining factor. In all these cases, it was not the insurrectionary proletariat but foreign armies that overthrew the existing regimes, whereupon the old internal democratic forces at last got the upper hand.

Of greater importance was the specifically capitalist art of industrialized warfare. The First World War was fought both with massive conscript armies and with whole civilian populations mobilized for military production. For this effort even the Wilhelmine Reich admitted the Social Democrats into the governmental machinery; against this background, too, the suffrage was extended in Belgium, Canada, Britain and the United States.

National unification and liberation have everywhere been seen by the bourgeoisie as a strategic necessity for the development and protection of trade and industry and the breaking of feudal dynastic power. And for these aims it has often found it invaluable to enlist popular support. The extension of suffrage in Denmark, Germany, Norway, Finland and Italy (for the imperialist Libyan expedition) formed part of a process of national unification.

Feverish development of the productive forces is another feature peculiar to the capitalist mode of exploitation. One of the main reasons why nineteenth- and early twentieth-century liberals could deny the compatibility of democracy with private property was their dread that popular legislatures and municipal bodies would greatly increase taxation. However, they were disregarding the elasticity and expansive capacity of capitalism. Higher levels of taxation have liquidated neither private property nor capital accumulation. Rises in productivity make possible a simultaneous increase of both rates of exploitation and real incomes of the exploited masses. This is, of course, not in itself conducive to democracy. But it is relevant in so far as it provides the bourgeoisie with an unprecedentedly wide room for manoeuvre in dealing with the exploited majority . . .

What makes capitalist democracy at all possible is a characteristic unique among known modes of production. Capitalism is an impersonal mode of exploitation, involving the rule of capital rather than personal domination of the bourgeoisie. It certainly does not function in the manner of an automatic machine, but it does operate as production for ever greater profit under conditions of impersonal market competition. The rule of capital requires a state—for both internal and external support and protection—but, as long as it upholds the separate realm of capitalist 'civil society,' this state does not have to be managed personally by bourgeois. And in the long history of democratization, bourgeois politicians have learnt the many mechanisms at their disposal to keep the state in harmony with the needs of capital.

This last-mentioned feature of capitalism may explain why the impersonal rule of a tiny minority is conceivable in democratic forms—why, for example, the rule of capital is compatible with a labour party government, whereas a feudal aristocracy cannot be governed by a peasant party. But a theoretical possibility is one thing, actual historical dynamics quite another. And the fight of the working class for universal suffrage and freely elected government was never by itself sufficient to enforce the introduction of bourgeois democracy.

This raises the question whether there are other internal tendencies of capitalism, which, under certain conditions, may generate forces of democratization apart from working-class struggle. One such tendency may be immediately identified. Capitalist relations of production tend to create an *internally competing, peacefully disunited ruling class*. In its development, capital is divided into several fractions: mercantile, banking, industrial, agrarian, small and big. Except in a situation of grave crisis or acute threat from an enemy (whether feudal, proletarian or a rival national state) bourgeois class relations contain no unifying element comparable to the dynastic kingship legitimacy and fixed hierarchy of feudalism. Furthermore, the development of capitalism has usually stimulated the expansion of petty commodity production, before tending to destroy it. Thus, the commercialization of agriculture transformed a self-subsistent peasantry into an agrarian petty bourgeoisie with distinct interests of its own.

In the absence of a single centre, some kind of elective, deliberative and representative political machinery became necessary. Therefore, propertied republics or parliamentary monarchies developed at an early stage in the formation of capitalist states—for example, the Italian, German and Swiss city republics, the United Provinces of the Low Countries, Britain, the United States, France and Belgium (the latter after 1830) . . .

Democratization and Class Struggle

Bourgeois democracy is no mere accident of history, and capitalism does contain a number of tendencies which are conducive to processes of democratization. Thus, it has frequently, and correctly, been observed that bourgeois democracy entails a competitive division within a basic framework of unity—even if this statement is interpreted in a naively idealistic way, by reference to ideology and varieties of "political culture." But the concrete economic and political dynamic of the rise of capitalism does involve the struggle for and development of a new divided unity. This appears as the *nation state*, freed of the barriers and boundaries of dynastic legitimacy, feudal enfiefment and provincial tradition . . .

Freedom of trade and industry created a network of divisive competitive relationships which ran through the new ruling class of the unified and sovereign states. The market replaced the hierarchical pyramid of medieval and Absolutist feudalism. And it was in this unity-division of national state and market that the process of democratization originated. This happened fundamentally in one of two different ways. In certain cases, democracy was first introduced for upper layers of the bourgeoisie (including commercialized landowners), who alone had the right to vote and form parliamentary or republican governments. Other sections of the bourgeoisie and petty bourgeoisie were subsequently included in this structure, according to widely varying tempos and modalities. However, where the bourgeois revolution stopped half way, democratization began as a constitutional compromise between the old landowning ruling class—including its apex, the dynasty—and the bourgeoisie. This system then developed either into a propertied democracy, as in Scandinavia, the Netherlands and Belgium, or into a still largely non-democratic form of government based on an extended franchise, as in Austria, Germany and Japan.

These are, of course, only the principal routes followed by the process, and specific detours such as the Jacobin régime of 1793 also have to be taken into account. But if these routes accurately express the general pattern, as I believe they do, then we may conclude that bourgeois democracy, in the same way as its Athenian predecessor, first arose as a democracy for male members of the ruling class alone. Only after protracted struggle were these rights extended to the ruled and exploited classes as well . . .

Leaving aside Switzerland, where armed male artisans and peasants won democratic rights in a series of violent struggles in the 1830s, '40s and '50s, neither of the two main processes of this first stage led to the establishment of democracy for all adult men, not to speak of the whole adult population. With this one partial exception, then, competitive capitalism has nowhere led to bourgeois democracy as a result of its own positive tendencies. A Marxist analysis of capitalism, however, must take up centrally the contradictions of the system. And it has been the development of the basic contradiction between capital and labour that has carried democracy beyond the boundaries of the ruling class and its props.

Thus, the second stage in the struggle for democracy was largely shaped by the emergence of the working class and the labour movement. The capitalist mode of production gives birth to an exploited class with capacities of organized opposition far superior to those of any previous one. In fact, the labour movement fought almost everywhere not only for higher wages and better working conditions, but also for political democracy—either as an end in itself (the British Chartists or the Australian and New Zealand trade-union movement) or as an integral part of the struggle for socialism (the parties of the Second International).

However, the working-class movement was nowhere capable of achieving democracy by its own unaided resources—and this tells much of the strength of bourgeois rule. From the Chartists in the 1840s to the Belgian Social Democrats just prior to, and the Japanese workers just after, the First World War such attempts always resulted in defeat. Only in conjunction with external allies were the non-propertied masses able to gain democratic rights; and it was above all the propertied minorities who in the end answered the critical questions of timing and form—of when and how democracy was to be introduced. Thus, the process of democratization unfolded within the framework of the capitalist state, congealing in the form of bourgeois democracy rather than opening the road to popular revolution and socialist transformation.

The most important allies of the working class in the struggle for democracy were the following: victorious armies of foreign bourgeois states, the small and the self-employed petty bourgeoisie, and a section of the ruling class itself. The role of these allies follows, of course, from other contradictions of capitalism—imperialist rivalry, national conflicts, the contradiction of competition and monopolization, and clashes between different fractions of capital.

In the space opened up by these contradictions, the weight of the working class could be brought to bear on the process of democratization, even in the absence of a significant labour movement. For example, the working-class vote could be utilized by bourgeois organizations and politicians for their own ends, as was most evidently the case in the United States. Here the political "machines" even found a place for new immigrant workers, excluded from the franchise by literacy tests, poll-taxes and registration statutes, by enlisting their support for the system of political graft—for a kind of city-level state capitalism. These machines were normally run by sections of the bourgeoisie distinct from established big capital.

[Conclusion:] The Two Paradoxes Explained

We are now in a position to confront the two paradoxes with which we started. For Marxists, it will be remembered, the problem appeared as one of explaining how a tiny social minority has come to rule predominantly in democratic forms; while for bourgeois liberal thought, it seemed an insoluble mystery that classical liberals were convinced of the incompatibility of capitalism and democracy, whereas contemporary bourgeois opinion maintains that *only* capitalism is compatible with democracy.

The solution to the Marxist problem is by now fairly clear. Bourgeois democracy has always and everywhere been established in struggle against (hegemonic fractions of) the bourgeoisie, but through political means and channels provided for by the capitalist state. Moreover, when it has been threatened or destroyed, the labour movement has taken up the struggle anew against the leading fraction of the ruling class (as in Austria, Finland, France, Germany and Italy). Thus, although bourgeois democracy is democratic government plus the rule of capital, its democratic component has been achieved and defended against the bourgeoisie.

The bourgeois paradox is resolved when we grasp a feature of the process to which classical liberalism quite naturally paid scant attention. Democracy developed neither out of the positive tendencies of capitalism, nor as a historical accident, but out of the *contradictions* of capitalism. Bourgeois democracy has been viable at all only because of the elasticity and expansive capacity of capitalism, which were grossly underestimated by classical liberals and Marxists alike . . . This leads on directly to further important areas of investigation: mechanisms of containment of the working class, development of the repressive apparatuses and the rise of anti-democratic forces. But our present contribution to analysis of the establishment of bourgeois democracy will end here.

Notes from the Editor

1. Australia, Austria, Belgium, Canada, Denmark, Finland, France, German Federal Republic, Italy, Japan, Netherlands, New Zealand, Norway, Sweden, Switzerland, United Kingdom, and United States.
2. In the original, this last paragraph appears before the preceding one. For the sake of clarity the editor has reversed the order.

Economic Development and Democracy
[The Role of Subordinate Classes]

Selections from the Work of
Evelyne Huber, Dietrich Rueschemeyer, and John D. Stephens

For a society to become democratic, the power balance in civil society has to shift. Civil society is the public sphere distinguished from the state, the economy and the web of family and kin relations. It comprises all social groups, associations and institutions that are not strictly production-related, nor governmental or familial in character. Since the major power resource of the many is collective organization, their chance to organize in associations, unions and parties gains critical significance.

Among social classes we focus in the first place on dominant and subordinate positions—on landlords and peasants in the agrarian sector and on major capital owners (classically labeled the bourgeoisie) and workers in the industrial sector. Independent small and medium farmers, craftsmen, merchants, and the new white collar employees—often collectively referred to as the middle-classes—stand in between; but before the attainment of democracy they, too, were in most countries excluded from political participation. Democratic participation in political decision-making will develop and be sustained only if the economic and cultural power of dominant groups is counterbalanced in civil society by the organizational power of subordinate classes.

The structure of the state and state-society relations are also clearly relevant for the chances in democracy. The state needs to be strong and autonomous enough to ensure the rule of law and avoid being the captive of the interests of dominant groups; the state's authority to make binding decisions in a territory and the state's monopoly of co-

Excerpts from Evelyne Huber, Dietrich Rueschemeyer, and John D. Stephens, "The Impact of Economic Development on Democracy," *Journal of Economic Perspectives* 7 (1993): 71–85. Reprinted by permission of the American Economic Association. Bracketed headings have been created by the editor of this volume.

ercion must be settled. The vote does not rule where it competes with the gun. However, the power of the state needs to be counterbalanced by the organizational strength of the civil society to make democracy possible; the state must not be so strong and autonomous from all social forces as to overpower civil society and rule without accountability. Thus, centralized state control over the economy and the presence of a large military and police apparatus are conditions inimical to a favorable power balance between state and civil society. The relation of the state to religious organization is another critical factor. Civil society gains strength from non-established religious movements, while an alliance of "crown and altar" strengthens the hand of the state.

The third power cluster involves international power relations. Aside from the impact of war (typically creating a need for mass support and discrediting ruling groups in case of defeat), we look especially into the role of economic and geopolitical dependence . . . We expected dependency to be an important factor but one without a clear-cut, unequivocal effect.

The three power clusters—relative class power, the role of the state, and the impact of transnational power structures—are closely interrelated. For instance, economic dependency can have long term effects on the structures of class; war and geopolitical factors can strengthen the role of the security forces within the state; and the results of power relations in civil society are crucially affected by differential access to the state apparatus.

Our central thesis, and indeed our most basic finding, can now be stated in stark fashion: Capitalist development is related to democracy because it shifts the balance of class power, because it weakens the power of the landlord class and strengthens subordinate classes. The working and the middle classes—unlike other subordinate classes in history—gain an unprecedented capacity for self-organization due to such developments as urbanization, factory production, and new forms of communication and transportation.

This thesis negates other explanations. The primary link between capitalist development and democracy is not found in an expansion of the middle classes . . . Democracy is not the creation of the bourgeoisie, the new dominant class of capital owners, as was claimed by both liberal and Marxist political theory. The bourgeoisie made important contributions to the move towards democracy by insisting on its share in political power in the form of parliamentary control of the state, but the bourgeoisie was also hostile to further democratization when its interests seemed threatened . . . It is also important to note that the bourgeoisie often comes around to support democracy once it turns out that its interests can be protected within the system.

Having stated the thesis bluntly, some warnings to the reader are in order. We are not arguing that the correlation between level of development and degree of democratization is unilinear or automatic. And we certainly are not arguing that class is all that matters. Although we consider the shift in the balance of class power to be the most important factor accounting for the positive correlation between development and democracy, our analysis leaves ample room for the other two clusters of power and for complex interactions among them. Perhaps the biggest complicating factor, given the centrality of the balance of class power in our overall interpretation of the association of development and democracy, is that class interests are not ahistorical givens; they are historically constructed by movements, organizations and leaderships that act in some particular environment of influences and oppositions, possible alliances and enmities . . .

The fact that class interests are historically constructed has crucial consequences for the analysis. It raises interclass relations to critical importance. One class may exercise hegemonic influence over another, and this will affect the alliance options among classes. The interests actually pursued by peasants and even by urban middle classes are often profoundly shaped by landlords, the bourgeoisie, and the state as well as state-affiliated churches. The alliance developments at the top—among landlords, bourgeoisie, and the state—can be decisive for the alliance options of other classes. This is of critical importance for the chances of democracy because the working class, even the European working class, was too weak on its own to succeed in the final push toward democracy with universal suffrage.

[Democratic Transition and Breakdown in Europe]

In 1870, only one European country, Switzerland, was a democracy. Many countries frequently thought to be democratic at this time such as Britain, Netherlands, and Belgium, had parliamentary government and competitive party systems, but the electorate was limited by income or property qualifications. By contrast, by 1920, almost all Western European countries were fully democratic. This period of transition to democracy in Europe was also marked by the arrival of the organized working class. The change in the underlying class structure as indicated by labor force figures is significant enough: between 1870 and 1910, the non-agricultural workforce grew by one-third to one-half, eventually reaching an average of 61 percent of the total workforce in the 13 European countries we studied.

The change at the level of class formation and class organization was even more significant: in 1870, in no country were the socialists a significant mass-based party, and the trade unions organized a minuscule proportion of the labor force. By the eve of World War I, the major socialist and labor parties garnered an average of 26 percent of the vote (despite suffrage restrictions in a number of countries) and the trade unions organized an average of 11 percent of the non-agricultural labor force. In the immediate postwar elections, the socialists' electoral share increased to an average of 32 percent, while trade union organizations grew spectacularly, increasing two and a half times. The organized working class was also the most consistently pro-democratic force in the period under consideration: at the onset of World War I, European labor movements had converged on an ideology which placed the achievement of universal suffrage and parliamentary government at the center of their program.

Though the working class was the main agent of democracy in Europe, it needed allies. It found them in the urban middle classes and the independent small farming population. Without these groups, the working class was too weak to press through full democracy. Indeed, in Switzerland and Norway, two countries which (like the north and west of the United States during the Jacksonian period) might be termed agrarian democracies, these groups were more important in the struggle for democracy than the working class. However, unlike the working class, both the urban middle classes and small farmers were not consistently pro-democratic: In some countries, they were ambivalent about the introduction to democracy and, in the interwar period, they provided mass support for fascism and other authoritarian movements which destroyed the new democratic regimes.

What was the role of the bourgeoisie, the class of the major

owners of capital? In only three of the 13 European countries studied—France, Switzerland, and Britain—did any significant segment
of the bourgeoisie play a leading role in promoting full democracy.
Significantly, in all three of these cases, the bourgeoisie did not face
a working class politically organized by socialist parties at the time
of democratic transition; in ten of the other eleven countries, it did
face such an opponent. Fear of challenges to property rights certainly played an important role in the reticence of propertied upper
classes to support political inclusion of the working class.

As Barrington Moore has argued, the existence of a powerful
class of landlords dependent on a large supply of cheap labor were
associated with significant problems for democracy: In four of the
five Western European countries in which large landholders played
a significant political role towards the end of the nineteenth century—Germany, Austria-Hungary, Spain and Italy—democratic regimes collapsed in the interwar period. In each of these countries,
the landed upper classes, in coalition with the state and the bourgeoisie, were crucially implicated in the weakness of the push toward democracy outside of the working class movement before World
War I and in the events that led to the demise of democracy in the
interwar period.

[Democratic Transition and Breakdown in South America]

Does Latin America show similar developments? Patterns for large
landholding and the existence of a powerful class of landlords with a
need for a large cheap labor force also posed significant problems for
democracy in South America. Breakthroughs to full democracy before the 1970s, even if temporary, were only possible where the large
landowners were primarily engaged in ranching and thus had lower
labor needs (Argentina and Uruguay), or where their economic power
was undermined or counterbalanced by the presence of a strong
mining export sector (Venezuela and Bolivia).

Like its counterpart in Europe, the bourgeoisie was not a pro-
moter of full democracy in South America. As in Europe, the forces
pushing for democracy were the organized segments of the subordinate classes, but the leadership roles were reversed. In South America
the middle classes were the driving force, but they mainly promoted

their own inclusion and thus often accepted restricted forms of democracy. For full democracy to be installed, the middle classes had to be dependent on working class support in their push for democracy, and they had to receive support from a working class which had some measure of strength. Peron's Argentina (1946–55) provides a dramatic illustration that the working class was not invariably pro-democratic, and could be attracted to support authoritarian rulers, if these rulers were the first ones to include the working class on a large scale and to promise to satisfy its material demands in a meaningful way.

The political history of 20th century Latin America is characterized by numerous breakthroughs to restricted or full democracies, then followed by breakdowns of democracy. Essentially, the economically dominant classes tolerated democracy only as long as what they perceived to be their vital interests were protected. Where the capacity of the state or political parties to channel and contain militant action of subordinate classes declined, economic elites turned to the military in search of allies to replace the democratic with authoritarian regimes.

State structure and state-society relations were inimical to democratization in Latin America in several ways. State consolidation had to be achieved in a much shorter period and later relative to economic development than in Europe, and without a consolidated state there could be no democracy. The independence wars (1810–25) and later wars over borders (for example, the War of the Pacific, Peru and Bolivia against Chile, 1879–83) left the societies with a strong legacy of militarism. Furthermore, rather than industrialization leading to urbanization and an export economy, as happened in Europe, Latin America saw the growth of the export economy and of urbanization preceding industrialization. This gave the state additional power, and in many cases led to attempts by the state to preempt an independent organization of the emerging industrial working class.

Finally, in the post-World War II period the state's coercive capacity grew stronger, in part due to the U.S. military assistance, as did the state's capacity to mobilize economic resources independent of domestic economically dominant classes. This gave the state greater autonomy from civil society and generated a new form of anti-democratic regimes, called bureaucratic-authoritarian regimes, in which the military as an institution exercised power and engaged in large-scale repression of labor movements and reformist political parties (as in Brazil after 1964, Chile after 1973, and Argentina after 1976).

These developments also involve the impact of the third power cluster, the ways in which the international economy and system of states were important for the trajectory of democratization in South America. The crucial role of the state as intermediary to international markets for goods, capital, and technology afforded the state significant autonomy from civil society. This autonomy was reinforced through external support for the security forces. The position of South American countries in the world economy as late and dependent developers, with imported technology, resulted in small industrial working classes compared to Europe at similar levels of economic development, and thus in class structures inimical to democratization. Economic dependence further meant high vulnerability to fluctuations in world markets, and the resulting economic instability made stabilization and legitimization of regimes difficult, whether those regimes were authoritarian or democratic . . .

[Conclusion]

[In conclusion:] The level of economic development is causally related to the development of political democracy. However, the underlying reason for the connection, in our view, is that capitalist development transforms the class structure, enlarging the working and middle classes and facilitating their self-organization, thus making it more difficult for elites to exclude them politically. Simultaneously, development weakens the landed upper class, democracy's most consistent opponent. The development of the class structure hardly accounts for all national differences in democratic development . . . but it is of central importance.

Some readers may be familiar with the argument that the bourgeoisie played an important role as the agents of democratic reform, and thus may be surprised at how little weight we give this factor. Surely, leading businessmen in contemporary advanced capitalist countries are rightly regarded as supporters of democracy. However, most of their predecessors in 19th century Europe and 20th century Latin America were not, because they feared that extending suffrage to workers would represent a threat to their material interests. As democracy was established during the 20th century and these fears proved to be exaggerated, the bourgeoisies of advanced capitalist societies gradually came to accept and then strongly to support democratic institutions . . . And one can hope that contemporary South America is experiencing the same phenomenon . . .

In the case of both workers and businessmen, our analysis shows that their political posture toward democratic institutions was motivated in no small part by their perception of how democracy would affect their material interests. On this account, one can say that the current economic problems in the Third World, economic stagnation and the crushing debt, are also a problem for democracy. There is no doubt that rapid economic growth, or a growing economic pie, facilitates compromise between capital and labor and that, conversely, slow growth makes it almost impossible to satisfy both parties. Under such conditions, demands for mere economic betterment on the part of workers become a threat to business.

The analysis leads us to expect some countries within the Third World to have better prospects for democratization than others. Most obviously, the prospects are brighter for those countries at higher levels of economic development. However, as our analysis made clear, it is not the mere rise in per capita income (created, for example, by mineral wealth) that is of greatest importance, but rather the changes in the class and social structure caused by industrialization and urbanization which are most consequential for democracy. In addition, the analysis of agrarian class relations leads us to the conclusion that democratic prospects are much better in Third World countries without a significant group of large landholders and with a significant agrarian middle class.

Part IV

Elites in Democracy and Democratization— New Analyses

Introduction

Field and his colleagues open their contribution to this volume with the claim that elites have come to be at the core of political analysis. This claim is borne out by the plethora of writings from which the selection for this part had to be made. In quantity, contemporary elite analyses certainly overshadow contemporary class analyses of democracy. Moreover, the recent vintage of this school of thought not merely enriches the theoretical literature, but also branches out into a large number of analyses of concrete transitions to democracy in various parts of the world.

In order to do at least partial justice to the embarrassment of riches in this field today, it was necessary to make this part the longest part of the volume. It starts with general elite analyses of democracy, or analyses which, though they pertain to a specific country, may be generalized to all democracies. It then moves on to analyses of specific democratic transitions in one or more areas/countries of the world.

Opening this part is a contribution by Dye and Zeigler, that is a modern descendant of the classical mainstream elite theory: it offers a skeptical view of democracy, albeit with a new twist. The pieces by Polsby and Sartori also add new twists to earlier theories and, at the same time, are responses to mainstream elite views of democracy, such as that by Dye and Zeigler. The contribution by Field, Higley and Burton and that by Karl and Schmitter, for their part, may be regarded as general frameworks for the more concrete analyses of transition to democracy, which follow in their wake.

Dye and Zeigler present an intriguing thesis on the "irony of democracy": democracy, which is ostensibly government by the people, survives because elites, not the people, govern. The preservation of democracy rests on the shoulders of elites, for they, not the people, are most committed to its values. The masses are ill-informed and apathetic, and democracy works best when they are only minimally involved in politics. Intriguing as this thesis is, it lays itself open to the charge of excessive cynicism.

Such a critique is, in fact, implied by Polsby and Sartori, who take a very different view of democracy. These authors' contributions may be referred to as pluralist-elitist. They are descended from the pluralist school, which held sway in the 1950s. It contended that power in a democracy was diffused among a plurality of interest groups that checked each other, and none of which possessed decisive power. Through their affiliation with such groups, all parts of the public could make themselves heard in the decision-making processes. These ideas were later discredited as overly naive, and even some of their own erstwhile advocates (such as Dahl) subsequently adopted more sophisticated views of democracy.[1] The contributions by Polsby and Sartori are examples of such sophisticated pluralist analyses: they adhere to the notion of pluralism, yet assign elites a more central role in a democracy than pluralists were wont to do before.

Thus, Polsby sees the United States (and by implication democracies in general) as moving toward greater pluralism. Yet he sees pluralism as embodied not in the dispersion and dissipation of power, but rather in the greater variety of linkages between leaders and their followers, the people. Sartori is committed to the pluralist view that democracies are characterized by a diffusion of power and an overload of conflicting demands, yet assigns a major democratic role to leaders, their responsiveness, and responsibility.

Have pluralist-elite analyses such as these still overestimated the diffusion of power in a democracy? This is the view implied by analytical schemes such as those by Field, Higley, and Burton, whose focus is chiefly on elite configurations and their impact on the structure of regimes. According to this scheme, disunified elites generate unstable regimes; ideologically unified elites (whose unity is imposed from above) give rise to stable autocratic regimes; consensually unified elites (that are divided ideologically, yet are unified by their agreement on the rules of the political game) produce representative democracies. Consensual elite unity is the result of historical elite settlements or convergences. While this framework contains some tautological elements (democracy prevails when elites agree to adhere to its rules) it is nonetheless very useful, as attested to by several studies in this volume, that do in fact utilize it (see below).

A partly diverging framework for democratic transitions is that by Karl and Schmitter. According to these authors, the mode that has most often resulted in democracy is transition "from above," by elite actors. This transition takes place either through the forcible imposition of democracy by elites, or through compromises resulting from agreements between contending elites, which define the rules of governance on the basis of mutual guarantees of their interests.

While the general perspectives on democracy or democratization are naturally of great importance, it is time now to turn to the nitty-gritty of actual democratic transitions in various parts of the world. Opening this type of analysis is the piece by Burton and Ryu, which successfully applies the Field-Higley-Burton scheme to the democratic transition in South Korea. This is followed by Morlino's analysis focusing on the strategic role of party elites in democratic transitions in Southern Europe.

Next, are two pieces on Latin America. The first, by O'Donnell, calls attention to a yet unexplored type of democracy prevalent in countries that have but recently undergone the first stages of democratization. This is delegative democracy, in which the leaders are elected, but subsequently eschew accountability to the public and to organized interests, and thereby lead their countries into increasingly severe democratic crises. The second piece, by Reis and Cheibub, reports on the attitudes of Brazilian elites to democracy, in an attempt to establish the extent to which they do (or do not) foster democracy in that country.

Last, is a piece on Eastern Europe, the latecomer to the scene of regime transitions. This, the concluding piece of Part IV, by Wesolowski, pertains to Poland. Here, the author identifies a type of elite agreement which, in contrast to that envisaged by Field-Higley-Burton, signals the death of one of the signatories. He further identifies a shortage of elites' transformative powers, which encumbers the transition to democracy.

All in all, elite analyses thus offer a rich tapestry of perspectives, counterperspectives, theoretical schemes, and descriptions of democratic reality and transitions. The very proliferation of such analyses constitutes at least *prima facie* evidence of their fruitfulness. Yet, once we have perused them—together with those in the previous parts of the volume—we are still left with the question: are class-impacts and elite-impacts on democracy and democratization either-or propositions? Are there not also some insights to be gained from viewing them side-by-side or in combination with each other? It is to these questions that the final part of this volume is devoted.

Note from the Editor

1.   See Dahl in this volume.

The Irony of Democracy

Thomas Dye and Harmon Zeigler

In an industrial, scientific, and nuclear age, life in a democracy, just as in a totalitarian society, is shaped by a handful of people. Major political, economic, and social decisions are made by tiny minorities, not the masses of people . . . Democracy is government "by the people," but the survival of democracy rests on the shoulders of elites. This is the irony of democracy: elites must govern wisely if government "by the people" is to survive. The masses do not lead; they follow. They respond to the attitudes, proposals, and behavior of elites . . .

The Meaning of Elitism

The central idea of elitism is that all societies are divided into two classes: the few who govern and the many who are governed . . . Elitism also asserts that the few who govern are not typical of the masses who are governed. Elites control resources: power, wealth, education, prestige, status, skills of leadership, information, knowledge of political processes, ability to communicate and organization . . . They come from society's upper classes, those who own or control a disproportionate share of the societal institutions: industry, commerce, finance, education, the military, communications, civic organizations, and law . . .

Elite theory admits of some social mobility that enables nonelites to become elites. In fact, a certain amount of "circulation of elites" (upward mobility) is essential for the stability of the elite system.

Excerpts from Thomas Dye and Harmon Zeigler, *The Irony of Democracy*, tenth ed. (Belmont, Calif.: Wadsworth, 1996), 1–4, 16–20. Copyright © Wadsworth Publishing Co. Reprinted by permission of the publisher. Bracketed headings have been created by the editor of this volume.

Openness in the system siphons off potentially revolutionary leadership from the lower classes; moreover, an elite system is strengthened when talented and ambitious individuals from the masses enter governing circles. However, social stability requires that movement from nonelite to elite positions be a slow, continuous assimilation rather than a rapid or revolutionary change. Only those nonelites who have demonstrated their commitment to the elite system itself and to the system's political and economic values can be admitted to the ruling class. Elites share a general consensus about the fundamental norms of the social system. They agree on the basic rules of the game, as well as on the importance of preserving the social system. The stability of the system, and even its survival depend on this consensus . . .

Public policy does not reflect demands "of the people" so much as it reflects the interests and values of elites. Changes and innovations in public policies come about when elites redefine their own values. However, the general conservatism of elites—that is, their interest in preserving the system—means that changes in public policies will be incremental rather than revolutionary. Public policies are often modified but seldom replaced.

Elites may act out of narrow self-serving interest or enlightened, "public-regarding" motives. Occasionally elites abuse their powers and position and undermine mass confidence in their leadership. At other times, elites initiate reforms designed to preserve the system and restore mass support. Elitism does not necessarily mean that the masses are exploited or repressed, although these abuses are not uncommon. Elitism means only that the responsibility for mass welfare rests with elites, not with masses.

Finally, elitism assumes that the masses are largely passive, apathetic, and ill informed. Mass sentiments are manipulated by elites more often than elite values are influenced by the sentiments of the masses. Most communication between elites and masses flows downward. Masses seldom make decisions about governmental policies through elections or through evaluation of political parties' policy alternatives. For the most part, these "democratic" institutions—elections and parties—have only symbolic value: they help tie the masses to the political system by giving them a role to play on election day. Elitism contends that the masses have at best only an indirect influence over the decision-making behavior of elites . . .

Elite theory suggests that accommodation and compromise among leadership groups is the prevailing style of decision making, not competition and conflict. Pluralism contends that competition among leadership groups protects the individual. But why should we assume that leadership groups compete with each other? More likely, each elite group allows other elite groups to govern in their own spheres of influence without interference. According to elite theory, accommodation rather than competition is the prevailing style of elite interaction: "You scratch my back and I'll scratch yours." . . .

Elite and Mass Threats to Democracy

It is the irony of democracy that the survival of democratic values—individual dignity, limited government, equality of opportunity, private property, freedom of speech and press, religious tolerance, and due process of law—depends on enlightened elites. The masses respond to the ideas and actions of elites. When elites abandon democratic principles, or the masses lose confidence in elites, democracy is in peril.

Yet democratic elites do not always live up to their responsibilities to preserve the system and its values. Elite behavior is not always enlightened and farsighted, but is instead frequently shortsighted and narrowly self-serving . . . Examples of narrowly self-serving elite behavior abound. Politicians resort to divisive, racial appeals or to class antagonisms—setting black against white or poor against rich—to win elections, knowing that these tactics undermine mass confidence in national leadership. Corporate officials sacrifice long-term economic growth for short-term, windfall, paper profits, knowing that the nation's competitive position in the world is undermined by short-sighted "bottom-line" policies. Banking and savings and loan executives finance risky ventures in search of quick profits, knowing that their failures will be paid for by depositors and taxpayers. Members of Congress in pursuit of personal pay and perks as well as lifetime tenure cater to the political activists in their home districts, with little regard for national concerns. Bureaucrats, seeking to expand their powers and budgets, create a regulatory quagmire and huge government deficits, disadvantaging the nation in global competition and burdening future generations with enormous debts . . .

In short, elites do not always act with unity and purpose. They all too frequently put narrow interests ahead of broader, shared values. These behaviors . . . are encouraged by the absence of any external checks on the power of elites in their various domains. The only effective check on irresponsible elite behavior is their own realization that the system itself will become endangered if such behavior continues unrestrained. So periodically elites undertake reforms, mutually agreeing to curb the most flagrant abuses of the system. The stimulus to reform is the restoration of mass confidence in elite government, and ultimately the preservation of the elite system itself. But reforms often succeed only in creating new opportunities for abuse, changing the rules but failing to restrain self-interested elites.

But mass politics can also threaten democratic values. Despite a superficial commitment to the symbols of democracy, the masses have surprisingly weak commitments to the principles of individual liberty, toleration of diversity, and freedom of expression when required to apply these principles to despised or obnoxious groups or individuals. In contrast, elites, and the better educated groups from which they are recruited, are generally more willing than the masses to apply democratic values to specific situations and to protect the freedoms of unpopular groups . . .

It is the irony of democracy that democratic values can survive only in the absence of mass political activism. Democratic values thrive best when the masses are absorbed in the problems of everyday life and involved in groups and activities that distract their attention from mass political movements. Political stability depends on mass involvement in work, family, neighborhood, trade union, hobby, church, group recreation and other activities. When the masses become alienated from home, work, and community—when their ties to social organizations and institutions weaken—they become vulnerable to the appeals of demagogues, and democratic values are endangered . . .

[Conclusion]

Elite theory is not an apology for elite rule; it is not a defense of official misdeeds or repression. Rather, it is a realistic explanation of

how democracy works, how democratic values are both preserved
and threatened, how elites and masses interact, how public policy is
actually determined, and whose interests generally prevail . . .

Elite theory neither endorses nor condemns elite governance,
but rather seeks to expose and analyze the way in which elites function in a democracy. It is true that elite theory denies the possibility
of ever abolishing elite rule. But, by providing a better understanding of how elites in a democratic society go about gaining, exercising, and maintaining power, elite theory identifies both the obstacles
and the opportunities for social progress . . .

Prospects for Pluralism
[Linkages Between Leaders and Followers
in the American Democracy]

*Selections from the Work of
Nelson W. Polsby*

What are the prospects for pluralism in the United States? . . . We
would have to consider the autonomous (self-governing) existence
of [interest] groups; the existence of rules of political conduct that
at the least prevent the suppression of, or, more generously, facilitate the formation or mobilization of such groups for political
purposes; and the access of some sizable portion of the population to such groups. By prospects, we might mean: Are there
trends that, if persisted in, will materially alter the political condition of groups of this sort in the United States over the next
decade or so?

[Questions to Be Considered]
In principle a polity shows its pluralistic character on at least three
levels. As to leaders: Are there, as in a federal system, different arenas
of decision making with many different decision makers? Is there a
circulation of leaders in and out of decision-making roles? Do leaders recognize restrictions on their authority, processes of accountability or checks and balances? Do such restrictions exist, regardless
of leaders' awareness of them? As to followers: Are there many different sorts of cleavages in society? Do people normally distribute
themselves into groups in such a way as to create large numbers of
groups with overlapping members? Are people—nominally or actively—members of many different groups? As to processes of intermediation between leaders and followers: Are there many possible

linkages between leaders and followers? . . . Are there varied means for followers to reach leaders with their concerns, and do followers avail themselves of these varied means?

A thorough consideration of the prospects for pluralism would discuss all three levels; I restrict myself here to the issue of intermediation. In discussing pluralism I am neither endorsing nor condemning it. Pluralism in a political system may conduce to democratic practices, as we understand them; I believe on the whole it does. [But] empirical study of a sort different from that which I undertake here is necessary to ascertain whether the contemporary United States is pluralistic or democratic enough to suit the preferences of observers of varied minds . . .

[Linkages Between Leaders and Followers]

In a pluralistic system we should expect that linkages between leaders and followers, between those to whom policy applies and those charged with formulating and applying policy would be diverse. The more diverse they are, the more pluralistic the system; the less diverse, the less pluralistic. Trends that encourage this diversity and that sustain varied institutions that maintain these varied linkages are trends favoring pluralism, and conversely.

What sorts of messages are supposed to flow back and forth between leaders and followers? Both variety and volume play a part, and a two-way street has to be present. Frequency of petition for redress of grievances in specific matters of business between individual citizens and the government would constitute a meaningful measurement of intermediation, but so, in the presence of dense follower-to-leader communication, would frequency of communication from leaders to followers in the form, for example, of congressionally franked mail.

[Linkages Between Congress and Constituents]

There are a large number of devices that in some respects facilitate intermediation between leaders and followers in the United States, and which would have to be included in any competent census of intermediation processes: The professionalization of congressional casework, for example, greatly extends the individual capacities of an aggrieved constituent to have a limited, but to the citizen, meaningful, impact on the execution of governmental policy. The cumulative effect of these encounters—and the spread of the propensity to make use of them—can be counted as a significant trend that is bound to leave more than a trace in the overall accounting.

The figures, insofar as they can be believed, are quite astounding. Official estimates suggest that over the decade 1972–81 the receipt of mail by members of Congress has grown fourfold, from 40 to 160 million pieces. Nobody knows how much of this reflects the revolution in electronic word processing, the mechanized orchestration of appeals. No doubt a lot of orchestrated demand shows up in figures of these kinds—just as a lot of impersonal response is reflected in the millions of pieces of mail sent out under the congressional frank. Willy-nilly, a lot of communication is going on by this means between leaders and followers. It takes skilled interpretation on both sides to make sense of the messages, but the channel is there and to an increasing degree is used.

[Litigation as Linkage]
Another small-scale institutional innovation that may well begin to add up is the steady increase in the number of public-sector organizations—e.g., state governments—using the services of an ombudsman. Litigation is seldom understood as an intermediation device, but it is one. Litigation is a form of interest group activity. The burgeoning of lawyers and the spread of their availability to wider segments of the population place within more and more hands the skills necessary to extract preferred outcomes from a political-legal system. Insofar as this is occurring, the prospects of American pluralism are changing. The numbers are daunting, and they suggest a major recent commitment of societal resources . . . bound to have overwhelming importance.

Despite, or in addition to, all these trends, the three great unofficial intermediation mechanisms of American politics deserve more extended consideration. In some respects they can be regarded as functionally alternative, in some respects as complementary, in some respects as competitive. It will, in any event, be our task to discuss in parallel the main trends affecting parties, interest groups, and the mass media.

[Parties as Linkages]

If the health of the American political system depended on the health of its parties, the system would be in sad shape. Intermittently, but more or less continuously at least since the beginning of the twentieth century, state and locally based organizations specializing in the staffing of the government by, in the first instance, winning elections—i.e., parties—have lost functions ancillary and instrumental to their central business and have even in recent years lost their capacity effectively to monopolize the making of nominations for key elective offices . . .

Political parties have changed. No longer are they welfare intermediaries, and less and less are they patronage intermediaries, although this picture still varies from place to place. Nevertheless parties retain at least two tasks of central importance to the maintenance of the political system: (1) Aside from those states and communities in which by law nonpartisan local elections are required, they monopolize the supply of labels that channel the preferences of voters. (2) Parties provide an organizational basis for the coordination of public officials within legislative bodies, and between elected legislative and executive officials within the same jurisdiction.

To provide these services, parties offer a setting for the promulgation and elaboration of public policies. They make nominations and conduct political campaigns. Despite all the things that have happened in American politics over the last half-century, and in spite of the fact that party leaders' control over the parties' central functions has been challenged and in some cases supplanted by interest group and mass media interventions, the contribution of parties to public-sector intermediation in the United States remains essential.

Consider, for example, the formulation and development of public policies. Interest groups and experts, think tanks, and law firms are all capable of dreaming up public policies and justifying them, using arguments that may range from the most crassly selfish to the most nobly altruistic. What they do not do is draw up such a program across the board, or relate programmatic trade-offs to some broadly based electoral clientele. Party politicians—elected officials, party leaders—do this as a matter of course . . .

[Another] task of a political party is to fashion electoral appeals that respond in at least some respects to the programmatic interests of broad numbers of potential voters. The party must find means for resisting commitment to those policies it does not intend to pursue and for advertising those it does intend to pursue, means for discovering and for shaping consensus, and means also for determining which public policies nevertheless to espouse about which there is division in the population at large. Parties must therefore receive, process, and disseminate information about popular preferences, as well as attempt to influence them.

Parties retain certain capacities in respect of which they have not yet been replaced by interest groups or the mass media—nor are they likely to be over the short run. Although at the national level party leaders have been greatly crippled in their ability to fulfill these functions by changes in the rules of presidential nomination vesting powers in the mass media, in prospective candidates, and in bureaucrats and technical specialists in candidates' entourages, parties have not been successfully supplanted by interest groups or the mass media. There has, rather, developed a disjunction between the power to nominate and the power to govern, between the forces that are most influential in the presidential nomination process and those that coordinate and harmonize legislative-executive relations. Over the short run, this disjunction seems likely to inhibit the capacity of political parties successfully to perform intermediation tasks . . .

[The Mass Media as Linkage]

The mass media have over the last couple of decades greatly increased their impact on public affairs. This is chiefly to be observed in the use of television, a phenomenon of immense significance that grew from a small influence to total saturation of the American population in a mere thirty years. Television is important because people pay attention to it. In the United States over the past three decades only a limited number of channels have increasingly claimed the attention of virtually the entire population.

Some of the political results have been astounding . . . Television is capable of creating a version of reality that follows its own rules of perspective, size, and immediacy. The theories—cognitive capacities as well as political prejudices—of those gatekeepers having independent access to television and who therefore hold in their hands the opportunity to program the rest of us, are in consequence of some interest. They are, however, of diminishing interest. The vast increase in channel capacity that now exists presages a sharp fragmentation in the attention patterns of American (and in due course European) TV watchers. This implies a multiplication in the number of gatekeepers and a significant dilution in the influence of each . . . This should lead to greater variety and less uniformity in the political views available to consumers of TV news, public affairs, and opinion; higher degrees of specialization in the material that is presented; and much smaller audiences for any single presentation.

[Interest Groups as Linkages]

The implications over the short run for interest groups of the decline of parties and the rise of mass media in politics are straightforward. Those interest groups tied to parties—specifically to state and local parties, geographically based and reliant on face-to-face interaction—have in recent years been relatively disadvantaged compared with interest groups tied to the approval and publicity of the mass media.

Over the short run this has meant the rise in the influence of groups with, oddly enough, few or no members but good public relations—examples would be various offshoots of Ralph Nader's operations—in comparison with groups having large memberships—trade unions are an example—but no particular skill at feeding the mass media the sorts of things they like to process . . . [Further], the interests that people maintain as producers and breadwinners [cannot] eclipse interests based on the status needs of a population increasingly differentiated by activities that run beyond the narrowly economic . . . Quite the reverse: as the cognitive and communicative capacities of Americans increase in conditions of relative prosperity, bedrock economic interests recede in importance and Americans will choose to align themselves in more and more intricate patterns of affiliation, creating the possibility, as well as other preconditions, for demands of all sorts—for recognition, access, subsidy, ancillary services—based on these affiliations.

A number of gross demographic and technological indicators over the last several decades point with unanimity to the increased capacities of Americans to choose (rather than merely inherit) the groups that express their lifestyles and interests in the political arena. These indicators relate to such things as more time and money, more geographic mobility, . . . release from the behavioral restrictions imposed by living within the confines of an extended family, or, for that matter, the nuclear family; release from restrictions on the maintenance of traditional gender roles, and so on.

That these overwhelming demographic facts should have both direct and indirect political consequences should occasion no surprise. Nor should it come as a surprise that there are costs as well as benefits attached to emerging possibilities in lifestyles and political styles: . . . political freedom and political instability; more alternatives in public policy but mistrust of political leaders; irresponsible leadership and ungovernable followers along with wider behavioral possibilities and room to explore them; more litigation along with fewer issues settled by the status relations of adversaries.

[Conclusion: Prospects for Pluralism and Its Costs]

I am now prepared to offer a tentative answer to the question of the prospects for American pluralism. First, as to major institutions of unofficial public-sector intermediation, the gains in influence of managers of the mass media have been balanced by the losses of leaders of the political parties. Interest groups associated with each have gained and lost influence accordingly. I do not expect political parties to go out of business because the necessity is very great for finding means to coordinate the activities of politicians in a separation of powers, multilevel system of government. Party leaders will nevertheless have great difficulty performing these functions so long as their influence on nominating processes remains shaky . . .

As to underlying conditions in the population at large making for multiple political demands, there are no signs of abatement of current trends: the proliferation of groups, the invention of new demands, and the consequent bureaucratization of intermediation as service agencies attempt to protect themselves against excessive claims. There will be plenty of work for lawyers, and it will be necessary to devise new forms of insurance—especially against malpractice—to spread the risks of public service. Trust between leaders and those led will be a rare commodity, and when it appears it may take the form of media-induced spasms of popularity rather than the rippling out of word-of-mouth information from people who know what they are talking about. This is one of the costs of participation in a very large and very heterogeneous society in which status, tradition, and habit come to mean less and less, and explicit decisions of various sorts—decisions to affiliate, to agree or disagree, to back or withhold backing—are spread more and more widely among a population whose members are increasingly eager to make choices for themselves.

What individuals cannot choose is a society in which they retain the right to move about as they like or need, exercising their options to change their jobs, marital status, geographic location, names, hair, lifestyles, political commitments, while others hold still and provide them with the comforting support systems—stable neighborhoods, lifelong friendships, personalized and unbureaucratic professional services—of a more settled, confining, and less resourceful age. This tragic fly in the ointment of modern American social life dooms traditionalists with democratic ideals to a certain amount of nostalgia, often mistaken for neoconservative crotchets. It seems to be inescapably the case that the price of more pluralism is a less orderly political life. This, no doubt, is one reason otherwise levelheaded analysts with liberal values occasionally observe that we are doing better and feeling worse.

Democratic Government by Leading Minorities, Responsiveness, and Responsibility

Selections from the Work of
Giovanni Sartori

It is time to look to democracy as a system of government and, more generally, to the vertical structuring of democracy—*vertical democracy*, for short . . . we may thus circumscribe our object of enquiry as follows: the extent and modality of the controlling power . . .

[Democracy as Leadership by Minorities]

When we come to the heart of the matter, we are currently apt to refer to what Dahl calls the *ruling elite model*. Actually, what is intended and discussed under this label is, above all, Mosca's law of the political class. Hence my preference is for saying "ruling class model."[1] In any event, what matters is the notion of rule . . . The controversy on the ruling elite model (or, as I prefer to say, on the law of the ruling class) [may] be formulated as follows: first, whether or not control groups (power minorities) add up, in any given setting, to a singular or a plural; second, and more precisely, whether or not such groups are —as in Meisel's (1962) three Cs formula— characterized by group consciousness, coherence, and conspiracy; third, and conclusively, whether or not in any given setting power minorities can be concretely nailed down. Depending on which side of these alternatives passes the test of verification, in one case the finding is appropriately summarized by speaking of *ruling class* in the singular, and in the other case by saying leadership and *leading minorities* in the plural . . .

If we assume that there is *one* ruling class, that a society is actually controlled by a power clique, then such an assumption cannot

Excerpts from Giovanni Sartori, *The Theory of Democracy Revisited*, 132, 142, 145–156, 163–167 (Chatham, N.J.: Chatham House, 1987). Reprinted by permission of the publisher. Bracketed headings have been created by the editor of this volume.

escape the burden of proof. For in such case a political class is not a mere category, a "class" resulting from a classification; we are imputing to it, instead, an operative, concrete existence—and an existent of this sort must be found to exist. The case is such, then, as to make it both feasible and imperative to trace down and identify *who is* the ruling class. Conversely, if the tracing fails, the assumption is disconfirmed . . .

If Mosca's law [concerning the ruling class] means that every political society shapes up, in its vertical structuring as a pyramid . . . then Mosca's law would verge on meaninglessness, for it is a platitude to assert that there will always be rulers and ruled, governors and governed. In order to escape triviality Mosca's law must be assumed to imply something more, to wit, that all political societies are ultimately controlled by *one minority*—and the question thus hinges on how "one" is to be intended. In Meisel's interpretation the minority in question is required to be self-conscious (of its group interest), cohesive, and characterized by solidarity in pursuing a common course of action.

While these conditions could be met, they were not put forward by Mosca for the obvious reason that he well realized that they can hardly be generalized. The generalizable condition must be, therefore, a lenient condition, namely, that one is "one," as long as it is not a fragmented multiplicity of antagonistic power groups. Empirically put, if one is to be "one" it must be identifiable and identified. If, conversely, this "one" cannot be concretely identified, the implication is that Mosca's law is falsified . . .

We are left with the question: What is the vertical power structure of democracies? Under . . . all the testable criteria devised thus far, democracies *are* characterized by diffusion of power—indeed by an extent of diffusion that baffles the "ruling class model." Clearly, therefore, the model that applies to democracies is another model. I wish to suggest that it is appropriate to describe it—in contradistinction to the other—as a *leadership by minorities* model characterized by a multiplicity of crisscrossing power groups engaged in coalitional maneuverings. To be sure, the fact that the processes of leading and influencing become, in democracies, enormously complex and elusive . . . should not be taken to imply that power minorities have little power or that they cancel themselves out among themselves.

Maybe; maybe not. At certain points in time we may find, as Riesman (1950) finds, a "veto group system." But at other points in time, let alone in space, we may find winning coalitions . . .

[Democratic Competition and the Leaders' Responsiveness to the Public]

Let us look at the interplay between antagonistic and competing [leading minorities]. Why and for whom do they compete? Clearly they compete for supporters, because their strength comes from the numbers that follow them. How do they compete? Evidently, and overtly, by promising benefits and advantages to their followers. The implication is that the unorganized majority of the politically inactive becomes the arbiter—and eventually the—*tertium gaudens*—in the contest among the organized minorities of the politically active . . . An overall democracy results from the sheer fact that the *power* of deciding between the competitors *is* in the hands of the demos . . .

The one who did see into this more clearly than anybody before him was Schumpeter . . . Schumpeter puts forward the classic definition of what is now called the competitive theory of democracy: "The democratic method is that institutional arrangement for arriving at political decisions in which individuals acquire the power to decide by means of a competitive struggle for the people's vote."[2] The noteworthy point is that Schumpeter confines his argument to the *input* side, or moment, of the overall process of democracy. Hence, it must be asked: How do we move on from the method to its democratic consequences, that is, from democracy in *input* to democracy in *output*?

The reply is afforded, I suggest, by Friedrich's (1941) principle or rule of "anticipated reactions." In the case at hand the rule can be spelled out as follows: Elected officials seeking reelection (in a competitive setting) are conditioned, in their deciding, by the anticipation of how electorates will react to what they decide. The rule of anticipated reactions thus provides the linkage between input and output. Let then the complete definition be: *Democracy is the by-product of a competitive method of leadership recruitment.* This is so because the power to elect also results, in feedback fashion, in the heeding of those elected to the power of their electors. *In short, competitive elections produce democracy.* And let the above be called—

within the ambit of the competitive theory—the feedback theory of democracy . . .

Descriptively, the "feedback model" can be rendered by saying that democracy is an *electoral polyarchy*. For Dahl[3] this label would be redundant, for his concept of polyarchy includes, by definition, free and competitive elections (and other properties as well). Yet, when labels succeed, they acquire a life of their own; their semantic inertia largely outweighs the conceptualization of their inventor. Now, semantically, "polyarchy" stands in contradistinction to "oligarchy." Therefore the term polyarchy, in and by itself, conveys only that an oligarchy is broken up, that it is transformed into a multiple, diffuse, and, at best, open constellation of power groups . . .

Therefore, a nonelective polyarchy will meaningfully afford a reciprocal delimitation and control *among* leaders, at least in the sense that its dispersion defies cartelization. However, this is still a far cry from democracy. Democracies too avail themselves of a reciprocal control among leaders; but after having established first the control *of* leaders *upon* leaders. The crux of the matter is, thus, that to restrain, control, and influence leaders, the demos must have the full and unfettered power to choose them—regular elections must regularly occur . . . My earlier descriptive definition was: Democracy is the by-product of a competitive method of leadership recruitment. It may now be explicated in full as follows: Large-scale democracy is a procedure and/or a *mechanism* that (a) generates an *open polyarchy* whose *competition* on the electoral market (b) attributes *power to the people* and (c) specifically enforces the *responsiveness* of the leaders to the led . . .

[Governmental Overload and the Leaders' Responsibility]

As the argument is placed in perspective, the timely question is: Where do the present and imminent dangers lie for democracy as a political form? In some kind of "minority rule"? I think not. For the plain fact is that democratic governments are all—some more some less—in loss of authority and clogged by too many demands that they are unable to process. Note that overload is not big government. While big government may be said to facilitate overload, certainly one can exist without the other.

So we live in a traffic jam, cross-pressured democracy characterized by low governing capability, to wit, by low resistance to demands and low capability to take and carry through decisions. More
often than not, the pattern of the 1960s and 1970s has been one of
indecision, shortsightedness, inefficiency and overspending. Not all
of this is displeasing. Actually it forcefully attests—against
the contrary claims of perfectionists, participationists, and populists—
that representative democracy is by no means a sham, a polity in which
people are deprived of their power. For all of this confirms the extent
to which the representative linkage has maximized *responsiveness*.

However, responsiveness is but one of the elements of representative government. A government that simply yields to demands,
that simply gives in, turns out to be a highly irresponsible government, a government that does not live up to its responsibilities. A
representative is not only responsible *to*, but also responsible *for*.
This is the same as saying that representation intrinsically consists of
two ingredients: responsiveness *and* independent responsibility. And
the more governments become responsive *to* at the detriment of being responsible *for*, the more we are likely to be misgoverned and/or
ungoverned. Which is equally to say that the more we have indulged
in responsiveness, the greater the need for *independent responsibility*—what leadership is really about.

We thus [turn] to the question . . . whether leadership is or is
not an integral element of democracy. The old but now rejuvenated
view is that leadership is needed only to the extent that the role of
the people remains secondary. This view easily gets the applause. Yet
if its propounders really believed in it, why not have leaders replaced
by "administrators" appointed by lot? Waiting for this alternative to
be put to the test, let me bring my own brief to a close . . .

[Conclusion]

If a headless society were at all possible, we could indeed rejoice; on
this score we have lately been doing very well. But if headlessness or
leaderlessness is no solution, then our current downgrading or fear
of elites is an anachronism that blinds us to the problems and perils
that confront us. The more we lose sight of democracy as a system of
government, the more our predicaments are aggravated—and the
more they are with us.

Notes from the Editor

1. See Mosca in this volume.
2. See Schumpeter in this volume.
3. See Dahl in this volume.

[References]

Friedrich, Carl. 1941. *Constitutional Government and Democracy*, second edition. Boston: Ginn.

Meisel, J. H. 1962. *The Myth of the Ruling Class*. Ann Arbor: University of Michigan Press.

Riesman, David. 1971. *The Lonely Crowd*. New Haven: Yale University Press.

National Elite Configurations and Transition to Democracy

Selections from the Work of
G. Lowell Field, John Higley, and Michael G. Burton

References to elites are ubiquitous in contemporary discussions of politics. Journalists and commentators speak routinely of elite circles, elite opinions, and elite conflicts when discussing events in Washington or Moscow, Beijing or Paris. Social scientists and historians just as routinely assign elites pivotal roles in analyzing political regimes, revolutions, social movements, democratic transitions and breakdowns, changing ideologies, and changing policies. Elites are thus at the core of the widely noted emphasis on "political" causation in contemporary political sociology, though analysts may use such roughly synonymous terms as leaders, rulers, power groups, power networks, parties, state actors, and ruling class fractions. Indeed, elites and elite-like entities bulk so large in popular and academic writing about politics today that one is entitled to speak of a "paradigm shift" from societally-centered pluralist and Marxian approaches toward an elite-centered approach.

This is not to say, however, that elite *theory* is flourishing. By and large, scholars have not followed up on the attempts of the early elite theorists—Gaetano Mosca, Vilfredo Pareto, and Robert Michels—to use the elite concept as the centerpiece in a general theory of political continuity and change . . . And though scholars often speak of "elite theory," no widely recognized body of interrelated concepts and propositions warranting the label exists . . .

The work of the early elite theorists promised more. Realizing that promise requires reconsidering and extending their basic con-

Excerpts from G. Lowell Field, John Higley, and Michael G. Burton, "A New Elite Framework for Political Sociology," *Revue Européene des Sciences Sociales* 28 (1990):149–182. Copyright © Droz. Reprinted by permission of the publisher. Bracketed headings have been created by the editor of this volume.

tentions about the importance of *variations in elite structure and functioning* for political continuities and changes, and the *interdependent relationship between elites and mass publics* in all modern societies. Taken together, these contentions suggest a decidedly more realistic theory of politics than the semi-utopian democratic and Marxian theories against which Mosca, Pareto, and Michels reacted. Each contention needs elaboration: to specify how elites vary and with what political consequences; and to reformulate the interdependence of elites and mass publics . . .

Elites are the principal decisionmakers in the largest or otherwise most pivotally situated organizations in a society . . . National elites [are] top position-holders in the largest or most resource-rich political, governmental, economic, military, professional, communications, and cultural organizations and movements in a society . . . Given this inclusive conception of national elites, relating variations in their structure and functioning to major political outcomes involves (1) identifying the basic configurations that national elites take, and (2) specifying the major political consequences of these configurations . . .

Configurations of National Elites

[There are] two basic but parallel dimensions in the structure and functioning of national elites: the extent of structural integration, and the extent of value consensus. Structural integration involves the relative inclusiveness of formal and informal networks of communication and influence among the persons, groups and factions in a national elite. Value consensus involves the relative agreement among these persons, groups and factions about formal and informal rules and codes of political conduct and about the worth of existing political institutions. Focusing on these dimensions, we can distinguish three basic configurations of national elites:

1. *Disunified:* Structural integration and value consensus are minimal in the sense that communication and influence networks do not cross factional lines in any comprehensive way; factions disagree on the rules and codes of political conduct and on the worth of existing institutions. Accordingly, elites tend to distrust each other deeply, to perceive political outcomes in zero-

sum terms, and to engage in unrestrained, often violent, struggles for dominance.

2. *Consensually Unified:* Structural integration is inclusive in the sense that overlapping and interconnected communication and influence networks encompass all elite factions and no single faction dominates these networks; value consensus is also inclusive in the sense that, while factions regularly and publicly oppose each other on ideological and policy questions, they share an underlying consensus about rules of the game and the worth of existing political institutions. Accordingly, factions tend to compete in terms of a restrained partisanship, to cooperate tacitly to contain especially explosive issues and conflicts, and to perceive decisional outcomes in positive-sum or politics-as-bargaining terms (Sartori 1987, p. 224).

3. *Ideologically Unified:* Structural integration is inclusive in the sense that communication and influence networks encompass all elite factions but run mainly through, and are sharply centralized in, a dominant faction and the party or movement it leads; value consensus is also inclusive in the sense that factions publicly express no deep ideological or policy disagreements and instead conform their public statements to a single, explicit ideology whose policy implications are officially construed by the uppermost leaders of the dominant faction. Accordingly, elite factions publicly manifest a monolithic ideological unity.

These configurations are ideal or pure types . . . In reality, national elites appear to vary along a continuum while nevertheless clustering around three fundamentally distinct forms. Disunified elites range from a thoroughly disunified, chaotic extreme, such as Lebanese or Ugandan elites in recent years, through an array of more organized, but still basically disunified configurations—such as the dichotomous divisions into highly antagonistic leftist and rightist camps of most European elites during the seventeenth and eighteenth centuries, and of all Latin American elites during the nineteenth and early twentieth centuries; or again, the trichotomous divisions into distinct leftist, centrist, and rightist camps of most European elites during the nineteenth and early twentieth centuries, and of most Latin American elites since about World War II.

Next along the continuum are consensually unified elites whose unity varies from tenuous, as in the Philippines before Marcos, or in Malaysia, Tunisia and perhaps Mexico today; to firmly established, as in Britain, the U.S., or the Netherlands for long periods; to virtually unchallenged, as in Sweden, Norway, Australia and New Zealand in recent decades. Finally, assorted elites display ideological unity in lesser or greater degrees, ranging from the Yugoslav and other East European elites since the 1960s, as well as the Soviet and Chinese elites very recently, to the more tightly unified Soviet and German elites under Stalin and Hitler, respectively . . . We now specify the political regime patterns apparently associated with these configurations.

Types of Political Regimes

The stability and instability of political regimes is one of the most visible and important variations among societies in the modern world . . . An *unstable regime* is one in which government executive power is subject to irregular seizures, serious attempted seizures, or widely expected seizures by open force. Concrete indicators of an unstable regime are revolutions, uprisings, or coups d'état aimed at changing the personnel controlling government executive offices and not primarily orchestrated by extra-national forces. A regime may be classified as unstable during periods when such seizures occur, are seriously attempted, or are regarded by informed observers as likely possibilities. If any of these indicators obtain, a regime's current mode of functioning, whether "democratic" or "authoritarian" or something else, is almost certain to be temporary.

Ordinarily, regime instability is clear-cut: Irregular, forcible power seizures are sufficiently frequent and visible, or expectations of them are sufficiently palpable that the analyst can readily recognize an unstable regime. Thus . . . Veliz (1967, p. 278) counts 80 successful military coups in 18 Latin American countries between 1920 and 1966 . . . and Macridis (1986, p. 225) lists 26 coups in 16 countries of Tropical Africa between 1970–1984 . . . In European history unstable political regimes usually took the form of strictly traditional monarchies. Royal courts encompassed most elite persons not in hiding, prison, or exile, and instability was manifest in constant intrigues and usurpations aimed at using monarchical power for factional or personal elite interests. More recently, various institutional patterns have coexisted with regime instability, including some that are formally representative and democratic. The key feature of these more recent patterns is that the military and associated civilian elites exercise de facto control over a regime's prospects. They have shown themselves willing, or are widely thought willing, to alter or overthrow by force any government that threatens their interests. So long as this situation persists, existing political institutions have few binding effects on elite and mass actors as they advance and defend their interests.

Political regimes lacking these features are stable—irregular, forcible seizures of government executive power have not occurred or been seriously attempted and are not widely expected by informed observers. But there are two basic types of stable regimes. One is the *stable representative regime* in which factions maneuver and compete for government executive power by appealing to various, somewhat conflicting mass interests and categories. The degree of representativeness varies widely, however.

In one variant, competing factions merely take turns wielding government executive power via their alternating dominance of a parliament or other deliberative body which is elected periodically by a sharply restricted electorate. Britain during the eighteenth and nineteenth centuries is an example. In another variant, members of a dominant ethnic or other cultural group enjoy political representation and participation while excluding one or more, perhaps larger, subordinate groups. Examples are the American South until recently, and South Africa throughout its independent existence. But today, a stable representative regime is usually indicated by successive, peaceful transfers of government executive power among competing factions on the basis of periodic and contested elections involving universal suffrage, as happens in the Western democracies.

The other basic type of stable regime may be termed *stable unrepresentative*. In this type, formally representative political institutions and processes may or may not exist, but representative politics are not actively practiced. Though elections may be held, they are not seriously contested and their outcomes do not determine the holders of government executive office or influence the main lines of government policy. Executive power is transferred among successive elite persons and groups via secret deliberations among the highest officials of the regime. In the main variant of this type, one party or movement monopolizes all political positions, and the public expression of conflicting interests and opinions is consistently repressed in favor of its ideology. Examples are the Soviet Union from the late 1920's, Nazi Germany after 1933, and China after 1949. In a second variant, criticisms of the regime and its policies are allowed limited public expression, but government offices are nevertheless monopolized by a single party or movement and there is no serious practice of representative politics. Examples are . . . most East European countries until 1989, and perhaps Iran since 1981 . . .

[Variations in National Elite Configurations and Political Regimes]

Regimes usually display some mixture of these features, but we can plausibly classify most regimes as preponderantly of one or another type, especially when their longer-term patterns are examined. In line with elite theory's basic contention that variations in elite structure and functioning are decisive for major political outcomes, our framework causally associates national elite configurations with political regime types as follows:

Elite Configuration	Regime Type
Disunified	Unstable
Consensually unified	Stable Representative
Ideologically unified	Stable Unrepresentative

As the causal variable, a national elite configuration always predates a regime type. A central question, therefore, is how do the different elite configurations come about? . . .

Origins of the Elite Configurations

The disunified, consensually unified, and ideologically unified configurations of national elites appear to originate only in a few sets of circumstances, events, and processes. Once created, moreover, each configuration strongly tends to persist despite many other changes in a society's makeup and functioning—elite transformations from one configuration to another are rare. It follows that the distinctive regime characteristics associated with each elite configuration are equally persistent, with changes from one regime type to another depending on a prior elite transformation. Putting aside the outcomes of international warfare, the elite configurations have originated in six ways.

Each of the national elite configurations has a "foundational" origin in nation-state formation. Forming a nation-state from disparate, at least partially autonomous political entities typically involves the forcible repression and subjugation of some elites by other elites who end up dominating the new nation-state. Unremitting fears, hatreds, and conflicts of the sort that define disunified elites are the usual result. This happened in all the European nation-states that emerged at the end of the medieval period, in all the nation-states that formed after the Spaniards and Portuguese were driven from Latin America, and in nearly all the postcolonial nation-states of Africa, the Middle East, and Asia during the contemporary period. Indeed, nation-state formation has so frequently left a legacy of elite disunity and resulting regime instability as to constitute the modal pattern of politics in the modern world.

Much less frequently, certain consensually unified elites have originated with nation-state formation. Where native or settler elites in a colonial or otherwise dependent territory have had prolonged opportunities to practice cooperative and conciliatory politics in "home rule" governments and/or in large and complex independence movements, consensually unified elites have sometimes emerged coterminous with the attainment of national independence. Clear examples are elites in Britain's American colonies before and during the War of Independence, elites in Britain's New Zealand, Canadian, and Australian colonies during the nineteenth century, as well as Indian and Israeli elites who forged consensus and unity while waging struggles for national independence . . . Where a consensually unified elite originates with nation-state formation . . . , a stable representative regime is established, and it persists as long as no transformation to a different elite configuration occurs.

In rare instances, ideologically unified elites have likewise originated in the formation of an independent nation-state: where native or settler elites in colonial territories have fought each other during a larger struggle for national independence and a particularly doctrinaire, tightly organized faction has triumphed, eliminating other factions and imposing its ideology and organization on all segments of the newly independent nation-state. An example is the victory by the Vietminh movement and the creation of an ideologically unified elite in North Vietnam after the French defeat in 1954. As this case illustrates, where an ideologically unified elite dates from the formation of an independent nation-state, the elite configuration and its attendant stable unrepresentative regime strongly tend to persist.

The long-term persistence of elite configurations that originate with nation-state formation highlights the pivotal importance of elite cooperation or conflict during that formative process. But while initial configurations usually last over long periods, subsequent *elite transformations* sometimes occur, and they account for most major, lasting political changes in nation-states.

Elite transformations from disunity to consensual unity have happened in two ways. The first is an *elite settlement* in which the warring factions of a disunified national elite suddenly and deliberately reorganize their relations by negotiating compromises on their most basic disagreements, thereby achieving consensual unity and laying the basis for a stable representative regime. Examples are: England's Glorious Revolution in 1688–89, Sweden's constitutional settlement in 1809, Mexico's formation of a relatively inclusive and consensually-based elite structure in 1929, Costa Rica's constitutional settlement in 1948, the explicit pacts negotiated by Colombian and Venezuelan elites in 1957–58, and Spain's constitutional settlement in 1978–79. Successful elite settlements occur only in extraordinary circumstances whose key features are a legacy of protracted but inconclusive elite conflict, a sudden crisis threatening the worsening of that conflict, an organization of elite factions which facilitates effective negotiations among their principal leaders, and considerable elite freedom from mass pressures against the compromises settlements require.

The other kind of transformation from disunity to consensual unity is an *elite convergence* in which some warring factions in a disunified elite discover that by forming a broad electoral coalition they can mobilize a reliable majority of voters, win elections repeatedly, and thereby protect their interests against the attacks of dissident and hostile elite factions by dominating government executive power. Successive electoral defeats may convince the major dissident and hostile elite factions that to avoid permanent exclusion from government executive power they must moderate their distinctive ideological and policy positions and compete for votes.

Such moderation gradually bridges the deep ideological chasms that mark disunified elites, and all important factions come to hold a tacit consensus about rules of the game and the worth of existing institutions while competing on the basis of a restrained partisanship. Examples are Norway and Denmark during the first third of this century, when radical social democratic and trade union elites moderated their positions to defeat previously dominant conservative and liberal elite factions, as well as West Germany, France, Italy, and Japan during the last thirty years, when previously disaffected socialist and/or communist elites moderated their ideological postures and policy programs to attract voters outside their customary class constituencies.

Elite transformations from disunity to ideological unity occur only through *revolutions:* Some extremist elite group seizes power, liquidates pre-existing elites, centralizes political activity in the party or movement it leads, and enforces its ideology as the only framework for political expression. Examples are Russia 1917–21, Italy 1922–26, Germany 1929–33, and perhaps Iran 1979–81. As these examples indicate, elite transformations from disunity to ideological unity have occurred through both egalitarian and anti-egalitarian revolutions . . .

Six indigenous origins of national elite configurations are thus specified: three "foundational" origins coterminous with nation-state formations, and three "transformational" origins involving elite settlements, elite convergences, or revolutions in societies with disunified elites . . . Of course, the open-endedness of history prevents flat statements about future possibilities, and our specification implies several other conceivable outcomes. Elite transformations could occur from either consensual or ideological unity to disunity, or from consensual to ideological unity and vice versa. Exploring some recent or current cases that may exemplify these additional possibilities . . . are key tasks in further elaborating the framework. These relationships between national elite configurations and regimes help account for much of the historical and contemporary political record. But our framework does not assume that elites alone run the political show . . .

The Interdependence of Elites and Mass Publics

The classical elite theorists dwelled heavily on the relationship between elites and masses, stressing two key processes: elite circulation and elite mobilization of mass support. They viewed elite circulation—the altering of elite social composition through gradual or sudden movements of persons from mass to elite statuses and vice versa—as crucial for a society's political stability and overall vitality . . . While elite circulation is important, elite mobilization of mass support is in our view the more central aspect of the relationship between elites and mass publics. What we inherit from the classical theorists is a valuable strategic conception of this aspect, but no workable scheme for applying it . . .

Classical elite theory's strategic conception of elite-mass interdependence is nevertheless sound: To carry out major initiatives and to perpetuate their statuses, elites need mass support. To win this support, elites must frame their appeals in accord with existing mass interests and political orientations. These mass interests and orientations are not created by elites but arise instead from some combination of human nature and life circumstances, though elites can often activate or muffle mass interests and orientations through well-couched appeals. But fundamentally, the necessity for elites to conform their appeals for support with independently existing mass interests and orientations limits what they can do or get away with. Failure to win mass support frequently shortens elite tenures or, at least, undermines elite effectiveness. In sum, mass interests and orientations constitute *parameters* within which elites can safely and effectively act. These parameters normally leave elites a range of choices, and the choices they make tend to be decisive for political outcomes . . .

Conclusion

Our new elite framework . . . stresses [some] distinct paths to [consensual elite unity and thereby to] stable democracy and highlights the fact that a number of Western countries are recent arrivals. Our framework also offers a promising approach to politics in non-Western, non-democratic countries . . . Regarding contemporary state-socialist regimes currently undergoing change, our framework identifies what has been their most distinctive feature—an ideologically unified elite—and it specifies what is required for a fundamental regime change, namely an elite transformation to consensual unity, producing a stable representative regime, or to disunity, producing an unstable regime. Regarding developing countries that have tended to oscillate between authoritarian and democratic regimes, our framework identifies the underlying basis of this oscillation—elite disunity—and it specifies how this pattern of instability could be broken: by an elite transformation to consensual unity, either through an elite settlement or an elite convergence, which would usher in a stable representative regime; or by an elite transformation to ideological unity through revolution, establishing a stable unrepresentative regime . . .

The contemporary political world is hardly a democratic one, and political continuities and changes are more independent of society-wide determinants than existing frameworks recognize. Looking at elite rather than mass phenomena is therefore a more useful route to political explanation. However, one must guard against going too far in this direction, and our framework does not depict elites as alone determining outcomes . . . Mass interests and orientations limit elite actions, and elites who ignore these mass limits do not remain elites for long.

References

Macridis, Roy C.1986. *Modern Political Regimes: Patterns and Institutions.* Boston: Little, Brown.

Sartori, Giovanni. 1987. *The Theory of Democracy Revisited.* Chatham, N.J.: Chatham Publishers.

Veliz, Claudio (ed.). 1967. *The Politics of Conformity in Latin America.* London: Oxford University Press.

Modes of Transition and the Emergence of Democracy in Latin America and Southern Europe

Selections from the Work of
Terry Lynn Karl and Philippe C. Schmitter

Let us start with the following (disputable) assumptions about contemporary politics: (1) polities undergoing regime change from autocracy do so by a variety of means; (2) these can be specified and clustered into a limited number of "modes of transition" [that are principal determinants of whether democracy will emerge]; (3) these modes, to a significant extent, determine which types of democracy will emerge; (4) whether or not they will be consolidated; and (5) what the long-range consequences will be for different social groups. This article will take (1) for granted and explore the plausibility of (2). Assumptions (3), (4) and (5) have been left for future speculation.

On the surface, these assumptions—especially (3), (4) and (5)—might seem dubious, if not counter-intuitive. As we shall see, the transition is a period of great political uncertainty. It is subject to unforeseen contingencies, unfolding processes and unintended outcomes. The "normal" constraints of social structures and political institutions seem temporarily suspended; actors are often forced into making hurried and confused choices; and the alliances they enter are usually fleeting and opportunistic. The result of these interactions is often not what any one group preferred initially. Why, then, should such an improbable and *under*determined "founding moment" have a lasting effect? Would it not be more plausible to assume that these "events" would prove epiphenomenal and that, ultimately, the polity will acquire the regime configuration that it

Excerpts from Terry Lynn Karl and Philippe C. Schmitter, "Modes of Transition in Latin America, Southern and Eastern Europe," *International Social Science Journal* 128 (1991): 269–284. By permission of the *ISSJ*. Bracketed headings have been created by the editor of this volume.

deserves, given its entrenched social structures, its standing citizen preferences, or its established constitutional history?

Our argument is not based on deductive principles of rational choice or historical inertia, but on inductive observation from a limited range of recent experiences in Europe and Latin America . . . In a sense, it bears a generic resemblance to the currently fashionable attention being paid to "chaos theory" and to "path dependency." Small differences and minor choices, whose relevance is often unknown to those experiencing them, may be capable of producing major effects and channelling a system in quite different and lasting directions . . .

[Modes of Transition]

Historically created structures may . . . determine the range of options available to decision makers . . . [Yet], once these links between pre-existing structures and contingent choice have been made explicit, it becomes apparent that the arrangements "crafted" by key political actors during a regime transition establish new rules, roles and behavioural patterns which may (or may not) represent an important rupture with the past. These, in turn, become the institutions shaping the prospects for regime consolidation in the future . . . The interaction of strategies may often result in outcomes that no one initially preferred, but nevertheless we believe that actors and strategies define the basic property space within which transitions can occur and that the specific combination of the two defines which type of transition has occurred.

In Figure 1, we have depicted the relevant space by cross-tabulating variation in strategy by variation in actors. Simplifying considerably on the *y*-axis, strategies of transition can vary along a continuum that runs from unilateral recourse to force to multilateral willingness to compromise. In between lies a muddled and ambiguous zone of action in which mutual threats are exchanged, acts of physical intimidation and coercion may be committed and substantial mobilizations of support may occur.

On the *x*-axis, we distinguish between cases in which most, if not all, of the impetus for change comes "from below," from actors in subordinate or excluded positions in the social, economic and political order of the *ancien régime*, and those in which elite actors "from above," i.e., from within the dominant institutions of authoritarian rule, social prestige and/or economic exploitation, play the leading role in moving the system towards some form of democracy. Again, we concede that the range of variation cannot be collapsed into a neat dichotomy and have left room for a "messy" intermediate category in which elites and non-elites mingle and compete for the direction of the transition. This is also an area where actors coming "from outside" may intervene directly and significantly—often because they have defeated the previous authoritarian regime in international warfare!

From the four "extreme" corners of the plot in Figure 1 emerge four ideal-types of regime transition: by *Pact* when elites agree upon a multilateral compromise among themselves; by *Imposition* when elites use force unilaterally and effectively to bring about a regime change against the resistance of incumbents; by *Reform* when masses mobilize from below and impose a compromised outcome without resorting to violence, and by *Revolution* when masses rise up in arms and defeat the previous authoritarian rulers militarily. In the capacious space in between the four extremes presumably lie a large number of situations in which both the identity of the relevant actors and the selection of strategies are "mixed." Violence is tempered by

Figure 1. *Modes of Transition: The Property Space*

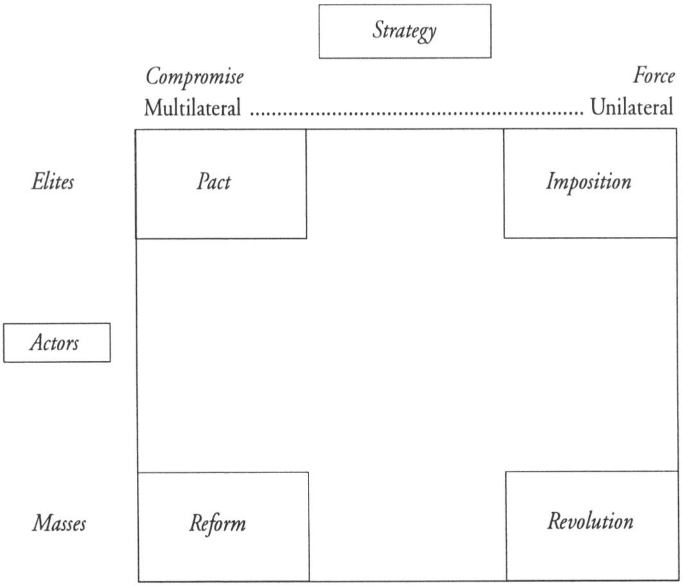

Figure 2. *Modes of Transition: The Distribution of Recent Cases*

		Strategy	
	Compromise		*Force*
	Multilateral .... Unilateral		
Elites	*Pact* [Venezuela 1958] [Colombia 1957] Spain Uruguay	[Costa Rica 1948] Chile	*Imposition* Turkey Brazil Ecuador Paraguay* El Salvador* Guatemala*
Actors		Argentina Peru Greece [Venezuela 1918]*	Portugal [Greece 1916]
Masses	*Reform* [Guatemala 1916]*	[Argentina 1946]	*Revolution* [Mexico 1910]* [Bolivia 1952]* [Cuba 1959]* [Nicaragua 1979]

*These countries either did not then become or have not yet become democracies.

compromise before it becomes dominant; masses are aroused and active, but still under the control of previous elites; domestic actors and strategies are significant, but the outcome hinges critically, on what foreign occupiers or intervenors do.

In Figure 2 we have attempted to "score" recent cases in Latin America and . . . Europe according to type of transition. In brackets [ ], we have included a few "representative" historical cases. These placements are, of course, tentative and subject to revision by specialists in the politics of the countries concerned. Moreover, they seek to resume in a single evaluation what is, in many cases, a very complex historical pattern . . .

Among the recent cases, some are relatively easy to classify. Spain and Uruguay are leading contemporary instances (and frequently taken as exemplary models) of pacted transition . . . In Turkey, Brazil and Ecuador, the change in regime was largely initiated from above and the coercive power of the state was consistently brought to bear to determine the timing, pace and content of change. Paraguay [was] a more ambiguous case in that actual violence was used and popular mobilization occurred in the process of ousting Stroessner, but incumbent elites retained subsequent control. In El Salvador since 1982, there has been an attempt to impose a transition via restricted elections, but protracted resistance by those excluded has prevented such an outcome. The revolutionary cases are well known: Mexico in 1910, Cuba in 1959, Nicaragua in 1979, with Bolivia in 1952 meriting a more ambiguous score.

Many cases are, however, even more difficult to classify. Take Portugal. It began its transition suddenly and unexpectedly by imposition—a *coup d'état* launched by junior military officers in the context of impending military defeat in Guinea-Bissau. Virtually overnight, the successful seizure of power triggered a mass response that first pushed the process in a reformist direction and, then, in the spring and summer of 1975 seemed to be leading toward a revolutionary outcome. The defeat of radical military elements in November prevented that and for some time the Portuguese polity remained suspended between reform and imposition (efforts to negotiate pacts failed), until the elections of 1987 and consequent changes in the constitution seemed at last to place the country on the road to consolidation. Chile is another hard case to classify. It was firmly (and protractedly) entrenched in the imposition mode until General Pinochet misjudged his capacity to win a key plebiscite in 1988. Since then, Chile's revived civilian politicians have opted for a pacted transition based on a "grand alliance" of all opposition parties . . .

At the very centre of our property space are three cases that literally defy classification: Argentina, Greece and Peru. Here, we find elements of imposition since important fragments from the previous autocratic regime—military in all three cases—played a key role in the transition, but in the context of considerable mobilization of urban masses and some resort to violence. In the former two cases, the scenario also included defeat in international war as the result of adventurous foreign policies, but without the subsequent occupation by foreign conquerors.

[Some Tentative Generalizations]

The first general observation is that all modes of transition have been tried, at one time or another, [but] revolutions have become less frequent . . . Latin America is particularly rich in the diversity of ways in which regime change has occurred, although that should be tempered by noting that few of these have given rise to any stable type of democracy. The Southern European cases are virtually all in the upper half of Figure 2, an indication of the dominant role played by elites there . . .

The second generalization stems from the distribution of asterisks (*) indicating that the transition in question did not or has not yet resulted in some form of stable democracy. Imposed and reformist transitions may or may not lead to democracies. Revolutions are less ambiguous; they may produce relatively enduring patterns of domination—witness Mexico since 1929, and Cuba since 1959— but they have rarely evolved into patterns of fair competition, unrestricted contestation, tolerance for rotation in power and free associability. This clashes frontally with the oft-cited generalization of Barrington Moore, Jr. that revolutions are necessary for democracy.[1] Admittedly, his assertion is based on different cases (Britain, the United States and France), and a longer time frame (almost a hundred years in the case of France and longer for the UK) . . . Nevertheless, our "sample" strongly suggests the contrary, i.e., that where authoritarian incumbents have been removed by force and replaced by a new elite representing mass constituencies, the subsequent emergence of political democracy is unlikely. We would note, however, that developments currently under way in Nicaragua and Mexico may (belatedly) be challenging this assertion.

The experience of the Latin American cases tentatively suggests a counter-intuitive conclusion: the reform mode of transition has rarely led to the consolidation of democracy. The prevailing wisdom has long been that peaceful pressure from below through the mobilization of excluded groups which compels ruling elites to expand rights of contestation and to extend the franchise is *the* most successful formula for democratization, especially where it occurs sequentially and gradually. This may have worked well in Chile prior to 1971–3, but not in response to the socialist reforms of Allende. Analogous experiences in Argentina (1946–55) and Guatemala (1946–54) resulted in regressions to authoritarian rule. It is important to note, however, that these failures of democratization took place in the context of the Cold War and were greatly influenced by it. With . . . Nicaragua currently well-ensconced in this mode of transition, we shall see whether in a different time-period and international context, this pessimism remains justified.

The modes that have most often resulted in the implantation of some type of political democracy are "transitions from above." In these cases, traditional rulers remain in control, even if pressured from below, and successfully use strategies of either compromise or force, or some mix of the two, to retain at least part of their power. Of these two modes of transition, democratization by pure imposition is the most common, especially if we include cases in which force or the threat of force is applied by foreign as well as domestic actors. Indeed, some of the most notoriously successful stable democracies were imposed upon defeated countries in the wake of the Second World War, although the Republic of Korea and the Philippines are witnesses to the possibility that the "formula" can fail. In Figure 2, the box labelled Imposition includes Brazil, Ecuador, Paraguay and Turkey, where the military used its dominant position to establish unilaterally the rules for eventual civilian governance. In [these] four cases, the transition has been drawn out, real limits have been placed upon the extent of democratization, and consolidation seems very difficult to reach, although no regression to autocracy has yet occurred . . .

Where democracies that have endured for a respectable length of time appear to cluster is in the cell defined by relatively strong elite actors who engage in strategies of compromise. This category includes the historical cases of Venezuela (1958–) and Colombia (1957–), and the recent redemocratizations in Spain (1975–) and Uruguay (1984–). What unites these otherwise diverse cases is the presence of foundational pacts, that is, explicit (though not always public) agreements between contending elites, which define the rules of governance on the basis of mutual guarantees for the "vital interests" of those involved . . .

These explicit, "foundational" pacts have several essential components. First, they are necessarily comprehensive and inclusive of virtually all politically significant actors. Because pacts are negotiated compromises in which contending forces agree to forego their capacity to harm each other by extending guarantees not to threaten each other's vital interests, they are only successful when they include *all* potentially threatening interests. Second, they are actually a series of accords that are interlocking and dependent upon each other. They necessarily include an agreement between the military and civilians over the conditions for establishing civilian rule, an agreement between political parties to compete under the new rules of governance, and a "social contract" between state agencies, business associations and trade unions regarding property rights, market arrangements and the distribution of benefits. Third, while they are ultimately both substantive (about the main tenets of policy) and procedural (about the rules of policy-making), they initially emphasize rule-making because "bargaining about bargaining" is the first and most important stage in the process of compromise.

Finally, foundational pacts serve to ensure survivability because, despite their inclusionary nature, they are also and simultaneously aimed at restricting the scope of representation in order to reassure traditional dominant classes that their vital interests will be respected. In essence, they are anti-democratic mechanisms, bargained by elites, which seek to create a deliberate socioeconomic and political contract that demobilizes emerging mass actors while delineating the extent to which all actors can participate or wield power in the future. They may accomplish this task by restricting contestation (as Colombian parties did in 1958 by agreeing to alternate in power regardless of the outcome of elections), by restricting the policy agenda itself (as Venezuelan parties did in 1958 by agreeing to implement the same economic programme), or by restricting the franchise (as Chilean elites did, beginning with the electoral law of 1874).

There are a number of cases that do not fit neatly into any of the ideal-typic categories which we have presented. Instead, they combine some of the features of these various types. For example, in Costa Rica in 1948 an opposition party militarily defeated the governing party in a short civil war, but then immediately resorted to pact-making to lay the foundation for an enduring democracy. In Chile, Pinochet's strategy of unilateralism was curbed by his defeat in the 1988 plebiscite and subsequently replaced by *pactismo* among civilian politicians. This intermediate ground between the two elitist modes—[is] a location that seems to bode well for a democratic outcome.

The same cannot be said for those cases which occupy positions *below* the elitist line. In Peru after 1978, the military's control over the timing and shape of the transition was strongly influenced by mass popular movement; in Guatemala (1984–) and El Salvador (1982–), an imposed transition led by civilian elites tied to the United States (and grudgingly tolerated by the armed forces) has been stalemated by the refusal of traditional elites to incorporate armed rebels and organized workers and peasants into the polity. In Argentina, placed right in the centre of Figure 2, one is hard pressed to imagine what dominant strategy could possibly dislodge it from permanent regime instability—whether of a democratic or an autocratic cast! Common to these cases is a loss of elite control and an inability of mass organizations successfully to impose a new coherent strategy for either domestic or external reasons . . .

[**Conclusion**]

In this article, we have explored the hypothesis that the mode of transition from autocratic rule is a principal determinant of whether democracy will emerge. Distinguishing between situations in which previous elites continued to dominate political life and those in which they were displaced by mass movements and between those in which actors chose strategies of multilateral compromise or unilateral imposition, we have concluded that "transitions by pact" are the most likely to lead to political democracy, followed by "transitions by imposition." Because of the nature of these two modes of transition, however, they are likely to produce restricted types of democracy.

Where incumbents lost control over the process of regime change and the new structures of power and authority emerged from below, either by reform or revolution, the probability of a successful outcome diminished—at least in the past. Most problematic were those situations which mixed elements of several modes of transition and from which no dominant winning strategy or coalition could emerge. Not only is the mode of transition a principal determinant of whether democracy will emerge, but it may also be a major factor influencing the specific type of democracy that will eventually be consolidated. That, however, is an argument that we must pursue elsewhere.

Note from the Editor

1.   See Moore in this volume.

South Korea's Elite Settlement and Democratic Consolidation

Michael G. Burton and Jai P. Ryu

Could a coup d'état happen now in South Korea? Korea meets the generally accepted criteria of procedural democracy, and it has high ratings on political rights and civil liberties. Can we say, therefore, that Korean democracy is consolidated? Not in the view of most scholars. Indeed, scholars overwhelmingly agree that Korean democracy *is not* consolidated. While some are optimistic about the *prospects* for consolidation, the most explicit and extensive treatments of the consolidation question, are decidedly pessimistic. They stress the weakness of political parties and other representative institutions, the lack of strong mass attachments to political parties, the concentration of power in the presidency, the continuing hold of Confucian culture, the privileged position of business elites, and persistent economic inequality (see e.g., Byung Kook Kim, 1994).

While these assessments reflect most leading theoretical perspectives on the conditions that are essential to democratic consolidation, the influential idea that consolidation depends primarily on the unity and cooperation of national elites has not been seriously explored. Applying this perspective to the political changes in Korea during the last decade, we find strong reasons for thinking that Korean democracy is consolidated. We concentrate on the idea that *consensual elite unity* is the most critical determinant of consolidated democracy, that is, of stable, procedural democracy. Consensually unified elites are characterized by inclusive communication and influence networks, and by broad agreement on political game rules, the most fundamental of which is the norm of restrained partisanship. How does such unity come about? This appears to have happened in two ways: elite settlements and elite convergences[1] . . .

Elite Disunity in Korean History

Elite disunity was deeply rooted in Korean history. Although the Yi dynasty (1392–1910) lasted more than five centuries, it was characterized by incessant, often bloody elite struggles for control of or proximity to the monarchy. Lacking significant ethnic, linguistic, religious, class, or other structural bases, elite conflict closely approximated purely personalistic factionalism. Factionalism persisted among the independence leaders who emerged during Japanese occupation (1910–1945), and then greatly escalated in the context of Cold War struggles over the future of the Korean peninsula after World War II. The Republic of Korea, formed with American backing under Syngman Rhee in 1948, was the product of three years of bloody conflict in which right-wing forces in the police and the military killed many leftists and moderates and drove the rest underground. Although Rhee became president under a quasi-democratic constitution, he regularly violated its modest restrictions over the next twelve years to hold onto the presidency and to suppress his opponents.

By the late 1950s, the Korean national elite displayed the basic configuration that persisted for the next thirty years. Essentially, it was polarized between forces supporting Rhee and his ruling Liberal Party and those backing the anti-government Democratic Party. Moreover, each camp was internally riven. Elite disunity during the next three decades was most clearly indicated by: the overthrow of Rhee in 1960 when the military refused to repress massive student protests against his fraudulent re-election; the military coup in May 1961 by Major General Park Chung Hee and a small clique of military officers; the growing authoritarianism of the Park regime in the 1970s and the emergence of a substantial democratic opposition movement; the assassination of Park in 1979 by his CIA director in an avowed effort to prevent a disastrous clash between regime and opposition forces; the December 1979 mutiny in the military in which General Chun Doo Hwan and several other young generals arrested and displaced their superior officers; and the coup d'état in May 1980 by the Chun group and their brutal repression of opposition forces.

The Chun Regime: Prelude to the Settlement

While repressive, the Chun regime enacted the new constitution of 1980. This retained many features of Park's authoritarian Yushin constitution, but it created a single-term, seven-year presidency and somewhat strengthened the legislature and judiciary by allowing a majority of the legislature to revoke an emergency decree, and by prohibiting the president from dissolving the assembly for three years. And Chun did not attempt to amend the constitution to keep himself in power as Rhee and Park had done . . .

Upon his inauguration as president in January 1981, Chun restated his commitment to a peaceful transfer of power in 1988. Nevertheless, over the next six years opposition to his regime mounted steadily, assisted by his vacillation on demands for democratization. Chun's liberalizing moves, such as lifting the five-year ban on former politicians in 1985, directly facilitated opposition mobilization, while his repressive measures, such as "campus stabilization," enraged his opponents and opened a rift within the ruling party . . . Now the party defending the existing government and constitution faced a strong and relatively unified (if only temporarily) camp of opponents who claimed the government was illegitimate and called for a new constitution . . .

Because the government party continued to dominate the National Assembly with its combination of 61 appointed and 87 elected deputies, the battle for democratization after 1985 was waged primarily on university campuses, in the streets, and at the factories by students, intellectuals, workers, and progressive Christians; and through public statements by prominent politicians, intellectuals, clergymen, and lawyers. The growth of opposition forces, along with Chun's repressive measures, deepened divisions between moderates and hardliners in the ruling party. At the same time, business elites became increasingly unhappy over Chun's demands for political contributions and his regime's intrusion in business decision-making. In this context, Chun announced in February 1986 his acceptance of the opposition demand for constitutional revision before the 1988 election. But the ensuing discussions soon deadlocked: the Chun government insisted on a parliamentary system with the chief executive elected by the legislature, and the opposition advocated a popularly elected presidency.

The 1987 Settlement

The impasse over constitutional revision continued into 1987, but it was widely reported in early March that Chun had given Roh Tae

Woo, head of the governing party, broad powers to seek resumption of the stalled talks. Mass opposition to the Chun regime and support for opposition elites was of course a key factor. Opposition intensified with the revelation in January that a Seoul National University student died of torture during police interrogation. Opposition leadership was now primarily in the hands of veteran dissidents Kim Dae Jung and Kim Young Sam. In April they defected from the New Korea Democratic Party (KNDP), because the nominal party head offered to compromise with the government, forming the Reunification Democratic Party (RDP). Also in April, Chun reacted to growing mass protest by reneging on his promise to allow a new constitution to be drafted before the 1988 presidential election, suspending constitutional discussions until after the elections and the 1988 Olympics, and placing Kim Dae Jung under house arrest. These actions sparked more protest demonstrations and seriously deepened the split between the increasingly moderate Democratic Justice Party (DJP) leadership and Chun and his lieutenants.

Chun responded in May with conciliatory moves: he replaced seven senior cabinet officials and the Prime Minister, who was Roh's main civilian rival for the DJP's presidential nomination. His new Prime Minister apologized to the nation for the student's death, and three senior police commanders were arrested on torture and corruption charges. By replacing Roh's chief rival, Chun appears to have been opening the way for Roh and moderate forces to take the lead. But these measures failed to mollify opposition elites and student protestors.

Mass protests reached unprecedented levels, with middle-class persons increasingly joining them after the June 10 announcement that the ruling DJP had selected Roh Tae Woo, Chun's right-hand man in the 1979 mutiny and the 1980 coup, as its presidential candidate. In a last-ditch effort to placate the opposition, Chun met with Kim Young Sam, head of the RDP, and offered to resume constitutional negotiations. Kim refused, calling publicly for an immediate referendum to choose between a presidential and a parliamentary system, the release of all political prisoners, and restoration of Kim Dae Jung's political and civil rights. Amid surging protests in Seoul and many other cities, the government freed Kim Dae Jung after 78 days of house arrest, and senior ruling party members told reporters they were considering compromises. On June 29, Roh Tae Woo announced a dramatic democratization plan that accepted all the opposition's demands, including speedy amendment of the constitution to allow for a directly elected presidency, amnesty and the restoration of rights for Kim Dae Jung, and free and fair elections by the end of the year. Government officials soon reported that Chun had agreed in principle to these concessions. Most analysts count Roh's June 29 announcement as the key moment in the democratic transition. We agree, and add that it was a major step in the elite settlement.

Following this victory, opposition leaders kept the pressure on, demanding and quickly winning the release of political prisoners and restoration of their political rights as a condition for further negotiations. However, as transition to a democratic presidential system appeared increasingly likely, the long-standing rivalry between Kim Young Sam and Kim Dae Jung resurfaced. Despite this growing fragmentation of the opposition, negotiations with the ruling party continued into the summer, spurred on by renewed anti-government demonstrations, including perhaps the largest in South Korea's history in Seoul in early July, and by waves of strikes and violent acts in July and August by workers at Hyundai, Daewoo, and other major factory sites.

The formal constitutional negotiations that began in early August were conducted by an eight-member committee consisting of four members from each of the two main parties . . . The constitutional committee held nineteen sessions, and on August 31 the committee—hastened by the knowledge that students would soon return to the campuses and renew their protests—announced agreement on the basic components of a new constitution: a single-term presidency of six years (subsequently changed to five), elimination of the president's right to dissolve the National Assembly, congressional endorsement of the president's Supreme Court nominees, congressional powers to investigate the government, a statement of the military's political neutrality, and guarantees of press freedom, the rights of habeas corpus, peaceful assembly, and collective bargaining.

The constitution reflected substantial concessions by both sides. The opposition abandoned demands for creating a vice-presidency, a statement in the preamble condemning the notorious Kwangju massacre in 1980, and a clause enjoining companies to share profits with workers. The ruling party accepted a statement in the preamble praising "the spirit of democracy" represented by the 1960 student uprising against Syngman Rhee—seen by the opposition as acknowledging the public's right to oppose an authoritarian regime—and a statement that: "The armed forces take it as their duty to perform the sacred duty of national security and territorial defense, and their political neutrality shall be observed." The new constitution was overwhelmingly approved, 254 to 4, by the National Assembly in mid-October and 93.1 percent of the voters endorsed it in a national referendum.

These agreements between the ruling and opposition parties constituted the visible part of a deeper elite settlement. Extensive private negotiations, deals, and promises among and within the various elite groups were required to produce the public agreement, but little of this has been studied and brought to light. It is widely believed that Roh assured Chun he would not be punished for the Kwangju massacre and other atrocities . . . Roh had consulted with fellow "softliners" in the military. So he clearly had considerable backing in the military and the ruling party. Indeed, Roh appears to have been the leader of moderate regime forces. That Chun himself had come under the influence of Roh and party moderates is suggested by his backing of Roh; and by a report that on June 19, after a night of violent demonstrations in which the police lost control, Chun was about to call troops into Seoul and other cities but was dissuaded at the last minute by party moderates. It appears that this event was a vital moment in the turn toward the democratic transition and the accompanying elite settlement.

Evidence of Chun's subsequent cooperation in the settlement, albeit reluctant, includes his replacement of the prime minister and eight cabinet officials during July in an avowed effort to make the government impartial during the transitional period, and his pledge in mid-August that the military would support the next president. Another sign of a basic shift in the stance of the ruling group was the very limited use of riot police against massive labor strikes during the summer—a major departure from past policies . . .

Thus, it appears that the main components of an elite settlement were in place by the end of August 1987, when the proposed constitution was announced . . . that amounted to a new code of political conduct for Korean elites. Despite, and probably because of, the opposition's great success, its internal divisions persisted into the fall of 1987. Neither Kim Young Sam nor Kim Dae Jung would forego a chance to win the presidency in the December 16 election. Thus, they split 45 percent of the vote almost evenly, enabling Roh Tae Woo to win with 36.6 percent. This election went a long way toward resolving the legitimacy issue that had plagued every government since the republic war formed. Despite some irregularities, it was an open election and each candidate was free to make his case and challenge the government. The results were generally accepted, although there was a good deal of public anger toward Kim Young Sam and Kim Dae Jung for splitting the opposition.

Solidifying the Settlement

Roh's presidency played an important role in ensuring that the settlement would last. It gave the military time to adjust to being on the political sidelines, and it gave all conservative elites time to develop confidence that democratic elections would not put radicals in power. Many military, political, and business elites would have been most uneasy if the opposition had won the presidency, as indicated by concerns expressed during the run-up to the election that the military might intervene if Roh lost. Moreover, Roh took a number of steps that reinforced the spirit of the settlement and advanced the democratization process. For example, he stated publicly that he should be the last president to come from the military, he dissolved the *honohae,* the elite army organization that played a key role in Chun's coup, and he redefined the Defense Security Command's mission to include preventing a military coup.

While non-threatening to conservative elites, the Roh government proved ineffective in the face of a parliament that was dominated by the opposition after the 1988 National Assembly elections. Although the opposition was split three ways, Roh's Democratic Justice Party could not command a legislative majority, resulting in a two-year deadlock: the government could pass no initiatives, and the opposition could do little more than create panels to investigate the 1979–1980 power seizures and subsequent abuses by the Chun regime. In January 1990, however, after six months of secret negotiations, the two opposition parties led by Kim Young Sam and Kim

Jong Pil merged with Roh's Democratic Justice Party to form the Democratic Liberal Party (DLP). Many in the opposition felt betrayed by the merger, Kim Young Sam was called a traitor, and thousands of protesting students hit the streets. Nevertheless, liberalization of the regime continued . . .

We lack a detailed account of the secret negotiations among leaders of the three parties during the six-month period leading up to the January 1990 merger, but the outcome indicated that substantial compromises were made all around . . . Whereas the three previous major political realignments in South Korea—in 1961, 1972, and 1980—were essentially carried out by the ruling camp, which virtually forced certain individuals in the opposition to join them, this merger entailed joint, party-to-party negotiations, no coercion was used, nearly all members of the two opposition parties went along, with many receiving important party posts, and the formation of the new party was preceded by dissolution of the ruling party. We would stress that consensual elite unity stemming from the 1987 settlement made this unusual event possible.

Kim Young Sam won the December 1992 presidential election with 42 percent of the vote. Kim Dae Jung got 34 percent, and Hyundai founder Chung Ju Young got 16 percent. It was the freest and the fairest election in Korean history. Roh prevented government officials from taking sides, the government put up portraits of each candidate in equal numbers, candidates were not allowed to do their own advertising, and editorialists were prevented from endorsing candidates. All candidates were civilians, and the losers accepted the outcome gracefully. Reasonably fair and free presidential elections have now produced two peaceful transfers of power, though the second elections were substantially freer of irregularities than the first. There has yet to be a transfer of government power to an opposition party—since the authoritarian regime's DJP was the biggest component of the three-party merger in 1990, and the resulting DLP still holds the presidency and dominates the legislature. However, it is significant that President Kim Young Sam was a longtime opposition leader who was imprisoned in 1961, placed under house arrest in 1980 and 1982, and banned from politics from 1980 to 1985. And since assuming the presidency Kim has enacted a number of the reforms he advocated as an opposition leader. Thus, de facto at least, part of the democratic opposition has won government executive power.

During Kim Young Sam's tenure, the military elite, which dominated all other elite groups after 1961, has given every indication of accepting subordination to civilian authorities, despite the fact that Kim moved to purge high-level officers for corruption or their involvement in the power seizures of 1979–1980. Kim also moved briskly to drive many members of the Chun and Roh governments from office . . . While aggressively pursuing such reforms, the Kim government also demonstrated the political restraint and conciliatory behavior that characterize a consensually unified elite. This was especially apparent in the handling of the highly sensitive "12/12 incident" in which generals Chun Doo Wan and Roh Tae Woo led the overthrow of their superiors in 1979. Joined by thirty-seven of his former colleagues, Chung brought charges of sedition under the Criminal Code against Chun, Roh, and thirty-two others. After more than a year of hearings, the government's chief prosecutor ruled on October 29, 1994, that Chun, Roh, and the others had committed mutiny, but he declined to indict them in consideration of the political and social impact. The deputy chief prosecutor was quoted as saying that while Chun and Roh were guilty, it was feared that indicting them would revive national divisiveness. The government stuck by this ruling despite street protests. When Lee Ki Tack, leader of the main opposition party, the Democratic Party (DP), threatened to quit parliament in protest, other DP members refused to follow him. Thus, it appears that most DP leaders are now unwilling to push the issue further.

In sum, by mixing significant reforms with conciliation and restraint, political and military elite factions peacefully transformed their basic relationships under the Chun, Roh, and Kim governments. Both the active military and the most controversial members of the authoritarian regime have left Korean politics . . . Business elites were clearly not harmed by the settlement and the democratic transition, and their prevailing view appears to be that stable democracy is now essential to Korea's success in the global economy.

While labor elites gained a stronger voice through the settlement, they remain somewhat marginal. The new constitution gave workers the right to collective bargaining but a number of restrictions persist. The government-sponsored Federation of Korean Trade Unions (FKTU) is recognized as the only legitimate national federation of unions, while two powerful independent federations are deemed illegal, even though they do not hold anti-system positions. Clearly, not all union leaders have become fully accepted members of the national elite. However, government repression of labor is much less than under the authoritarian regime, and the FKTU has recently been acting more like an independent labor federation by pushing for removal of legal barriers to union political activities . . .

Like labor elites, journalists, progressive intellectuals, students, and church leaders were not direct parties to the elite settlement, and many have criticized the relatively conservative nature of the new democratic regime. Yet these groups now possess the basic freedoms that are essential to their success—to publish, speak out, and form associations—and very few of their members advocate anti-system views. It thus appears that their situations are not fundamentally different from those of their counterparts in consolidated democracies . . .

Conclusion

Because elite settlements are typically underpinned in part by secret agreements and tacit understandings, and because some elite groups are usually more directly engaged in the process than others, elite settlements are rarely if ever clearcut, unequivocal events. This was certainly true in the Korean case, and we therefore stress the hypothetical nature of our conclusions.

The events of 1987 and subsequent patterns of elite behavior are consistent with the conclusion that Korean elites fashioned a settlement in 1987, transforming their basic relations from disunity to consensual unity. This has resulted in basic political stability, irregular power seizures have become highly unlikely, and it appears to have provided a framework of value commitments and interaction patterns that assure all major elite factions access to governmental decision-making. While difficult to achieve, such a configuration of interelite relations tends to persist because elites find that it enables them to pursue their interests in relative security and they come to value its basic principles. For these reasons, we think Korean democracy is consolidated . . .

A number of contextual factors that doubtless facilitated elite unification also bode well for continuing unity, and thus the stability of Korean democracy. They include a strong and growing economy, a substantial and growing middle class, a high level of education, the spread of democratic values within the general population, the absence of serious ethnic or other cultural cleavages that coincide with geographic divisions, the unifying effects of the threat from the North, and an international climate that accepts only democracy as a legitimate form of government.

However, these conditions did not ensure an elite settlement and they do not guarantee continuing elite unity. Most are subject to reversal, and even if reversals do not occur, elite unity could conceivably collapse from excessive factionalism, which has long been a feature of Korean politics. Moreover, it is impossible to know how the seemingly inevitable resolution of the North-South division will occur and what impact it will have on South Korea's elite structure. Nevertheless, it seems undeniable that consensual unity makes South Korea's elites better prepared than ever before to manage future crises while preserving political stability and democracy.

Note from the Editor

1.   On consensual elite unity and elite settlements and convergences, see Field, Higley, and Burton in this volume.

References

Byung Kook Kim. "Politics of Democratic Consolidation in Korea." Paper presented at the International Political Science Association Conference, Berlin, August 1994.

Party Elites and Democratic Consolidation in Southern Europe

Leonardo Morlino

In the democratic consolidations of Southern European countries, such as Italy, Spain, Portugal and Greece, parties and party elites, played a key role. Although the Italian experience encompasses the late 1940s and 1950s, whereas the other three took place in the 1970s and 1980s, they all may be defined as *consolidation through parties*. As a result, in each of these countries party government, in weaker or stronger form, was established. In all cases a predominant party system was also instituted, though we should make some qualifications regarding Greece. Certain mechanisms of an organizational or institutional kind account for the different processes and outcomes. They include a developed party organization, [and] a strong role played by parties vis-à-vis pressure groups. In the four cases under study, however, those factors are combined differently . . .

The "point of departure" we have chosen is the moment when once the approval of a constitutional charter has been achieved. This was 1947 for Italy, 1974 for Greece, 1976 for Portugal, and 1978 for Spain. The final moment to be considered is more approximate, but on the whole the focus is on the first years after the installation as the core period of consolidation. The "point of arrival" for Italy is the end of the 1950s; and for Portugal, Spain and Greece, basically the end of the 1980s.

Excerpts from Leonardo Morlino, "Party Elites and Democratic Consolidation in Southern Europe," *International Political Science Review* 16 (1995): 145–167. Reprinted with permission from *International Political Science Review*, Elsevier Science Ltd., Butterworth Heineman imprint, Oxford, England. Bracketed headings have been created by the editor of this volume.

What Is Democratic Consolidation?

In this article, consolidation is defined as the process by which the structures and norms of democracy have been firmly established and supported by the general public so that the regime gains persistence and the capability to overcome possible challenges . . . [and] crises. If adaptation and firm establishment are the main modes by which consolidation is achieved, a review of our cases suggests that the two main characteristics of the process are the legitimation of the institutions and the self-strengthening of the actors supporting the regime . . .

Thus, to understand democratic consolidation in the different countries, the *top-down* relationships between parties and party system vis-à-vis the general society must be explored, since these relationships determine how parties *control* society. At the same time, the *bottom-up* relationships between people and parties . . . have to be considered, since they represent the *consensual* [legitimatory] component of the consolidating process. Thus, our main starting point is that consolidation emerges from the interweaving of consensus and control, which bring about the characteristic "mixture" of consolidation in each country; the same factors are always present, but to different degrees, as a side effect of institutional control, and of flexibility, which is an effect of consensus.

Legitimation

All four cases present a process of legitimation, though at different speeds and with different features. In Italy, from the end of the 1940s through the 1950s, the process was very slow. Even in the early 1960s, legitimacy was limited, with anti-regime forces on both the Right, the neofascist Movimento Sociale Italiano (MSI), and the Left, the Partito Communista Italiano (PCI), which together took about 30 percent of the vote. By the early 1960s, the forces that only partially supported the regime, such as the Socialists, with 13–14 percent of the vote, had been integrated. This meant that during the first fifteen years after 1948 these forces basically overlapped with those participating in the governmental coalition formed by Christian Democrats (DC) Liberals (PLI), Republicans (PRI) and Social Democrats (PSDI). In other words, there was an internal party system that excluded fringe parties, Socialists included, and a broader party system with its more radical patterns of competition.

If placed on a sort of continuum, the Spanish case is very distant from the Italian one, much closer to the opposite pole. After the first election, in 1977, the extreme Right disappeared. A formation of the Right (Alianza Popular) found it very difficult to become established and achieved a resounding success only in 1982, thanks to the crisis of the Union de Centro Democrático (UCD) and its parallel transformation from a semi-proregime force to a more integrated party. The Communist Left showed a great deal of moderation at an elite level and, in spite of deep internal political conflict and a crisis in the leadership, it was fully integrated into the regime from the beginning. The legitimation of regionalist forces was much slower.

Greece and Portugal, which also differ from one another in important respects, are closer to the experience of Spain. In Greece, the Right was very supportive of the newly installed regime, which was created by Karamanlis and Nea Democratia (ND). After the first years, in Portugal as well, the Right also supported the regime. As for the Left, the Greek and Portuguese processes differed. The integration of Greek Communists originated from the weaknesses of the two Communist parties that were caught in an ancillary position vis-à-vis the Socialists after the electoral success of the Panhellenic Socialist Movement, PASOK, in 1981. The process of legitimation ended in 1989–90 when the government formed an alliance with Nea Democratia. In spite of the transformations of all Communist parties in Western and Eastern Europe, in Portugal the Communist leadership was able to maintain its position, all the while keeping the party midly in support of the regime and condemning it to a declining electoral trend. Thus, on the whole, the experience of Greece is closer to that of Spain, and in the early 1990s there has been no serious challenge to the legitimacy of either democracy.

To the issue of legitimacy, other important elements should be added. First, in three of the four countries the process has not been linear. In Italy, it basically remained frozen during the most oppressive years of the Cold War (1948–56), until the Hungarian revolt. In Spain, after the installation of democracy, there was a difficult period between 1979 and 1981 with public disenchantment and a crisis in and breakdown of the Union de Centro Democratico (UCD), the main actor in the democratic installation; these were also the years of Basque terrorism, with support coming from different separatist groups that had gained votes in national and regional elections. In Portugal, until the first important constitutional revision in 1982, there was a long phase during which it was not even clear what kind of democracy should be installed and considered legitimate: a radical socialist regime or a pluralist democracy closer to European models. Only in Greece was the process basically linear: in fact, the legitimation concerned Communists only and there were no important moments of backsliding . . .

[Party Organization in Relation to Society]

How is consolidation still possible if after a few years there is only a limited legitimacy, as in the Italian case? . . . The development of party organization and of the relationships that are established between interest groups and parties, seem to be a plausible answer. These two factors may be considered the main means for controlling society from a party's perspective . . .

The main purpose of organizational structuring is to maintain and enlarge a stable electorate that shares the ideology, values and programs of parties. It is well known, however, that a better, more articulated organization is achieved in special conditions where the ideological dimension is an important feature of the political conflict in the country. At the same time, its main thrust also comes from the logic of party competition: the electoral dynamics, above all, induce parties to create organizational resources to win more votes and maintain their electorate . . .

A stable, developed organizational structure of one or more parties in a party system may be a condition for democratic consolidation. [For] the *control* of society by political elites, in order to consolidate their power, may also be achieved through [such] party organization. Our cases, however, suggest that this is not the only way of gaining this sort of control. A second possibility lies in the establishment of relationships between the parties and more or less organized interest groups or sectors of society through the processes of decision making, the distribution of state resources, or in other ways. In this case the links with the public stem not from ideology and organization, but from economic interest. This is the party control over organized and non-organized interest groups, individuals and micro-interests, directly or through the public sector.

A way of looking at relationships and links between parties and interest groups, or individuals, is to see whether parties and the party system as a whole are able to perform a "gatekeeping" role in controlling access to the decisional arena. If so, for interest groups, party intermediation is the best way to protect their interests. Gatekeeping may become one of the main aspects in the process of consolidation, since it causes the most relevant sectors of the public to accept the role of parties and their control over them . . .

Empirical Patterns of Democratic Consolidation

With regard to the bottom-up consensual relationship toward institutions, legitimation plays a crucial role in different domains, not only at the level of parties (and the party system). The two poles consist of an incomplete, limited legitimation (*exclusive legitimation*) and a full legitimation (*inclusive legitimation*) of institutions through parties (and the party system). Thus, in Italy, about fifteen years after the democratic inauguration, the legitimacy achieved was partial and limited. If the positions of the Right and of most of the Left are considered, this may be labeled an *exclusive legitimacy*. Greece represents the opposite case, above all from the moment when the Communists participated in a government with Nea Democratia (1989–90). Largely *inclusive legitimacy* may also be defined as that achieved by Spain, in which some local anti-regime forces may be ignored by the end of the 1980s. Because of the position of the Communists, Portugal still presents some limitation of legitimacy. Thus, the Portuguese case is a *quasi-inclusive legitimacy*.

When the second dimension of the process, *control*, is considered, there are two main possibilities:

(i) institutions attain a firm control over society up to the point of dominating it through parties (and their organization), state institutions or both (*dominance* [or occupation]); or

(ii) a more active, autonomous, society and/or a situation of low development in party organization gives society more autonomy vis-à-vis state institutions and parties (*neutrality*).

Thus, with regard to internal party organization, Italy stands out as a case in which ideology, initial mass mobilization and bipolarization brought about a more developed party organization, thanks also to Catholic groups, authentic ancillary associations for Christian Democracy. In Spain the opposite is true. The combination of a long, traditional anti-party propaganda under Franco, the waning of ideology, and the modernization of a complex society were strong obstacles to party organization. The development of mass media and other techniques in a modern society led party leaders to appreciate other party models and to transform the old organization based on cells and sections. Greece and Portugal are in the middle, but closer to the Italian case than the Spanish one. After all, strong bipolarization and some ideological tenets contributed to the organizational development of PASOK and, later on, to the transformation and organizational development of Nea Democratia. The same applies to the Portuguese Social Democrats in their competition with the Socialists.

Although to a different degree, in all four countries there was a partisan occupation of the state: the phenomenon was relatively smaller in Spain, but greater in the other three countries. Thus, *neutrality* characterizes the relationships between parties and interest groups in Spain; party *dominance* is typical of Italy; in Greece a more accentuated *occupation* during the PASOK decade was the rule; and Portugal again lay between Italy and Greece. Therefore, in the end the hypotheses suggested by our cases seem to be the following:

(i)   When legitimacy is restricted, if some forms of elite stabilization, party organization and/or control of organized and nonorganized groups is not clearly achieved, then even a weak consolidation is not possible, and sooner or later a crisis will occur.

(ii) If, on the contrary, there is widespread democratic legitimacy from the beginning, or shortly thereafter, less party control of society is necessary to achieve consolidation.

(iii) If, in addition to widespread legitimacy, there is a partisan control of society, the second phenomenon is not decisive for consolidation, but it is still important in characterizing both the process of consolidation and the pattern of consolidated democracy . . .

At this point the main patterns of consolidation may be sketched.

If the legitimation of institutions is only partially achieved, then the role of parties and even of other institutions, which penetrate and dominate society, is a necessity for consolidation. Thus, party structures essentially organize and at the same time maintain internal divisions by encapsulating them. When this is the case, party-based consolidation or *party consolidation* is achieved.

In the case of wide legitimation, party structuring is unnecessary; if there is widespread support for democratic values, the role played by elites may be central and quite sufficient for achieving a flexible pattern of consolidation, where adaptation and change is always possible without a serious crisis. This is the elite-based consolidation, or *elite consolidation*.

There are two other possibilities. One involves wide legitimation and the control of society through a large public sector, as well as parties rooted in society which bring about a process of consolidation that is defined here as state-based consolidation or *state consolidation*. When, however, the traditions of the country, historical timing and other features do not allow either a strong control of society or a wide legitimation of democratic institutions, there is only *maintenance*. No consolidation is possible, and a crisis is always likely. Exclusive and weak legitimacy, no party dominance, a fairly developed party system, but one that lacks strong links with various sectors of society would be the main characteristics of this model. In this pattern, only an international context favorable to democracy will allow the existence of such a regime. That is, in this fourth case, the international aspects, which have deliberately been excluded from the picture, may become crucial to the resulting pattern (and the continuation of the regime).

If limited legitimacy and partisan dominance are stressed, the Italian experience may be labeled a *party consolidation*. In Spain, the process has developed in a very different way. Here, there is . . . no structuring of parties. However, the Socialist Party and its leader, Felipe González, occupy a key position in the party system and, at the same time, a widespread legitimacy has been achieved in a limited number of years. Therefore, from the point of view of the main actors in the process, Spain features an *elite consolidation*.

In Greece and Portugal some aspects are more similar to the first model and others are closer to the second one. Particularly in Greece there is a . . . fairly strong internal party organization and, at the same time, the control of civil society by the incumbent party and a great role played by the public sector, which additionally strengthens that control. The extent of legitimacy grows to the point where it is very close to the Spanish case. Thus, the best definition seems to be *state consolidation.*

Finally, in Portugal, there are various concurrent elements: . . . a relatively developed internal party organization, party dominance and a strong role played by the public sector until the end of the 1980s, when a reform of the Constitution (1989) permitted some development of private enterprise, quasi-legitimacy, but without the complete integration of the Communist Party. Thus, we again have *state consolidation* with an important role played by the old corporatist authoritarian tradition.

The whole picture is roughly sketched in Figure 1. This figure shows that the strong role of parties may be complemented by limited legitimacy. And also, that widespread legitimacy may be complemented by a weaker intervention of parties in society. But it also stresses that at the same time parties, state resources, and legitimacy may contribute to consolidation. To conclude, this analysis provides support to the hypothesis that there are at least two different patterns of consolidation: one achieved through legitimation and a limited control of society and another through a stronger control that compensates for the limited legitimation . . .

[Recent Developments and Prospects]

Confirmation that the process discussed here has definitely been concluded in Portugal, Greece and Spain and that the main aspects

Figure 1. *Models and Cases of Democratic Consolidation*

		Legitimation	
		Exclusive	Inclusive
Control	Dominance	party consolidation *Italy*	state consolidation *Portugal Greece*
	Neutrality	maintenance	*Spain* elite consolidation

of Italian consolidation are changing, is provided by the following facts. In Greece the new government of Nea Democratia seems to have inaugurated a new phase of politics in 1990, so that the main elements that characterized PASOK governments have changed. In addition, PASOK again won the 1993 elections and was returned to power. In Portugal, after 1989, the Social Democratic government made a number of decisions aimed at opening and enlarging the private sector and, thus, in this country also some of the most important features of the past few years will disappear. In Spain, the Socialists lost their majority in the 1993 election, but they remained in power, supported by other forces. In this way, one of the most characterizing elements of Spanish consolidation disappeared.

Finally, in Italy, after so many years and recurring crises, the most important features of consolidation have recently been disappearing or changing: party organization is fading away; the planned privatization of a number of agencies, banks and industries will shrink the public sector; parties are no longer able to dominate interest groups; a new party system is emerging. Actually, since the end of the 1980s Italy has entered a new phase of deconsolidation and crisis, which will culminate in the transformation of the present democracy. The approval of two new electoral (quasi-majority) laws for the Senate and Chamber of Deputies in early August 1993 is only the first step in this direction.

Delegative Democracy

Guillermo O'Donnell

Here I depict a "new species," a type of existing democracies that has yet to be theorized. As often happens, it has many similarities with other, already recognized species, with cases shading off between the former and some variety of the latter. Still, I believe that the differences are significant enough to warrant an attempt at such a depiction . . .

[The Main Points of the Argument]

Let me briefly state the main points of my argument: (1) Existing theories and typologies of democracy refer to *representative* democracy as it exists, with all its variations and subtypes, in highly developed capitalist countries. (2) Some newly installed democracies (Argentina, Brazil, Peru, Ecuador, Bolivia, Philippines, Korea, and many postcommunist countries) *are* democracies in the sense that they meet Robert Dahl's criteria for the definition of polyarchy.[1] (3) Yet these democracies, are not—and do not seem to be on the path toward becoming—representative democracies; they present characteristics that prompt me to call them *delegative* democracies (DD). (4) DDs are not consolidated (i.e., institutionalized) democracies, but they may be *enduring*. In many cases, there is no sign either of any imminent threat of an authoritarian regression, or of advances toward representative democracy. (5) There is an important interaction effect: the deep social and economic crisis that most of these countries inherited from their authoritarian predecessors reinforces certain practices and conceptions about the proper exercise of political authority that lead in the direction of delegative, not representative democracy.

The following considerations underlie [this] argument: The installation of a democratically elected government opens the way for a "second transition," often longer and more complex than the initial transition from authoritarian rule. This second transition is supposed to be from a democratically elected *government* to an institutionlized, consolidated, democratic *regime*. Nothing guarantees, however, that this second transition will occur. New democracies may regress to authoritarian rule, or they may stall in a feeble, uncertain situation. This situation may endure without opening avenues for institutionalized forms of democracy. The crucial element determining the success of the second transition is the building of a set of institutions that become important decisional points in the flow of political power.

For such a successful outcome to occur, governmental policies and the political strategies of various agents must embody the recognition of a paramount shared interest in democratic institution building. The successful cases have featured a decisive coalition of broadly supported political leaders who take great care in creating and strengthening democratic political institutions. These institutions, in turn, have made it easier to cope with the social and economic problems inherited from the authoritarian regime. This was the case in Spain, Portugal (although not immediately after democratic installation), Uruguay, and Chile. In contrast, the cases of delegative democracy mentioned earlier have achieved neither institutional progress nor much governmental effectiveness in dealing with their respective social and economic crises . . .

[The Leader and Democratic Institutions in Delegative Democracy]

Delegative Democracies rest on the premise that whoever wins election to the presidency is thereby entitled to govern as he or she sees fit, constrained only by the hard facts of existing power relations and by a constitutionally limited term of office. The president is taken to be the embodiment of the nation and the main custodian and definer of its interests. The policies of his government need bear no resemblance to the promises of his campaign . . .

Typically, winning presidential candidates in DDs present themselves as above both political parties and organized interests. How could it be otherwise for somebody who claims to embody the whole of the nation? In this view, other institutions—courts and legislatures, for instance—are nuisances that come attached to the domestic and international advantages of being a democratically elected president. Accountability to such institutions appears as a mere impediment to the full authority that the president has been delegated to exercise.

DD is not alien to the democratic tradition. It is more democratic, but less liberal, than representative democracy. DD is strongly majoritarian. It consists in constituting, through clean elections, a majority that empowers someone to become, for a given number of years, the embodiment and interpreter of the high interests of the nation. Often, DDs use devices such as runoff elections if the first round of elections does not generate a clear-cut majority. This majority must be created to support the myth of legitimate delegation.

Furthermore, DD is strongly individualistic, but more in a Hobbesian than a Lockean way: voters are supposed to choose, irrespective of their identities and affiliations, the individual who is most fit to take responsibility for the destiny of the country. Elections in DDs are a very emotional and high stakes event: candidates compete for a chance to rule virtually free of all constraints save those imposed by naked, noninstitutionalized power relations. After the election, voters/delegators are expected to become a passive but cheering audience of what the president does . . .

The leader has to heal the nation by uniting its dispersed fragments into a harmonious whole. Since the body politic is in disarray, and since its existing voices only reproduce its fragmentation, delegation includes the right (and the duty) of administering the unpleasant medicines that will restore the health of the nation. For this view, it seems obvious that only the head really knows: the president and his most trusted advisors are the alpha and the omega of politics . . . In the meantime, it is "obvious" that resistance—be it from congress, political parties, interest groups, or crowds in the streets—has to be ignored . . . The president isolates himself from most political institutions and organized interests, and bears sole responsibility for the successes and failures of "his" policies . . .

In DDs, parties, the congress, and the press are generally free to voice their criticisms. Sometimes the courts, citing what the executive typically dismisses as "legalistic, formalistic reasons," block unconstitutional policies. Workers' and capitalists' associations often complain loudly. The party (or coalition) that elected the president despairs about its loss of popularity, and refuses parliamentary support for the policies he has "foisted" on them. This increases the political isolation of the president, his difficulties in forming a stable legislative coalition, and his propensity to sidestep, ignore, or corrupt the congress and other institutions.

Here it is necessary to elaborate on what makes representative democracy different from its delegative cousin. Representation necessarily involves an element of delegation: through some procedure, a collectivity authorizes some individuals to speak for it, and eventually to commit the collectivity to what the representative decides. Consequently, representation and delegation are not polar opposites. It is not always easy to make a sharp distinction between the type of democracy which is organized around "representative delegation" and the type where the delegative element overshadows the representative one.

[But] representation entails accountability: somehow representatives are held responsible for their actions by those they claim to be entitled to speak for. In institutionalized democracies, accountability runs not only vertically, making elected officials responsible to the ballot box, but also horizontally, across a network of relatively autonomous powers (i.e., other institutions) that can call into question, and eventually punish, improper ways of discharging the responsibilities of a given official . . . Vertical accountability, along with the freedom to form parties and to try to influence public opinion, exists in both representative and delegative democracies. But the horizontal accountability characteristic of representative democracy is extremely weak or nonexistent in delegative democracies. Furthermore, since the institutions that make horizontal accountability effective are seen by delegative presidents as unnecessary encumbrances to their "mission," they make strenuous efforts to hamper the development of such institutions . . .

Because policies are carried out by a series of relatively autonomous powers, decision making in representative democracies tends to be slow and incremental and sometimes prone to gridlock. But, by this same token, those policies are usually vaccinated against gross mistakes, and they have a reasonably good chance of being implemented: moreover, responsibility for mistakes tends to be widely shared . . . DD gives the president the apparent advantage of having practically no horizontal accountability. DD has the additional apparent advantage of allowing swift policy making, but at the expense of a higher likelihood of gross mistakes, of hazardous implementation, and of concentrating responsibility for the outcomes on the president. Not surprisingly, presidents in DDs tend to suffer wild swings in popularity: one day they are acclaimed as providential saviors, and the next they are cursed as only fallen gods can be . . .

The Cycle of Crisis

Now I will focus on some South American cases of delegative democracy—Argentina, Brazil, and Peru. There is no need to detail the depth of the crisis that these countries inherited from their respective authoritarian regimes. Such a crisis generates a strong sense of urgency and provides fertile terrain for unleashing the delegative propensities that may be present in a given country. Problems and demands mount up before inexperienced governments that must operate through a weak and disarticulated (if not disloyal) bureaucracy . . .

The longer and deeper the crisis, and the less the confidence that the government will be able to solve it, the more rational it becomes for everyone to act (1) in a highly disaggregated manner, especially in relation to state agencies that may help to alleviate the consequences of the crisis for a given group or sector (thus further weakening and corrupting the state apparatus); (2) with extremely short time horizons; and (3) with the assumption that everyone else will do the same. In short, there is a general scramble for narrow, short-term advantage. This . . . is the exact opposite of the conditions that foster both strong democratic institutions and reasonably effective ways of dealing with pressing national problems. Once the initial hopes are dashed and the first packages have failed, cynicism about politics, politicians, and governments becomes the pervading mood . . .

How does one win election and how, once elected, does one

govern in this type of situation? Quite obviously—and most de-structively in terms of the building of public trust that helps a de-mocracy to consolidate—by saying one thing during the campaign and doing the contrary when in office. Of course, institutionalized democracies are not immune to this trick, but the consequences are more devastating when there are few and weak institutions and a deep socioeconomic crisis afflicts the country. Presidents have gained election in Argentina, Bolivia, Ecuador, and Peru by promising ex-pansionary economic policies and many other good things to come with them, only to enact severe stabilization packages immediately or shortly after entering office. Whatever the merits of such policies for a given country at a given time, their surprise adoption does nothing to promote public trust, particularly if their immediate and most visible impact further depresses the already low standard of living of most of the population. Moreover, the virtual exclusion of parties and congress from such momentous decisions has malign consequences. When the executive finally, and inevitably, needs leg-islative support, he is bound to find a congress that is resentful and feels no responsibility for policies it had no hand in making . . .

From Omnipotence to Impotence

If we consider that the logic of delegation also means that the execu-tive does nothing to strengthen the judiciary, the resulting dearth of effective and autonomous institutions places immense responsibil-ity on the president. Remember that the typical incumbent in a DD has won election by promising to save the country without much cost to anyone, yet soon gambles the fate of his government on poli-cies that entail substantial costs for many parts of the population. This results in policy making under conditions of despair: the shift from wide popularity to general vilification can be as rapid as it is dramatic. The result is a curious mixture of governmental omnipo-tence and impotence. Omnipotence begins with the spectacular en-actment of the first policy packages and continues with a flurry of decisions aimed at complementing those packages . . . The other side of the coin is extreme weakness in making those decisions into effec-tive long-term regulations of societal life . . .

In DDs we [also] witness a decision making frenzy, what in Latin American we call *decretismo* . . . In the midst of a severe crisis and increasing popular impatience, the upshot is usually new flurries of decisions which, because of the experience many sectors have had in resisting the previous ones, are even less likely to be implemented . . . As failures accumulate, the country finds itself stuck with a widely reviled president whose goal is just to hang on until the end of his term. The resulting period of passivity and disarray of public policy does nothing to help the situation of the country.

Given this scenario, the "natural" outcome in Latin America in the past would have been a successful coup d'état . . . At the moment, however—for reasons mostly linked to the international context, which I cannot discuss here—DDs exhibit a rather remarkable capacity for endurance. With the partial exception of Peru, where the constitutional breakdown was led by its delegative president, no successful coups d'état have taken place.

The economic policy undertaken by DDs is not always condemned to be widely perceived as failure, particularly in the aftermath of the hyperinflation or long periods of extremely high inflation. This is the case in Argentina today under President Menem, although it is not clear how sustainable the improved economic situation is. But such economic achievements, as well as the more short-lived ones of Collor (Brazil), Alfonsin (Argentina), and Garcia (Peru) at the height of the apparent successes of their economic packages, can lead a president to give the ultimate proof of the existence of a delegative democracy. As long as their policies are recognized as successful by electorally weighty segments of the population, delegative presidents find it simply abhorrent that their terms should be constitutionally limited; how could these "formal limitations" preclude the continuation of their providential mission? Consequently, they promote—by means that further weaken whatever horizontal accountability still exists—constitutional reforms that would allow their reelection or, failing this, their continuation at the apex of government as prime ministers in a parliamentary regime . . .

[This] begs the question of how long the bulk of the population will be willing to play this sort of game. [An] optimistic scenario would have a decisive segment of the political leadership recognizing the self-destructive quality of those [patterns], and agreeing to change the terms on which they compete and govern. This seems to me practically the only way out of the problem, but the obstacles to such a roundabout but ultimately happy outcome are many.

Note from the Editor

1.   See Dahl in this volume.

Elites' Political Values and Democratic Consolidation in Brazil

Elisa P. Reis and Zairo B. Cheibub

This paper discusses the values and attitudes of the Brazilian elites and explores the possible consequences that these may have on democratic consolidation. What we intend to do in the following pages is move beyond the democratic-versus-authoritarian-regime debate that has for so long motivated academic discussions; our concern is with the models of democracy involved in the current Brazilian political scene and, particularly, with the chances that a more inclusionary democratic order may become the norm.

While based upon Brazilian data, we believe this discussion relevant to other experiences in consolidating democracy. In many national contexts today, the question appears to be just what type of democracy may arise after a longer or shorter period of transition away from authoritarianism. Across these various cases, the processes of democratic construction may range in nature from the institutionalization of more socially integrated and inclusionary political orders to the institutionalization of more restrictive political orders.

Elites' Values, Political Choices, and Democratic Consolidation

It is our contention that the cognitive and normative perceptions of society are crucially significant for the scope and nature of the type of democracy under consolidation. Although we have chosen in this paper to focus on the values and attitudes of the elites, it should not be concluded that we deem either values in general or the attitudes of the elites in particular to be the sole determinants of eventual democratic outcomes. Yet, although we are fully aware of the multitude of factors shaping a political order, there can be little doubt that those who have command of scarce resources play a strategic role in societal life.

Although from the perspective of class theories those who rule are perceived as mere role-players, it is nevertheless clear that the values and beliefs, as well as the actual behavior, of members of the elite have the power either to preserve or to reverse the status quo. It does not matter if class theorists conceive of these values and attitudes as mere reflections of something else, nor that they reduce behavior to structural factors. Insofar as politics and policies involve some margin of choice and deliberation, there is no doubt but that the cognitive and normative perceptions of those who make decisions will to some extent contribute to forming reality.

Moreover, Brazil's social, political, and economic resources have historically been highly concentrated. There can thus be little argument that the country has very powerful elites, some with de facto veto power over particular paths to political and economic development. In this sense, even the chances for incremental change in Brazil are dependent to a considerable degree upon the acquiescence of the elites. While democratization itself contributes to making the elites more responsive to organized popular movements and parties, if we are to assess the most likely outcomes of ongoing political conflicts, there still remains a critical need to investigate just how the most powerful and influential sectors of society respond to such pressures for change.

The riddle of how the elites may respond to pressures for change can be approached from different angles and using different tools of sociopolitical analysis, insofar as the actual behavior of the elites depends upon different factors, such as institutional arrangements, economic interests, and strategic calculations. In order to further press home the relevance of our chosen emphasis on values, we would like to suggest that the cultural-ideological dimension—where values and beliefs take shape—constitutes a set of variable structured patterns, much as one can speak of the institutional context as being a structured environment. In this sense, identifying the views that the elites typically hold about society and policy helps us better understand their choices and actions, thus shedding light on the ongoing process of democratization.

In this paper we concentrate mainly on values and beliefs regarding social rights and distribution. As Seymour Martin Lipset's recent (1994) reappraisal of the question indicates, growth and distribution are among the prerequisites of democracy. Current levels of poverty and social inequality, which rank Brazil among the most unequal societies in the world, and the levels of social destitution experienced by a large part of the Brazilian population, may imply a drastic shrinking of the public arena, with serious consequences for social solidarity. The combined effect of acute poverty and accentuated inequality is to engender such dissimilar life chances and cognitive experiences that split political cultures result.

Under these circumstances one is led to conclude that the chances for democratic consolidation in Brazil, as in other Third World societies, will be greatly affected by the prospects for socially and politically incorporating the worse-off. That the strategic elites are the ones who make decisions of great relevance about these matters suggests to us that we have much to gain from coming to understand those values and beliefs that are among the parameters informing their decisions.

Accordingly, this paper presents data about members of the Brazilian elites' values and opinions concerning democracy, poverty, social inequality, and related issues. The data comes from a research project carried out at Instituto Universitário de Pesquisas do Rio de Janeiro, Brazil. Interviews were conducted in 1993 and encompassed a sample of 320 individuals, members of four elites usually identified as key policy actors in the Brazilian political economy: top public officials, elected politicians, business leaders, and union leaders.

Perceived Obstacles to Democracy

Let us first examine what the elites have to say about obstacles to the consolidation of democracy in Brazil. The first thing to be observed is that for the majority of the elite members interviewed (about two-thirds), Brazil is already a democracy. Moreover, they see no indications that this democratic order faces any direct threat of a return to authoritarianism. Based on responses to a fixed-choice question, we see a generalized belief that a return to military rule is inconceivable. Not only does no one claim to perceive the possibility of military intervention as a major obstacle to democracy, but nearly half the respondents affirm that the major roadblocks are social rather than economic or, strictly speaking, political. Thus, the two most often chosen obstacles were the population's lack of education and poverty/inequality.

Perceived Characteristics of Democracy

If, for the elites, Brazil is already a democracy, albeit threatened by its poor social record, what meaning do they ascribe to the term "democratic order"? Table I, based on a fixed-choice question, provides some clues.

Table I. *Main Characteristics of Democracy (Percentage)*

Characteristic	Total Sample	(1)*	(2)*	(3)*	(4)*
Civil/Individual Liberties	30.8	32.0	22.5	39.1	29.9
Political Participation	20.5	16.0	25.8	13.0	26.0
Equality of Opportunity	9.4	6.0	20.2	7.6	1.3
Equality of Rights	5.8	8.0	5.6	3.3	7.8
Pluralism/Tolerance	5.5	8.0	4.5	6.5	3.9
Various Institutional Features†	4.9	4.0	3.4	8.7	2.6
Respect for Majority Rule	3.9	4.0	3.4	5.4	2.6
Socioeconomic Equality	3.6	2.0	1.1	2.2	9.1
Representation	3.6	4.0	5.6	2.2	2.6
Respect for Law and Government	3.2	4.0	3.3	2.2	3.9
Liberty/Equality	2.3	2.0	1.1	—	6.6
Power Transparency	1.9	4.0	1.1	3.3	—
Others	4.5	6.0	2.2	6.5	3.9
Total	99.9	100.0	99.8	100.0	100.2
	(*n*=308)	(*n*=50)	(*n*=89)	(*n*=92)	(*n*=77)

* (1) Deputies and Senators (2) Top Public Officials (3) Businessmen (4) Labor Union Leaders

† Party organizations; secret ballot; power alternance and the like.

We can conclude from the data that the majority of the elites define democracy in classic liberal fashion: first comes respect for liberty and then political participation. For the bureaucratic elites, equality of opportunities, another liberal tenet, also stands out as a defining characteristic.

Our survey further explored this issue by inquiring about the expediency of enhancing conditions that could lead to "fair equality of opportunities." When we asked the elite members if they believed that historically disadvantaged groups should be granted legal privileges that would help foster true equality of opportunities, most respondents disagreed. Across the different sectors surveyed, indications are that the elites are unwilling to accept affirmative action programs.

Going back to the data in Table I, despite the previously observed salience of the socioeconomic dimension, equality along this axis was not ranked high among the defining characteristics of democracy. Even among union leaders, the incidence of answers placing emphasis on the socioeconomic dimension is not that great (9 percent).

How can we interpret this distinct tendency to define democracy along classic liberal lines when viewed in conjunction with the elites' tendency to stress the socioeconomic threats to democracy? Should we conclude that the apparent social sensitivity displayed by the elites in point of fact reflects a pragmatic concern with maintaining order, an attitude which does not necessarily imply adherence to a social-democratic model? Further analysis is needed before we can reach a conclusion.

Perceived National Problems

Table II shows that the elites also express a notable concern with the social dimension when the question (open-ended in this case) addresses national problems as such and not democratic stability per se.

Table II. *Brazil's Most Important Problems (Percentage)*

Problem	Total Sample	(1)*	(2)*	(3)*	(4)*
Inflation	17.5	22.2	13.8	25.5	8.9
Education/Health	15.9	13.0	23.0	17.0	8.9
Poverty	14.3	16.7	10.3	8.5	24.1
Governability	11.5	11.1	12.6	18.1	2.5
Income Distribution	8.3	3.7	11.5	5.3	11.4
Other Political Issues	8.3	3.7	8.0	12.8	6.3
Other Economic Issues	5.4	1.9	6.8	3.2	8.9
Corruption	4.8	9.3	3.4	1.1	7.6
Recession and Unemployment	4.1	9.3	2.3	2.1	5.1
Behavior of the Elites	3.5	—	1.1	5.3	6.3
Foreign Dependence	3.2	3.7	2.3	—	7.6
Moral Crisis	2.2	3.7	3.4	1.1	1.3
Other Social Issues	1.0	1.9	1.1	—	1.3
Total	100.0	100.2	99.6	100.0	100.2
	(n=308)	(n=50)	(n=89)	(n=93)	(n=76)

* (1) Deputies and Senators (2) Top Public Officials (3) Businessmen (4) Labor Union Leaders

Also interesting are the variations between elite sectors. For example, the inflation problem ranks number one overall but does not appear to be such a major concern among union leaders or even among bureaucrats. In turn, poverty, ranking third overall, revealed an inverse pattern: about one-fourth of the union leaders assert that this problem is paramount, whereas only a minority of the business leaders give the same opinion.

Our speculation that this seeming social sensitivity might in fact reflect an interest in maintaining order seems to gain support if we consider the relative importance placed on governability problems by some of the elite sectors, particularly business leaders. The only ones who paid scant attention to this issue were union leaders, the "least elite" among the elites.

Perceived National Policy Objectives

Be that as it may, displaying sensitivity to the size or relevance of a problem does not necessarily mean that this particular problem will be placed at the top of the country's policy agenda. We also asked the elite members to rank a compiled list of policy objectives. Table III summarizes the patterns that emerged.

Table III. *Main National Goal in the Medium Run (Percentage)*

Goal	Total Sample	(1)*	(2)*	(3)*	(4)*
Increase Educational Levels	23.0	14.8	24.7	29.8	18.5
Reduce Size of State	18.2	22.2	13.5	33.0	3.7
Eradicate Poverty and Reduce Inequality	17.6	25.9	19.1	9.6	19.8
Increase Popular Participation in Political Decisions	16.4	5.6	14.6	5.3	38.3
Preserve the Democratic Regime	11.3	20.4	7.9	8.5	12.3
Guarantee Economic Growth	9.7	7.3	14.6	10.6	4.9
Integrate the Economy into International Market	2.2	1.9	2.2	3.2	1.2
Keep Order	0.9	1.9	2.2	—	—
Further Integrate the Country into Mercosur	0.3	—	1.1	—	—
Protect the Environment	0.3	—	—	—	1.2
Total	99.9	100.0	99.9	100.0	99.9
	(n=318)	(n=54)	(n=89)	(n=94)	(n=81)

* (1) Deputies and Senators (2) Top Public Officials (3) Businessmen (4) Labor Union Leaders

Once again the educational issue comes in first place. Nearly one-fourth of the respondents identified the socioeconomic objective of increasing the nation's educational levels as the number-one target for the near future. Over 41 percent of the respondents identified the socioeconomic objectives of either increasing educational levels or eradicating poverty and reducing inequality as the number one target. Another aspect of Table III that merits attention are the dissimilarities between elite sectors. The second most-chosen goal, downsizing the state, received greatest mention from business leaders, followed by politicians and bureaucrats, in that order; barely any union leaders, however, chose it as a major goal. On the other hand, while a large number of politicians, union leaders, and bureaucrats say the priority should be fighting poverty and reducing inequalities, for the business elites such issues are apparently of much less concern. Last but not least, popular participation beyond the polls was not ranked high by these elite members, except for union leaders.

Concluding Comments

As we saw, the Brazilian elites voice a clear concern with social problems. In their expressed views, poverty, social misery, lack of education, income concentration, and other forms of inequality should rank high as national priorities, and overcoming such problems is stated to be important to laying the groundwork for democratic consolidation. Moreover, the majority of those interviewed identify a series of ameliorative programs as both desirable and viable. This framing of the social dimension as central reveals an apparent sensitivity to the nation's acute problems regarding social incorporation. Yet one does not observe these same elites undertaking any concerted efforts to attempt to change the situation.

This brings us immediately to two questions: first, where should we look for explanations for this lack of correspondence between an ostensibly acute perception of social problems by individual members of the elite and a lack of collective initiatives aimed at overcoming poverty and/or acute inequality? Second, what consequences may this contradiction have for the future of Brazilian democracy? While we have no ready answers to these questions, it may be that the model of social incorporation the elites have in mind does not entail the idea of a fair equality of opportunities. We can even cite evidence pointing in this direction, such as, for example, a widespread rejection of affirmative action programs expressed in these interviews. But above all, the most crucial problem seems to be that of building collective responsibility.

As so nicely summarized by E. Giannetti da Fonseca (1993), the term "Brazilian paradox" can be used to characterize this clash between (1) a generalized feeling—experienced by everyone individually—that the social status quo is unjust, perverse, and intolerable, and (2) an equally generalized individual feeling that one is not part of the establishment and is not responsible for what is going on in Brazil today. The author adopts the common approach of looking for explanations for this paradox in our historical-cultural tradition. Brazil's Iberian colonial legacy and slave past are often recalled in this context. While historical factors certainly form part of the explanation, our concern must be to search for the factors that may have contributed to re-activating the tradition. In contrast with the above assumptions, we suggest that it is the interplay of cultural, political, and economic factors that actively remolds values and beliefs into a tradition.

To close on a more optimistic note, we suggest that exploring variations in values and beliefs across sectors of the elites might help us identify possible ways of bringing this stalemate to an end and perhaps of overcoming collective paralysis as well. In the findings we have presented, a few data indicate significant variations in the way different sectors of the elites identify problems and rank priorities. Although we have not explored these differences here, we believe they merit careful attention. The next research step is to delve into these variations and discuss their potential implications in terms of inter-elite competition. And it may be precisely this competition that eventually terminates the deadlock, thereby clearing the way at last for the establishment of a more inclusive political order and a well-consolidated democracy.

References

Giannetti da Fonseca, E. 1993. *Vícios Privados, Benefícios Públicos?* Sao Paulo: Companhia das Letras.
Lipset, Seymour Martin. 1994. "The Social Requisites of Democracy Revisited." *American Sociological Review* 59:1–22.

The Role of Political Elites in the Transition from Communism to Democracy
The Case of Poland

Wlodzimierz Wesolowski

This paper analyzes the disintegration of communism in Poland and the formation of a new socioeconomic and political system. The actions of the political elite were pivotal in this process.

[A New Type of Transition: Elite Agreement and the Death of a Signatory]

The formation of parliamentary democracy in Poland began with the Round Table negotiations [between communist and oppositional elites] of February-March 1989 . . . The Round Table agreements— not only those in Poland, but similar ones throughout Eastern Europe—belong in the same general category as the pacts entered into by the military juntas and democratic forces in Latin America. Compared with these pacts, however, the "Eastern" agreements have their own character, which is the product of differences in both the political actors involved and the economic background . . .

A characteristic that is specific to the evolution of Eastern Europe becomes evident when we compare this evolution with Field, Burton and Higley's thesis concerning "elite settlements."[1] To be sure, the abandonment of communism began with an agreement similar to the one outlined [by these authors]. But if we examine the historical examples that provide the basis for their model, e.g., England, Sweden, and more recently Spain, one important characteristic cannot be ignored. Societies in which elites came to an unprecedented agreement had stable class differentiation and

Excerpts from Wlodzimierz Wesolowski, "The Role of Political Elites in the Transition from Communism to Democracy: The Case of Poland." *SISYPHUS* 2 (1992): 77–100. Reprinted by permission of the journal. Bracketed headings have been created by the editor of this volume.

stable elite articulation, which remained unchanged after the agreement.

The situation in Eastern Europe is different. The agreement there prompted profound, though gradual, changes in economic class structure because of the reinstitution of private property. It also led to a major transformation in the positions of the political elites who joined the agreement. The changes were such that one group, the Communist Party elite, both fell from power and lost its political identity. The agreement, unlike any of those analyzed by Field, Higley and Burton, proved to be a death sentence for one of its signatories . . .

Shortage of Transformative Powers: Resources and Instruments

[In addition,] the beginnings of the new system . . . revealed something that was not clearly perceived before, namely, the overwhelming shortages of transformative powers within the polity and society. I would like to discuss [two of] these shortages: (1) absence of a mature and stable party structure . . . and (2) lack of dynamic, self-assertive attitudes among the population. The first deficiency points to a shortage of adequate transformative resources. The second deficiency points to a shortage of adequate transformative instruments (means).

[Fragmentation of the Party Structure and Deficiencies in Elite Consensus]

The first shortage is the absence of a mature, stable, party structure. This makes the whole political scene fluid, unreliable, and unable to influence the transformative processes within the country. The missing link is a lack of specific programming and a lack of deliberate attempts at generating support of specific strata of the population.

Changes of governments make creation of definite programs difficult. Government coalitions are unstable. Political parties exist mostly at the level of parliament, not within the society. Hence they are rather parties of would-be leaders than real parties with strong roots in society (from that assessment only the peasant party can be excluded). Only few of them have chapters in local communities. Their structure ends mostly at the level of "county leadership," which is composed mostly of deputies to the parliament from that county. Moreover, several deputies have changed their party affiliations, moving rather unexpectedly to another group of politicians or creating their own, esoteric group. Consequently, a strong political link between society and the politicians at the top has not been created. We have excessive pluralism of parties with vague programs and unknown popular support.

[Some] intellectuals thought that it would be possible to keep the united Solidarity political movement and the unified Solidarity Trade Union as two political pillars of the government and of the whole political structure of the country during the transitional period. However, the "war at the top," initiated by Walesa in his electoral campaign of 1990, divided politicians into a variety of orientations. Somehow, parties emerged as an unhappy result of that war. Pluralization of the political scene has continued since then. Excessive pluralization developed into wars between leaders of small parties, mostly wars on symbolic issues, like the role of the Church in public life, the unification of Europe or the defense of national interests, etc. Excessive pluralization of parties gave birth to personalization of political conflicts.

Looking at the political scene from Giovanni Sartori's perspective we have in Poland a polarized party system (Sartori 1976), though no party claims that it disagrees with the market economy or political democracy, or that it aims at overthrowing the system. This is the paradox of the Polish polarized system. I tend to call it polarized because the aim of several parties is to kill other parties and eliminate them from the political scene . . .

On the theoretical level one can argue that the formation of democracy, that begins with the agreement of communist and oppositional elites, shortly and abruptly faces deep divisions between victors. Democracy is retained, but consensus vacillates. Such a situation provides material for a modification of the "settlement" thesis developed by Field, Higley and Burton. It seems that at least various kinds of "consensus" need to be elaborated.

In a sense, the political parties do not perform their basic political function: forming a stable majority in parliament and generating programs for the transformative processes. This function is left to successive governments, but the chaotic political scene behind the government does not help it in the difficult job of steering the governmental machinery in a desirable direction. The trap of excessive pluralization of the political scene consists in the fact that it neither contributes to the better representation of opinions of the electorate nor to more thorough, carefully conducted, and effective debates over programs. On the whole, its most detrimental effect is the delay in the formation of effective powers to transform the economy . . .

Fragmented party structure is a common feature of all post-communist countries in Central and Eastern Europe, and in all of them it rather hampers than speeds up the process of transformation. None of the post-communist countries made their political system an efficient instrument of change. Because it is the prime instrument of change, one can venture a hypothesis that politics and its institutions are responsible for insufficient reforms and the slow pace of change which have been achieved until now.

[Demobilization of the Population]

The second shortage is the absence of dynamic and assertive attitudes among the population. A free market economy based on private property assumes and requires an individual, who is active in planning and pursuing his goals in the economic sphere. It also requires the formation of groups, which promote and defend their interests. These interests push people to activity in the public arena. The "civil society" and "politically articulated society" is perceived by many theories and doctrines as a necessary requirement for making markets and democracy operative.

Historical examples of mature democracies indicate that the activity of the population in bringing about transformative changes is a requirement difficult to measure quantitatively. Nonetheless there always exists a qualitative critical threshold above which private activities must be elevated in the formation of a market economy and public activity. The question is whether Polish society has moved above that threshold. The second question is whether the programs and practical actions of the political elite contributed to moving Polish society above the critical threshold.

Looking back, one has to state that the level of popular mobilization, which existed in 1980–81, has never emerged again. The period of marshal law dispersed the mobilization potential. The brief period of political battles at the "Round Table" showed only a lim-

234 Wlodzimierz Wesolowski

activation of the population in strikes and demonstrations.
Democracy was won in Poland in 1989 without the required new
politicization and activation of the population.

There were a few new causes of the relatively low level of popular activity. Victory over communism was achieved without overt
battles. The opposition took over the government without aiming
at activating people, because activation could mean interference in
the process of peaceful and orderly take-over of governmental power.
Most importantly, the question emerged whether the new economic
order, foreseen for the future and actively pursued by the government, was consistent with the former ways of activating people. A
free market economy requires individual activity based on individual
resources, risk taking, and planning. Self-reliance of the individual
is becoming a model and a major requirement. Group activity is
considered secondary in importance.

The existence of the strong Solidarity trade union suggested the
possibility of economically-oriented activity among the population,
such as collective bargaining or collective take-over of enterprises.
However, the two-year period between 1989 and 1991 may be seen
in Poland as an extremely important time that brought about important psychological changes at both levels: the elites and the masses.
The elites moved to the acceptance of economic laissez-faire principles and political liberalism, emphasizing the freedom of individual
rights. But the programmatic postulate of "res publica of self-gov-
ernments," which was written into the program of Solidarity in 1981,
has been abandoned and forgotten. The masses have reluctantly and
unconsciously accepted the course of history. They started to concentrate on everyday life, solving the emerging hardships, and securing "food and shelter" for the family . . .

However, one can state briefly that demobilization has turned
into two separate phenomena. The first is that . . . the victorious
spirit of the Solidarity Trade Union is gone forever. The current ethos
of the Solidarity Trade Union, has become one of an efficient and
well-organized trade union, acting under extremely unfavorable conditions of systemic changes, which require curbing the appetites and
controlling the powers of employees.

The second psychological stream is the growing disillusionment
of the population at large. Walesa promised in his presidential cam-

paign to speed up economic and social changes, to provide everybody with resources to sustain the present standard of living or to open a new business. [However,] the resources for starting a new life were not available for employees, as it quickly turned out. Former working-class families and employees' families have no resources to establish a private firm. For them, the ideal of a free man, responsible for his own well-being, cannot be included in rational planning. Hence, the fear of the future has started to dominate the perception of the transformative processes. Uncertainty seems to take the upper hand for many families. The same uncertainty is reflected in the dominant mood. Creeping disillusionment undermines the very possibility of being involved in changes either individually or collectively. In some areas the elite undercut possibilities for group activism. This happened in factories, in which workers' councils were discouraged from preparing plans for group employee ownership.

The net result, which was produced by all of the above-mentioned developments, was a passive population . . . There is only one successful segment of the population which consists of businessmen. They are really very actively taking their future in their own hands. However, this stratum is not large enough and does not like public activity . . . They do not imprint their mood and their attitudes on the psychological situation in the country . . .

It seems that the political elite did not comprehend fully the significance of this overwhelming disactivation of the population . . . The idea of involving people in practical changes of the old system appeared only recently as a result of the negative lesson learned over a two-year period. In this sense, the initial mistaken approach, the neglect of the transformative potential of employees and more broadly, ordinary citizens, has been only recently perceived and acknowledged. If one considers the activity of the population as an important vehicle of systemic transformation, this vehicle moved in Poland with very little power and did not increase the speed nor the volume of changes . . . The low level of the citizens' participation in transformation processes is the common feature of the situation in all Central and East European, post-communist countries . . .

[The Elite's Problems in Democratic Institution Building]

The continuous debate in Poland over the role of elites in the transformation process has centered on a single issue: whether the elite of the Solidarity movement (intellectuals and leaders of the workers' movement, and later politicians who came to power via election), was successful in preparing a sufficiently clear, comprehensive, and practical vision for the change of the system, and whether it was determined enough in translating that vision into workable programs. A predominant opinion has emerged that in Poland, similarly to other East European countries, the gigantic task has not been matched by Giants. However, the shortage of transformative powers indicates that the elite faced problems which were extremely difficult. A balanced assessment could be that the political elite did not exploit all intellectual and pragmatic possibilities in the creation and execution of comprehensive programs for the crucial processes of change. It lacked sufficient imagination to comprehend the need for systematic institution building . . .

One illustration of delays in institution building is seen in the political sphere. The political elite has not been able to prepare and pass a constitutional bill. Therefore, prerogatives of the most important institutions: the president, the parliament and cabinet are provisional and, moreover, overlapping. Politicians are unable to agree whether Poland needs a presidential system, a parliamentary-cabinet system or a combination of both. They are unable to agree upon the kind of electoral system to be implemented: should it be the proportional one, or a first-past-the-post system. There are many other constitutional questions left unsolved. The existing bill of how a political party could be established and financed has many flaws. The role of the Catholic Church in public life has been regulated vaguely. The rights of minorities are waiting for their formulation and legalization. The inconclusiveness of the constitutional debates seems to be almost an unavoidable result of the number of official or semi-official actors participating in them.

[Conclusion: Fragmentation and the Role of the Political Elite]

The most damaging disease of the Polish political system is the fragmentation of its party system. It exerts a negative influence on the programmatic work of the elite, on the malfunctioning of state organs and administration. Lilliputian pluralism does not work . . .

The fragmentation of parties has passed the limit up to which politics may be fully effective for the society and transformative processes. The delays in the constitutional institution building also seem to have a detrimental impact. Hence, the political elite has to make order within its structure to be able to increase its efficiency in programming, coordinating, and stimulating change . . .

The political sphere retains its primacy in the transitional period because it is the source of all other changes. Particular institutions and processes receive from that sphere definite impulses that later, combined with more spontaneous developments, will shape the socio-economic and political order. The initial actions of the political elite as well as its failures will be imprinted in the future political order.

Notes from the Editor

1. See Field, Higley, and Burton in this volume. See also Higley and Gunther (1992).

References

Higley, John, and R. Gunther. 1992. *Elites and Democratic Consolidation in Latin America and Southern Europe.* Cambridge: Cambridge University Press.

Sartori, Giovanni. 1976. Parti*es and Party Systems: A Framework for Analysis, vol. 1.* Cambridge: Cambridge University Press.

Part V

Classes and Elites in Democracy and Democratization

Introduction

The writings on classes and those on elites in a democracy are many; hence, even the brief selections from the most outstanding of these had to be divided into four separate parts. The writings on the role of both classes and elites in a democracy are few, and could be brought together in this part of the volume. Among these, some address themselves to the separate roles of classes and elites. Thus the writings that take up the role of classes *versus* the role of elites, or the relations *between* classes *and* elites, in a democracy, are even fewer.

Some selections are by scholars who have their roots in class theory, including Miliband, Block, and Tilly. Others are by authors who generally adhere to (pluralist or other) elite theory, and they include Michels, Dahl, and Etzioni-Halevy. Still others are by authors who seem to strive for a balance between the two: Huntington, and Diamond and Linz. All, in their way, make some contribution to the convergence of class and elite theory of democracy.

One of the writings by an elite theorist, which clearly makes such a contribution by exploring the relationship between classes, elites, and democracy, is that by Michels. Known as one of the trio of classical elite theorists, and as a contemporary of Pareto and Mosca,

Michels's main claim to fame lies in his formulation of the iron law of oligarchy. By this law, even in a political party that is formally democratic, "who says organization, says oligarchy." Less attention has been paid to the fact that Michels also offers an analysis of the relationship between the working class and its elites. This, however, is what he does, concluding that the elites heading working class organizations—labor parties and unions—lose their accountability to it and abandon its interests in favor of their own.

The next contribution is that by Miliband, who offers a Marxist class analysis of the democratic capitalist state. In this he is not, of course, different from other Marxists, such as Althusser or Poulantzas (in previous parts of the volume). What earns Miliband a place here, is that he pays more attention than Marxists are wont to do, to the role of elites vis-à-vis classes in a democracy. Although Miliband's theoretical orientation is almost diametrically opposed to that of Michels, the conclusion he reaches is not dissimilar: he, too, believes that the elites that ostensibly have the interests of the working class at heart, in fact do not. Leaders of all—including working-class— parties are committed to upholding capitalism, by which that class is exploited. If the picture is one of profound controversy, which suggests that electors—by choosing between different parties—decide nothing less than the future of their country, this is merely the semblance of democracy, camouflaging the reality of capitalism.

A critique of such formulations, which reduce the state to a mere instrument of capitalist interests, comes from Block, who is himself a Marxist, yet realizes that elites, or state managers, play a role of their own in the capitalist democratic state. Thus, capitalist class interests prevail as an outcome of the maneuvering among three sets of actors: the capitalists (who promote their individual interests for profit), the state managers (who must placate the capitalists so as to maintain business confidence), and the working class (whose struggles to improve its lot result in the rationalization of capitalism). While it is more sophisticated, Block's analysis still reaches the traditional Marxist conclusion that in capitalist democracy, capitalist interests are inevitably victorious.

Descended from a different ancestry—that of pluralism—is the contribution by Dahl. Its ancestry includes earlier writings by Dahl himself, from which it inherits the terms *polyarchy* and *pluralist de-*

mocracy. Polyarchy refers to the political system of contemporary pluralist democracy, in which leaders are fairly elected and freedom of organization and civil liberties prevail. To this, Dahl now adds a concern with the dilemma of this pluralist democracy: the autonomy of organizations (including political parties and business enterprises) is required for the fair election of leaders and for the insurance of civil liberties, yet enhances economic class inequality. Dahl's continued concern with pluralism, combined with his newborn concern with economic inequality, has earned his (and similar recent conceptions) the title of neo-pluralism. Although it has some affinity to Marxism, neo-pluralism has attracted Marxist strictures for failing to realize that the problem it reveals has no solution within the confines of capitalism.

Turning from democracy to democratization, we encounter Tilly's conceptualization of democracy as resembling a lake, which may form in a variety of ways. One of these, for which democratization in Britain serves as an illustration, involves class coalitions, the weakening of the landholding class through removal of its control over military activities, subordination of the military elite to state (civilian) control, and representation of the people with respect to the collection of taxes.

Moving from past to present, Huntington devotes his attention to what he terms the "third wave": an almost irresistible global tide of democratization in recent years. Among its many causes are economic growth and the expansion of the middle class, which makes democracy possible, and elite compromise—involving the trade-off of participation in return for moderation—which makes it real.

Turning the limelight to Latin America, Diamond and Linz consider that while extensive economic class inequalities form obstacles to democratization, previously restricted but competitive elite oligarchy fosters the later development of full democracy. So, too, does an elite democratic political culture and elite acceptance of the autonomous expression of new popular interests.

In sharp contrast to Latin America (and other parts of the world) stands East/Central Europe, which, according to Offe—is unique in the difficulties faced by its regime transition. For it is only here that political reform is interspersed with economic reform and with the deliberate creation of a new class of economic entrepreneurs.

This occasions a dilemma: democratic procedures are necessary to legitimize the elite-initiated emergence of economic class cleavages; yet such procedures presuppose already existing class cleavages, which alone can generate a diversity of interests worth processing through the democratic machinery. This process also requires that the public muster tolerance for economic class inequality, in order not to interfere with democratization, even though by making use of its new democratic rights, it would be capable of doing so.

Meanwhile in the West, democracy has not been standing still. With this in mind, Etzioni-Halevy explores the changing relations between the working class and elites there. Despite the glaring economic inequalities it incorporates, she contends, democracy may still lead to decreases in such inequalities. And in distinction to Michels's and Miliband's stress on working-class elites' betrayal of that class, she argues that, historically, a coupling between that class and elites, involving certain democratic arrangements, in fact led to an empowerment of that class and thereby to decreasing economic inequalities. In recent years, with the emergence of the "postmodern" society, however, there has been a reversal of this trend: a partial uncoupling between the working class and elites, and a weakening of previous democratic arrangements. And it is this which has led to increases in economic inequalities.

Whether (following Dahl and others) we may say that there is pluralism—or neo-pluralism—in democracy, there is certainly much pluralism (old as well as new) in the *analysis* of democracy. Even the pieces in this part of the volume are exceedingly variegated. While they all take account of the role of both classes and elites in a democracy, they have little else in common. Whether this attests to a spurt of original creativity, or to an immaturity of the field, which has yet to develop some common core ideas on the relations between classes and elites in democratization and democracy, must be left for the reader to decide.

The Oligarchical Tendencies of Working-Class Organizations

Selections from the Work of
Robert Michels

Democracy is, on principle, responsible to the community at large for the prevailing conditions of rule, of which it is the sole arbiter . . . The life of political parties must, in theory, necessarily exhibit an even stronger tendency towards democracy than that which is manifested in the state . . . [In fact], the democratic external form which characterizes the life of political parties may readily veil from the superficial observers the tendency towards oligarchy, which is inherent in all party organization.

[The Oligarchical Tendencies of Socialist Labour Parties]

If we wish to obtain light upon this tendency, the best field of observation is offered by the intimate structure of the democratic parties, and, among these, of the socialist and revolutionary labour party. In the conservative parties, except during elections, the tendency to oligarchy manifests itself with that spontaneous vigour and clearness which corresponds with the essentially oligarchical character of these parties. But the parties which are subversive in their aims exhibit the like phenomena no less markedly. The study of the oligarchical manifestations in party life is most valuable and most decisive in its results when undertaken in relation to the revolutionary parties, for the reason that these parties, in respect of origin and of programme, represent the negation of any such tendency, and have actually come into existence out of opposition thereto. Thus the

Reprinted with the permission of The Free Press, a division of Simon & Schuster from *Political Parties* by Robert Michels, trans. Eden and Cedar Paul (Glencoe, Ill.: Free Press, 1915), 4–14, 25–41, 54–93, 103–11, 139–44, 179–195, 217–220, 381–390, 417. Copyright © 1962 by The Crowell-Collier Publishing Company. Bracketed headings have been created by the editor of this volume.

appearance of oligarchical phenomena in the very bosom of revolutionary parties is a conclusive proof of the existence of immanent oligarchical tendencies in every kind of human organization which strives for the attainment of definite ends. In theory, the principal aim of socialist and democratic parties is the struggle against oligarchy in all its forms. The question therefore arises how we are to explain the development in such parties of the very tendencies against which they have declared war . . .

[The Need for Organization of the Working Class]

Democracy is inconceivable without organization . . . A class which unfurls in face of society the banner of certain definite claims, and which aspires to the realization of a complex of ideal aims deriving from the economic functions which that class fulfills, needs an organization . . . Organization is the weapon of the weak in their struggle with the strong . . . The importance and the influence of the working class are directly proportional to its numerical strength. But for the representation of that numerical strength organization and coordination are indispensable. Yet . . . organization is, in fact, the source from which the conservative currents flow over the plain of democracy, occasioning there disastrous floods and rendering the plain unrecognizable . . .

[Impossibility of Direct Government by the Working Class]

The practical ideal of democracy consists in the self-government of the masses in conformity with the decisions of popular assemblies . . . The most formidable argument against the sovereignty of the masses is, however, derived from the mechanical and technical impossibility of its realization. The sovereign masses are altogether incapable of undertaking the most necessary resolutions. The impotence of direct democracy, like the power of indirect democracy, is a direct outcome of the influence of number . . . Above all in the great industrial centres, where the labour party sometimes numbers its adherents by tens of thousands, it is impossible to carry on the affairs of this gigantic body without a system of representation . . .

Originally . . . all the offices are filled by election . . . At the outset, the attempt is made to depart as little as possible from pure democracy by subordinating the delegates altogether to the will of the mass, by tying them hand and foot . . . Gradually, however . . . extensive organization renders necessary what is called expert leadership. Consequently the power of determination comes to be considered one of the specific attributes of leadership, and is gradually withdrawn from the masses to be concentrated in the hands of the leaders alone. Thus the leaders, who were at first no more than the executive organs of the collective will, soon emancipate themselves from the mass and become independent of its control . . .

Every solidly constructed organization, whether it be a democratic state, a political party, or a league of proletarians for the resistance of economic repression, presents a soil eminently favourable for the differentiation of organs and of functions. The more extended and the more ramified the official apparatus of the organization . . . , the less efficient becomes the direct control exercised by the rank and file . . . As organization develops, not only do the tasks of the administration become more difficult and more complicated, but, further, its duties become enlarged and specialized to such a degree that it is no longer possible to take them all in at a single glance . . . In theory, the leader has to carry out the orders of the mass. But in actual fact, as the organization increases in size, this control becomes purely fictitious . . .

It is indisputable that the oligarchical . . . tendency of party organization is a matter of technical and practical necessity. It is the inevitable product of the very principle of organization . . . The more solid the structure of an organization becomes, the more marked becomes the tendency to replace the emergency leader by the professional leader . . . For democracy, however, the first appearance of professional leadership marks the beginning of the end . . .

[Apathy and the Need for Leadership Felt by the Working Class Mass]

There is no exaggeration in the assertion that among the citizens who enjoy political rights the number of those who have a lively interest in public affairs is insignificant . . . In the life of the modern democratic parties we may observe signs of similar indifference. It is only a minority which participates in party decisions, and sometimes that minority is ludicrously small. The most important resolutions taken by the most democratic of all parties, the socialist party, always emanate from a handful of the members . . . The majority of the members are as indifferent to the organization as the majority of the electors are to parliament . . .

[Thus,] though it grumbles occasionally, the majority is really delighted to find persons who will take the trouble to look after its affairs. In the mass, and even in the organized mass of the labour parties, there is an immense need for direction and guidance. This need is accompanied by a genuine cult for the leaders, who are regarded as heroes . . . This peculiarity, common to all classes not excepting the proletariat, furnishes a psychological soil upon which a powerful directive hegemony can flourish luxuriantly . . .

[Incompetence of the Working Class and Superiority of the Leaders]

Long experience has shown that among the factors which secure the dominion of minorities over majorities . . . the first place must be given to the formal instruction of the leaders. Now the most superficial observation shows that in the parties of the proletariat the leaders are, in matters of education, greatly superior to the led . . .

[Moreover], whilst their occupation and the needs of daily life render it impossible for the masses to attain a profound knowledge of the social machinery, and above all of the working of the political machine, the leader of working class origin is enabled, thanks to his new situation, to make himself intimately familiar with all the technical details of public life, and thus to increase his superiority over the rank and file . . . Thus the gulf between the leaders and rest of the party becomes ever wider, until the moment arrives in which the leaders lose all true sense of solidarity with the class from which they have sprung, and there ensues a new class-division between ex-proletarian captains and proletarian common soldiers. When the workers choose leaders for themselves, they are with their own hands creating new masters whose principal means of dominion is found in their better instructed minds . . .

The leader's principal source of power is found in his indispensability . . . [For] the incompetence of the masses is almost universal throughout the domains of political life, and this constitutes the most solid foundation of the power of the leaders . . . Since the rank and file are incapable of looking after their own interests, it is necessary that they should have experts to attend to their affairs . . .

[The Indefinite Retention of Working Class Leaders]

In almost all the socialist parties and trade unions the officers are elected for a brief term, and must be re-elected at least every two years. The longer the tenure of office, the greater becomes the influence of the leader over the masses and the greater therefore his independence. Consequently a frequent repetition of election is an elementary precaution on the part of democracy against the virus of oligarchy . . . It must, moreover, be a natural endeavour not to leave the same comrades too long in occupation of important offices, lest the holders of these should stick in their grooves, and should come to regard themselves as God given leaders. But in those parties which are solidly organized, the actual state of affairs is far from corresponding to this theory . . . Leadership is indefinitely retained, simply because it is already constituted . . . The re-election demanded by the rules becomes a pure formality . . .

An explanation of this phenomenon is doubtless to be found in the force of tradition. But there is an additional motive in operation . . . In the working class organization, just as much as in the life of the state, it is indispensable that the official should remain in office for a considerable time, so that he may familiarize himself with the work he has to do, for he cannot become a useful official until he has been given time to work himself into his new office. Moreover, he will not devote himself zealously to his task . . . , if he is likely to be dismissed at any moment . . . Appointment to office for short terms is democratic, but is quite impractical alike on technical and psychological grounds . . .

In proportion as the chiefs become detached from the mass they show themselves more and more inclined, when gaps in their own ranks have to be filled, to effect this not by way of popular election, but by cooptation . . . Instead of allowing their successors to be appointed by the choice of the rank and file, the leaders do all in their power to choose these successors for themselves . . .

[The Leaders' Control of the Press and the Opposition]

The press constitutes a potent instrument for the conquest, the preservation, and the consolidation of power on the part of the leaders . . . This means is frequently employed by the leaders in order to gain or retain the sympathy of the masses, and to enable them to keep the guidance of the movement in their own hands. The democratic press is also utilized by the leaders in order to make attacks upon their adversaries . . . In all cases the press remains in the hands of the leaders and is never controlled by the rank and file . . .

The mistrust of the leaders is directed above all against those who aspire to command their own organizations . . . Here we have a struggle, as the Americans put it, between the "ins" and the "outs" . . . The leaders, those who already hold the power of the party in their hands, make no concealment of their natural inclination to control as strictly as possible the freedom of speech of those of their colleagues from whom they differ . . . They go as far as to exercise a censorship over any of their colleagues whom they suspect of rebellious inclinations, forcing them to abandon independent journals, and to publish all their articles in the official organs controlled by the leaders . . .

In order to combat the new chiefs, who are still in a minority, the old leaders of the majority instinctively avail themselves of a series of underhand methods through which they often secure victory, or at least notably retard defeat . . . If the leaders of the opposition within the party are dangerous because they have a large following among the masses, and if they are at the same time few in numbers, the old party leaders endeavour to hold them in check and to neutralize their influence by conciliatory methods. The leaders of the opposition receive high offices and honours in the party, and are thus rendered innocuous—all the more so seeing that they are not admitted to the supreme offices, but are relegated to posts of the second rank which give them no notable influence . . . On the other hand, they divide with their ancient adversaries the serious weight of responsibility which is generated by common deliberations and manifestations, so that their activities become confounded with those of the old leaders . . .

Doubtless the labour movement furnishes certain examples of leaders who have been deposed . . . Such cases are, however, rare, and . . . the profit for democracy of such a substitution is practically nil . . . As soon as the new leaders have succeeded . . . in overthrowing the odious tyranny of their predecessors and in attaining to power in their turn, we see them undergo a transformation which renders them in every respect similar to the dethroned tyrants . . . The revolutionaries of today become the reactionaries of tomorrow . . .

[The Metamorphosis of Working-Class Leaders]

The apathy of the masses and their need for guidance has as its counterpart in the leaders a natural greed for power . . . The consciousness of power always produces vanity . . . In the leader, the consciousness of his personal worth, and the need which the mass feels for guidance . . . awake in addition, that spirit of command which exists in the germ in every man born of woman . . . When the leaders are not persons of means and when they have no other source of income, they hold firmly to their positions for economic reasons, coming to regard the functions they exercise as theirs by inalienable right. Especially is this true of manual workers who, since becoming leaders, have lost the aptitude for their former occupation. For them, the loss of their position would be a financial disaster, and in most cases it would be altogether impossible for them to return to their old way of life . . . Their hands have lost the callosities of the manual toiler, and are likely to suffer from writer's cramp . . .

[The Conservative Basis of the Working-Class Organization]

At this point in our inquiry . . . we have to further examine whether the oligarchical nature of the organization be not responsible . . . for the production of an oligarchical policy. The analysis here made shows clearly that the internal policy of the party organization is today absolutely conservative, or is on the way to become such . . . Generated to overthrow the centralized power of the state, the party of the workers . . . organizes the *framework* of the social revolution. For this reason it continually endeavours to strengthen its positions, to extend its bureaucratic mechanism, to store up its energies and its funds . . . [But] instead of gaining revolutionary energy as the force and solidity of its structure has increased, the precise opposite has occurred: . . . a continued increase in the prudence, the timidity even, which inspires its policy. The party, continually threatened by the state upon which its existence depends, carefully avoids (once it has attained to maturity) everything which might irritate the state to excess . . .

The history of the international labour movement furnishes innumerable examples of the manner in which the party becomes increasingly inert as the strength of its organization grows . . . The party is endowed with a bureaucracy; . . . the treasuries are full . . . A bold and enterprising tactic would endanger all this: the work of many decades, the social existence of thousands of leaders and sub-leaders, the entire party would be compromised . . . Thus from a means, organization becomes an end . . . Henceforward the sole preoccupation is to avoid anything which may clog the machinery . . . We have now a finely conservative party . . . Having become an end in itself, endowed with aims and interests of its own, it undergoes detachment . . . from the class which it represents . . .

[Final Considerations: The Iron Law of Oligarchy]

If we leave out of consideration the tendency of leaders to organize themselves and to consolidate their interests . . . and the general immobility and passivity of the masses, we are led to conclude that the principal cause of oligarchy in the democratic parties is to be found in the technical indispensability of leadership . . . At the outset leaders arise *spontaneously;* their functions are *accessory* and *gratuitous.* Soon, however, they become *professional* leaders, and in this second stage of development they are *stable* and *irremovable.*

It follows that the explanation of the oligarchical phenomenon which thus results is partly *psychological;* oligarchy derives, that is to say, from the psychical transformations which the leading personalities in the parties undergo in the course of their lives. But also, and still more, oligarchy depends upon what we may term the *psychology of organization itself,* that is to say, upon the tactical and technical necessities which result from the consolidation of every disciplined political aggregate. Reduced to its most concise expression, the fundamental sociological law of political parties . . . may be formulated in the following terms: "It is organization which gives birth to the dominion of the elected over the electors . . . of the delegates over the delegators. *Who says organization says oligarchy.*" . . .

State Leaders as Promoters of Capitalist Interests in Democracies

Selections from the Work of
Ralph Miliband

The reason for attaching considerable importance to the social composition of the state elite in advanced capitalist countries lies in the strong presumption which this creates as to its general outlook, ideological dispositions and political bias. In the case of the governments of these countries, however, we can do much more than merely presume: after all, hardly a day goes by in which political leaders in charge of the affairs of their country do not press upon the public their ideas and beliefs. Much of this may conceal as much as it reveals. But a great deal remains which, together with much other evidence, notably what governments actually do, affords a clear view of what, in large terms, they are about.

[The Illusion: State Leaders' Fundamental Controversies]

At first sight, the picture is one of endless diversity between succeeding governments, and indeed inside each of them; as also between governments of different countries. Presidents, prime ministers and their colleagues have worn many different political labels (often wildly misleading), and belonged to many different parties, or occasionally to none. This diversity of views, attitudes, programmes and policies, on an infinite number of subjects, is certainly very striking and makes for lively political debate and competition. And the impression of diversity and conflict is further enhanced by the insistence of party leaders, particularly at election time, on the wide and almost

Excerpts from Ralph Miliband, *The State in Capitalist Society* (London: Weidenfeld and Nicolson, 1969), 68–83. Reprinted by permission of the publisher. Bracketed headings have been created by the editor of this volume.

impassable . . . gulf which separates them from their opponents and competitors.

The assertion of such profound differences is a matter of great importance for the functioning and legitimation of the political system, since it suggests that electors, by voting for one or other of the main competing parties, are making a choice between fundamental and incompatible alternatives, and that they are therefore, as voters, deciding nothing less than the future of their country.

[The Reality: State Leaders' Consensus over the Virtues of Capitalism]

In actual fact, however, this picture is in some crucial ways highly superficial and mystifying. For one of the most important aspects of the political life of advanced capitalism is precisely that the disagreement *between those political leaders who have generally been able to gain high office* have very seldom been of the fundamental kind these leaders and other people so often suggest. What is really striking about *these* political leaders and political office holders, in relation to each other, is not their many differences, but the extent of their agreement on truly fundamental issues—as they themselves, when occasion requires, have been wont to recognise, and as large numbers of people among the public at large, despite the political rhetoric to which they are subjected, recognise in the phrase "politicians are all the same." This is an exaggeration, of course. But it is an exaggeration with a solid kernel of truth, at least in relation to the kind of men who tend to succeed each other in office in advanced capitalist countries. Marxists put the same point somewhat differently when they say that these men, whatever their political labels or party affiliations, are bourgeois politicians.

The basic sense in which this is true is that the political office-holders of advanced capitalism have, with very few exceptions, been agreed over what Lord Balfour, in a classical formulation, once called "the foundations of society," meaning above all the existing economic and social system of private ownership and private appropriation— Marx's "mode of production." Balfour was writing about Britain, and about the Whig and Tory administrations of the nineteenth century. But his point applies equally well to other capitalist countries, and to the twentieth century as well as to the nineteenth.

For it is no more than a matter of plain political history that the governments of these countries have mostly been composed of men who beyond all their political, social, religious, cultural and other differences and diversities, have at least had in common a basic and usually explicit belief in the validity and the virtues of the capitalist system, though this was not what they would necessarily call it; and those among them who have not been particularly concerned with that system, or even aware that they were helping to run a specific economic system, much in the way that they were not aware of the air they breathed, have at least shared with their more ideologically-aware colleagues or competitors a quite basic and unswerving hostility to any socialist alternative to that system.

There have, it is true, been occasions . . . when men issued from working-class and formally socialist parties have occupied positions of governmental power, either alone or more commonly as members of coalitions, in many capitalist countries. But even though these men have quite often professed anti-capitalist convictions, they have never posed—and indeed have for the most part never wished to pose—a serious challenge to a capitalist system . . . whose basic framework and essential features they have accepted much more readily than their pronouncements in opposition, and even sometimes in office, would have tended to suggest.

In this sense, the pattern of executive power has remained much more consistent than the alternation in office of governments bearing different labels and affecting different colorations has made it appear: capitalist regimes have mainly been governed by men who have either genuinely believed in the virtues of capitalism, or who, whatever their reservations as to this or that aspect of it, have accepted it as far superior to any possible alternative economic and social system, and who have therefore made it their prime business to defend it. Alternatively, these regimes have been governed by men who, even though they might call themselves socialists, have not found the commitment this might be thought to entail in the least incompatible with the ready, even eager, acceptance of all the essential features of the system they came to administer . . .

However, even if we leave out for the present the particular role of formally socialist power-holders, it must be stressed that this basic consensus between bourgeois politicians does not preclude genuine and important differences between them, not only on issues other than the actual management of the economic system, but on that issue as well. Thus it has always been possible to make an important distinction between parties and leaders, however committed they might be to the private enterprise system, who stood for a large measure of state intervention in economic and social life, and those who believed in a lesser degree of intervention; and the same distinction encompasses those parties and men who have believed that the state must assume a greater degree of responsibility for social and other kinds of reform; and those who have wished for less.

This quarrel between strong interventionists and their opponents has been and remains a perfectly genuine one. No doubt, no serious politician—however bourgeois and convinced of the virtues of private enterprise—would now wish or be able to dismantle the main structure of state intervention; and indeed it is often the most capitalist-oriented politicians who see most clearly how essential that structure of intervention has become to the maintenance of capitalism. Even so, sufficient differences endure about the desirable extent, the character and incidence of intervention, to make the debate around such questions (and around many others as well) a serious and meaningful one, upon whose outcome depends much which affects many aspects of public policy and many individual lives. From this point of view at least, competition between these men is by no means a complete sham.

But the fact nevertheless remains that these differences and controversies, even at their most intense, have never been allowed by the politicians concerned to bring into question the validity of the "free enterprise" system itself; and even the most determined interventionists among them have always conceived their proposals and policies as a means, not of eroding—let alone supplanting—the capitalist system, but of ensuring its greater strength and stability. To a much greater extent than appearance and rhetoric have been made to suggest, the politics of advanced capitalism have been about different conceptions of how to run the *same* economic and social system, and not about radically different social systems. *This* debate has not so far come high on the political agenda.

[**State Leaders as Defenders of Capitalist Class Interests**]

This consensus between political office holders is clearly crucial . . . The fact that governments accept as beyond question the capitalist context in which they operate is of absolutely fundamental importance in shaping their attitudes, policies and actions in regard to the specific issues and problems with which they are confronted, and to the needs and conflicts of civil society . . . However, political office holders themselves do not all see their commitment to the capitalist enterprise as involving any element of class partiality. On the contrary, they are the most ardent and eloquent exponents of the view of the state, and of themselves, as above the battles of civil society, as classless, as concerned above all to serve the whole nation, the national interest, as being charged with the special task of subduing special interests and class-oriented demands for the supreme good of all . . . even when they appear to others to exhibit the most blatant class bias in their policies and actions . . .

Opponents of capitalism believe it to be a system whose very nature nowadays makes impossible the optimum utilisation of resources for rational human ends; whose inherent character is one of compulsion, domination, and parasitical appropriation; whose spirit and purpose fatally corrode all human relations; and whose maintenance is today the major obstacle to human progress . . . But the governments which manage "liberal democracy" are mostly composed of men who *cannot* see the system in this guise, who attribute the deficiencies in it which they perceive as separate and specific "problems," remediable within its confines—in fact *only* remediable within its confines. . . .

Given their view of that system, it is easy to understand why governments should wish to help business in every possible way, yet do not at all feel that this entails any degree of bias towards particular classes, interests and groups. For if the national interest is in fact inextricably bound up with the fortunes of capitalist enterprise, apparent partiality towards it is not really partiality at all. On the contrary, in serving the interests of business and in helping capitalist enterprise to thrive, governments are really fulfilling their exalted role as guardians of the good of all. From this standpoint, the much derided phrase "What is good for General Motors is good for

America" is only defective in that it tends to identify the interests of one particular enterprise with the national interest. But if General Motors is taken to stand for the world of capitalist enterprise as a whole, this slogan is one to which governments in capitalist countries do subscribe, often explicitly. And they do so because they accept the notion that the economic rationality of the capitalist system is synonymous with rationality itself, and that it provides the best possible set of human arrangements in a necessarily imperfect world . . .

The commitment which governments in advanced capitalist countries have to the private enterprise system . . . has immense policy implications. For the resolution, or at least the alleviation of a vast range of economic and social problems requires precisely that governments *should* be willing to act in "fundamental opposition" to these interests. Far from being a trivial matter, their extreme reluctance to do so is one of the largest of all facts in the life of these societies . . . Governments acting in the name of the state, have in fact been compelled over the years to act against *some* property rights . . . to help redress *somewhat* the balance between capital and labour, between property and those who are subject to it . . .

As against this, however, must be set the very positive support which governments have generally sought to give to dominant economic interests. Capitalist enterprise . . . *depends* to an ever greater extent on the bounties and direct support of the state, and can only preserve its "private" character on the basis of such public help. State intervention in economic life in fact largely *means* intervention for the purpose of helping capitalist enterprise. In no field has the notion of the "welfare state" had a more precise and apposite meaning than here: there are no more persistent and successful applicants for public assistance than the proud giants of the private enterprise system.

Nor need that assistance be of a direct kind to be of immense value to capitalist interests. Because of the imperative requirements of modern life, the state must, within limits imposed upon it by the prevailing economic system . . . assume responsibility for many functions and services which are beyond the scope and capabilities of capitalist interests. As it does so, however . . . "the bias of the system" ensures that these interests will automatically benefit from state intervention . . . Governments may be solely concerned with the better running of "the economy." But . . . what is being improved is a *capitalist* economy; and this ensures that whoever may or may not gain, capitalist interests are least likely to lose . . .

[State Leaders, Capitalist Interests, and Organised Labor]

The same considerations apply to government intervention in "industrial relations," the consecrated euphemism for the permanent conflict, now acute, now subdued, between capital and labour. Whenever governments have felt it incumbent, as they have done more and more, to intervene directly in disputes between employers and wage earners, the result of their intervention has tended to be disadvantageous to the latter, not the former. On innumerable occasions, and in all capital countries, governments have played a decisive role in defeating strikes, often by the invocation of the coercive power of the state and the use of naked violence; and the fact that they have done so in the name of the national interest, law and order, constitutional government, the protection of "the public," etc., rather than simply to support employers, has not made that intervention any the less useful to these employers . . .

Governments are deeply involved, on a permanent and institutionalised basis, in that "routinisation of conflict," which is an essential part of the politics of advanced capitalism. They enter that conflict in the guise of a neutral and independent party, concerned to achieve not the outright defeat of one side or the other but a "reasonable" settlement between them. But the state's intervention in negotiations occurs in the shadow of its known and declared propensity to invoke its powers of coercion, against one of the parties in the dispute rather than the other, if "conciliation" procedures fail. These procedures form, in fact, an additional element of restraint upon organised labour, and also serve the useful purpose of further dividing the trade union ranks. The state does interpose itself between the "two sides of industry"—not, however, as a neutral but as a partisan.

Nor is this nowadays only true when industrial disputes actually occur. One of the most notable features in the recent evolution of advanced capitalism is the degree to which governments have sought to place new and further inhibitions upon organised labour in order to prevent it from exercising what pressures it can on employers (and on the state as a major employer) in the matter of wage claims. What they tend to achieve, by such means as an "incomes policy," or by deflationary policies which reduce the demand for labour, is a *general* weakening of the bargaining position of wage earners . . .

Quite naturally, this partiality of governments assumes an even more specific, precise and organised character in relation to all movements, groupings and parties dedicated to the transformation of capitalist societies into socialist ones. The manner in which governments have expressed this antagonism has greatly varied over time, and between countries, assuming here a milder form, there a harsher one; but the antagonism itself has been a permanent fact in the history of all capitalist countries. In no field has the underlying consensus between political office holders of different political affiliations, and between the governments of different countries, been more substantial and notable—the leaders of all governmental parties, whether in office or in opposition, and including nominally "socialist" ones, have always been deeply hostile to the socialist and militant left . . . Governments, in other words, are deeply concerned, whatever their political coloration, that the "democratic process" should operate within a framework in which left-wing dissent plays as weak a role as possible . . .

The Ruling Class Does Not Rule
[State Managers, Capitalists, and the Working Class in Capitalist Democracies]

Selections from the Work of
Fred Block

The Marxist theory of the state remains a muddle despite the recent revival of interest in the subject. Substantial progress has been made in formulating a critique of orthodox Marxist formulations that reduce the state to a mere reflection of economic interests. However, the outlines of an adequate alternative Marxist theory are not yet clear . . . This essay proposes [some] elements of an alternative Marxist theory of the state.

Despite its fundamental irrationality, capitalism in the developed world has shown a remarkable capacity to rationalize itself in response to the twin dangers of economic crisis and radical working-class movements . . . The traditional Marxist explanation of capitalist rationality is to root it in the consciousness of some sector of the ruling class. In this light, capitalist reform reflects the conscious will and understanding of some sector of the capitalist class that has grasped the magnitude of the problem and proposes a set of solutions. The alternative framework being proposed here suggests that the capacity of capitalism to rationalize itself is the outcome of a conflict among three sets of agents—the capitalist class, the managers of the state apparatus, and the working class. Rationalization occurs "behind the backs" of each set of actors so that rationality cannot be seen as a function of the consciousness of one particular group . . .

[State Managers and the Capitalist Class]

The major development in the Marxist theory of the state in recent

Excerpts from Fred Block, "The Ruling Class Does Not Rule: Notes on the Marxist Theory of the State," *Socialist Review* 33 (1977): 6–27. Reprinted by permission of the journal. Bracketed headings have been created by the editor of this volume.

years has been the formulation of a critique of instrumentalism. A number of writers have characterized the orthodox Marxist view of the state as instrumentalism because it views the state as a simple tool or instrument of ruling class purposes ... The critics of instrumentalism propose the idea of the relative autonomy of the state as an alternative framework. In order to serve the general interests of capital, the state must have some autonomy from direct ruling class control ...

The basic problem in formulations of "relative autonomy" is the conceptualization of the ruling class. Relative autonomy theories assume that the ruling class will respond effectively to the state's abuse of that autonomy. But for the ruling class to be capable of taking such corrective actions, it must have some degree of political cohesion, an understanding of its general interests, and a high degree of political sophistication. In sum, the theory requires that the ruling class, or a portion of it, be class conscious, that is, aware of what is necessary to reproduce capitalist social relations in changing historical circumstances. Yet if the ruling class or a segment of it is class-conscious, then the degree of autonomy of the state is clearly quite limited ...

The way out of this theoretical bind ... is to reject the idea of a class conscious ruling class. Instead of the relative autonomy framework the key idea becomes a division of labor between those who accumulate capital and those who manage the state apparatus. Those who accumulate capital are conscious of their interests as capitalists, but in general they are not conscious of what is necessary to reproduce the social order in changing circumstances. Those who manage the state apparatus, however, are forced to concern themselves to a greater degree with the reproduction of the social order because their continued power rests on the maintenance of political and economic order.

In this framework, the central theoretical task is to explain how it is that despite this division of labor, the state tends to serve the interests of the capitalist class. It is to this task—the elaboration of a structural theory of the state—that I will [now] turn ...

[State Managers and the Maintenance of Business Confidence]

A viable structural theory of the state must do two separate things. It must elaborate the structural constraints that operate to reduce the likelihood that state managers will act against the general interests of capitalists . . . But a structural theory must also explain the tendency of state managers to pursue policies that are in the general interests of capital. It is not sufficient to explain why the state avoids anti-capitalist policies; it is necessary to explain why the state has served to rationalize capitalism. Once one rejects the idea of ruling-class class consciousness, one needs to provide an alternative explanation of efforts at rationalization.

Both tendencies can be derived from the fact that those who manage the state apparatus—regardless of their own political ideology—are dependent on the maintenance of some reasonable level of economic activity. This is true for two reasons. First, the capacity of the state to finance itself through taxation or borrowing depends on the state of the economy. If economic activity is in decline, the state will have difficulty maintaining its revenues at an adequate level. Second, public support for a regime will decline sharply if the regime presides over a serious drop in the level of economic activity, with a parallel rise in unemployment and shortages of key goods. Such a drop in support increases the likelihood that the state managers will be removed from power one way or another. And even if the drop is not that dramatic, it will increase the challenges to the regime and decrease the regime's political ability to take effective actions.

In a capitalist economy the level of economic activity is largely determined by the private investment decisions of capitalists. This means that capitalists, in their collective role as investors, have a veto over state policies in that their failure to invest at adequate levels can create major political problems for the state managers. This discourages state managers from taking actions that might seriously decrease the rate of investment. It also means that state managers have a direct interest in using their power to facilitate investment, since their own continued power rests on a healthy economy. There will be a tendency for state agencies to orient their various programs toward the goal of facilitating and encouraging private investment. In doing so, the state managers address the problem of investment from a broader perspective than that of the individual capitalist. This increases the likelihood that such policies will be in the general interest of capital.

This is, of course, too simple. Both sides of the picture—constraints and rationalization—must be filled out in greater detail to make this approach convincing. One problem, in particular, stands out—if capitalists have a veto over state policies, isn't this simply another version of instrumentalism? The answer to this question lies in a more careful analysis of the determinants of investment decisions. The most useful concept is the idea of business confidence.

Individual capitalists decide on their rate of investment in a particular country on the basis of a variety of specific variables such as the price of labor and the size of the market for a specific product. But there is also an intangible variable—the capitalist's evaluation of the general political/economic climate. Is the society stable; is the working class under control; are taxes likely to rise; do government agencies interfere with business freedom; will the economy grow? . . . The sum of all these evaluations across a national economy can be termed the level of business confidence. As the level of business confidence declines, so will the rate of investment . . . Business confidence is, however, very different from "ruling-class consciousness." Business confidence is based on an evaluation of the market that considers political events only as they might impinge on the market. This means that it is rooted in the narrow self-interest of the individual capitalist who is worried about profit. Business confidence . . . does not make subtle evaluations as to whether the regime is serving the long-term interests of capital . . .

[When Leftist Governments Are Elected]

The dynamic of business confidence as a constraint on the managers of the state apparatus can be grasped by tracing out a scenario of what happens when left-of-center governments come to power through parliamentary means and attempt to push through major reforms. The scenario distills a number of twentieth century experiences including that of Chile under Allende. From the moment the left wins the election, business confidence declines. The most important manifestation of this decline is an increase in speculation against the nation's currency. Reformist governments are always under suspicion that they will pursue inflationary policies; a high rate of inflation means that the international value of the nation's currency will fall. Speculators begin to discount the currency for the expected inflation as soon as possible.

This association between reformist governments and inflation is not arbitrary. Reformist policies—higher levels of employment, redistribution of income toward the poor, improved social services—directly or indirectly lead to a shift of income from profits toward the working class . . . The reformist government, faced with the initial speculative assault on its currency, has two choices. It can reassure the international and domestic business community, making clear its intention to pursue orthodox economic policies. Or it can forge ahead with its reform program. If it pursues the latter course, an increased rate of inflation and an eventual international monetary crisis is likely. The international crisis results from the combination of continued speculative pressure against the currency and several new factors. Domestic inflation is likely to affect the nation's balance of trade adversely, leading to a real deterioration in the nation's balance of payments account. In addition, inflation and loss of confidence in the currency leads to the flight of foreign and domestic capital and increased foreign reluctance to lend money to the afflicted nation . . .

If the government is [still] committed to defending its programs, it will have to act to insulate its economy from the pressures of the international market by imposing some combination of price controls, import controls, and exchange controls. Escalation in the government's attempts to control the market sets off a new chain of events. These new controls involve threats to individual capitalists. Price controls mean that firms lose the ability to manipulate one of the major determinants of profit levels. Import controls mean that a firm may no longer be able to import goods critical to its business. Exchange controls mean that firms and individuals no longer are able to move their assets freely to secure international havens. The fact that assets are locked into a rapidly inflating currency poses the possibility that large fortunes will be lost.

These are the ingredients for a sharp decline in domestic business confidence. Why should business owners continue to invest if they must operate in an environment in which the government violates the fundamental rules of a market economy? A sharp decline in business confidence leads to a parallel economic downturn. High rates of unemployment coexist with annoying shortages of critical commodities. The popularity of the regime falls precipitously. The only alternative to capitulation—eliminating controls and initial reforms—is sharp forward movement to socialize the economy. The government could put people back to work and relieve the shortages by taking over private firms. However, the political basis for this kind of action does not exist, even where the leaders of the government are rhetorically committed to the goal of socialism. Generally, the reformist government has not prepared its electoral supporters for extreme action; its entire program has been based on the promise of gradual transition . . .

The outcome of this impasse is tragically familiar. The government either falls from power through standard parliamentary means—loss of an election, defection of some of its parliamentary support—or it is removed militarily. Military actions that violate constitutionality meet formidable obstacles in liberal capitalist nations, but when economic chaos severely diminishes the legitimacy of a regime, the chances of a military coup are enhanced . . . Naturally the removal of the reformist government leads to a rapid revival of business confidence simply because order has been restored . . .

The key point in elaborating this scenario is that the chain of events can unfold without any members of the ruling class consciously deciding to act "politically" against the regime in power . . . Conspiracies to destabilize the regime are basically superfluous, since decisions made by individual capitalists according to their own narrow economic rationality are sufficient to paralyze the regime . . .

[The Role of Class Struggle in the Rationalization of Capitalism]

The dynamic of business confidence helps explain why governments are constrained from pursuing anticapitalist policies. It remains to be explained why governments tend to act in the general interests of capital. Part of the answer has already been suggested. Since state managers are so dependent upon the workings of the investment accumulation process, it is natural that they will use whatever resources are available to aid that process . . .

There is one major difficulty in this formulation—the problem of explaining the dynamic through which reforms that increase the rationality of capitalism come about. Almost all these reforms involve an extension of the state's role in the economy and society, either in a regulatory capacity or in the provision of services. The difficulty is that business confidence has been depicted as so short-sighted that it is likely to decline in the face of most efforts to extend the state's role domestically, since such efforts threaten to restrict the freedom of individual capitalists and/or increase the tax burden on capitalists. If the state is unwilling to risk a decline in business confidence, how is it then that the state's role has expanded inexorably throughout the twentieth century? . . .

There is a line of argument [which explains this] . . . It depends on the existence of another structural mechanism—class struggle. Whatever the role of class struggle in advancing the development of revolutionary consciousness, class struggle between proletariat and ruling class in Marx's view has another important function. It pushes forward the development of capitalism—speeding the process by which capitalism advances the development of the productive forces . . . Class struggle produces this result most clearly in conflict over wages. When workers are able to win wage gains, they increase the pressure on the capitalists to find ways to substitute machines for people . . . This, in turn, diminishes the capacity of workers to win wage gains, until the economic boom again creates a labor shortage. While this description applies particularly to competitive capitalism, the point is that workers' struggles . . . play an important role in speeding the pace of technological innovations. *Class struggle is responsible for much of the economic dynamism of capitalism.*

This pattern goes beyond the struggle over wages. From the beginning of capitalism, workers have struggled to improve their living conditions, which also means upgrading their potential as a labor force. For example, unbridled early capitalism, through child labor and horrendously long working days, threatened to destroy the capacity of the working class to reproduce itself—an outcome not in the long-term interests of capitalists. So working people's struggles against child labor, against incredibly low standards of public health and housing, and for the shorter day, made it possible for the class to reproduce itself, providing capitalism a new generation of laborers. In each historical period, the working class struggles to reproduce itself at a higher level of existence. Workers have played an important role, for example, in demanding increased public education. Public education, in turn, helped create the educated labor pool that developing capitalism required. Obviously, not every working class demand contributes to the advance of capitalism, but it is foolish to ignore this dimension of class struggle.

In its struggles to protect itself from the ravages of a market economy, the working class has played a key role in the steady expansion of the state's role in capitalist societies. Pressures from the working class have contributed to the expansion of the state's role in the regulation of the economy and in the provision of services. The working class has not been the only force behind the expansion of the state's role in these areas. Examples can be cited of capitalists who have supported an expansion of the state's role into a certain area either because of narrow self-interest—access to government contracts, or because government regulation would hamper competitors—or because of some farsighted recognition of the need to coopt the working class. However, the major impetus for the extension of the state's role has come from the working class and from the managers of the state apparatus, whose own powers expand with a growing state . . .

[Conclusion]

Where there is strong popular pressure for an expansion of social services or increased regulation of markets, the state managers must weigh three factors. First, they do not want to damage business confidence, which generally responds unfavorably to an expansion of the government's role in providing social services and in regulating the market. Second, they do not want class antagonisms to escalate to a level that would endanger their own rule. Third, they recognize that their own power and resources will grow if the state's role is expanded. If the state managers decide to respond to pressures with concessions, they are likely to shape their concessions in a manner that will least offend business confidence and will most expand their own power. These two constraints increase the likelihood that the concessions will ultimately serve to rationalize capitalism . . .

The Dilemma of Pluralist Democracy
[Autonomy Versus Equality]

Selections from the Work of
Robert A. Dahl

[Democracy and Polyarchy]

The term "democracy" is like an ancient kitchen midden packed with assorted leftovers from twenty-five hundred years of nearly continuous usage. From a number of possible ways to conceive democracy, I shall pick two that bear most closely on the problem of democratic pluralism. The first conceives of democracy as an ideal or theoretical system, perhaps at the extreme limit of human possibilities or even beyond. According to this interpretation an ideal democratic process would satisfy five criteria:

1. Equality in voting: In making collective binding decisions, the expressed preference of each citizen . . . ought to be taken equally into account in determining the final solution.

2. Effective participation: Throughout the process of collective decision making, including the stage of putting matters on the agenda, each citizen ought to have adequate and equal opportunities for expressing his or her preferences as to the final outcome.

3. Enlightened understanding: In the time permitted by the need for a decision, each citizen ought to have adequate and equal opportunities for arriving at his or her considered judgment as to the most desirable outcome.

4. Final control over the agenda: The body of citizens (the demos) should have the exclusive authority to determine what matters

Excerpts from Robert A. Dahl, *Dilemmas of Pluralist Democracy* (New Haven: Yale University Press, 1982), 4–11, 26–47, 197–205. Copyright © Yale University Press. Reprinted with permission of the publisher. Bracketed headings have been created by the editor of this volume.

are or are not to be decided by means of processes that satisfy the first three criteria . . .

5. Inclusion: The demos ought to include all adults subject to its laws, except transients . . .

The ideal criteria are so demanding that no actual regime has ever fully met them. Possibly none ever will . . . The kitchen midden of democratic ideas furnishes several accounts of actual democratic regimes, however, each with rather different political institutions. Of these, two are particularly germane. Historically, the first to appear were the regimes of relatively democratized city-states. Very much later came the second, the regimes of relatively democratized nation-states . . . [Here] political institutions developed that, taken together, distinguish the regimes of modern democratic countries from all other regimes, including those of the relatively democratized city-states. Seven institutions in particular, taken as a whole, define a type of regime that is historically unique:

1. Control over government decisions about policy is constitutionally vested in elected officials.
2. Elected officials are chosen in frequent and fairly conducted elections in which coercion is comparatively uncommon.
3. Practically all adults have the right to vote in the election of officials.
4. Practically all adults have the right to run for elective offices in the government, though age limits may be higher for holding office than for the suffrage.
5. Citizens have a right to express themselves without the danger of severe punishment on political matters broadly defined, including criticism of officials, the government, the regime, the socio-economic order, and the prevailing ideology.
6. Citizens have a right to seek out alternative sources of information. Moreover, alternative sources of information exist and are protected by law.
7. To achieve their various rights, including those listed above, citizens also have a right to form relatively independent associations or organizations, including independent political parties and interest groups . . .

Countries can be classified according to the extent to which their political institutions approximate these criteria. In ordinary usage, countries in which the political institutions most closely approximate these criteria are democratic. In order to emphasize the distinction between regimes like these and democracy in the ideal sense, they may also be called polyarchies. I use several terms interchangeably: modern democratic regimes, democratic countries, large-scale democracy, polyarchy and so on. None of these terms is meant to imply, of course, that these regimes are democratic in the ideal sense . . .

[Pluralist Democracy and the Relative Autonomy of Organizations]

An organization is relatively autonomous if it undertakes actions that (a) are considered harmful by another organization and that (b) no other organization, including the government of the state, can prevent, or could prevent except by incurring costs so high as to exceed the gains to the actor from doing so . . . I am going to lump [organizations] into three untidy heaps, on which I want to stick the labels governmental, political, and economic. As to the first, whatever constitutional theory may prescribe, in every democratic country the major institutions of government—the chief executive, the bureaucracies, the parliament, the judiciary—are in important respects independent of one another. Although the legislature and the chief executive are probably more independent of one another in countries where the doctrine of separation of powers is explicitly enshrined in constitutional theory and practice (like the United States), some independence exists among the major institutions of the national government in all democratic countries . . . The extent of independence permitted to parties and interest groups is a characteristic of modern democratic regimes that distinguishes them . . . from authoritarian regimes . . .

Economic organizations, mainly business firms and trade unions, are also deeply implicated in the problem of autonomy and control. Their autonomy is at once a fact, a value, and a source of harm. In all democratic countries, business firms make important decisions that are not fully controlled by government; even state-owned firms usually enjoy a significant measure of autonomy in relation to parliament, cabinet and central bureaucracies . . . Independent trade unions that exercise the right to strike exist in all democratic countries . . . In exercising the right to strike, trade unions are relatively autonomous in relation both to employers and to the government itself . . .

Of the more than one hundred and fifty countries in the world today, the institutions of polyarchy exist in about thirty. In these countries, some important governmental, political and economic organizations are relatively autonomous in relation to one another. In this sense, all democratic countries are also pluralist . . . [Hence] the problem of democratic pluralism exists in all democratic countries.

[The Dilemma of Pluralist Democracy]

The problem of democratic pluralism is . . . [that] independent organizations are highly desirable and at the same time their independence allows them to do harm . . . In large political systems independent organizations help to prevent domination and to create mutual control. The main alternative to mutual control in the government of the state is hierarchy. To govern a system as large as a country exclusively by hierarchy is to invite domination by those who control the government of the state. Independent organizations help to curb hierarchy and domination . . .

[In addition], the rights required for democracy on a large scale make relatively autonomous organizations simultaneously possible and necessary. For example, elections cannot be contested in a large system without organizations. To forbid political parties would make it impossible for citizens to coordinate their efforts in order to nominate and elect their preferred candidates and thus would violate the criteria of voting equality and effective participation. To forbid all political parties save one would be to grant exceptional opportunities to the members of one party in comparison with other citizens . . .

Desirable as independent organizations are for these reasons, they also appear to be implicated in problems of democratic pluralism: they may help to stabilize injustices, deform civic consciousness, [and] distort the public agenda . . . Even when the institutional guarantees of polyarchy exist and the political system of a country is democratic to this extent, organizational pluralism is perfectly consistent with extensive inequalities. Moreover, the influence and power of organizations does more than simply register existing inequalities in other resources. Organization is itself a resource. It confers advantage directly on its leaders and often indirectly on at least some members. Although organization is indispensable for offsetting the universal tendency toward domination, the pattern of pluralism in a particular country, even while checking domination may help to sustain inequalities of various kinds, including inequality in control over the government of the state. For example, when organizations are not broadly inclusive in their membership, political inequality is a likely consequence, for, other things being equal, the organized are more influential than an equivalent number of unorganized citizens . . .

[Corporate Autonomy and Inequality]

In a democratic country the autonomy of private business firms is on a rather different footing from the autonomy of the other kinds of organizations, and particularly their nearest analogues, political, governmental, and trade union organizations. For the political rights necessary to the democratic process directly require a substantial measure of independence for organizations that facilitate the exercise of these rights, such as political parties, interest groups, lobbies, newspapers, magazines, and so on. A certain measure of independence over some range of matters for local elected governments might also be derived from a right of citizens to establish smaller democratic units for making decisions that essentially affect only themselves—though social interdependence considerably diminishes the zone of rightful local autonomy. Independent trade unions are problematical; yet a strong case can be made that they are necessary both to democratic rights and to freedom of choice . . .

But privately owned and controlled economic enterprises, particularly in the form of very large corporations, are a different story. For a large corporation is a political system, analogous in important ways to the government of the state. Yet the government of a large corporation differs radically from the government of the state in a democratic country, because neither in theory nor in practice are corporate governments democratic. Is the autonomy of large corporations justified, however, as necessary to fundamental rights?

It might be argued that by decentralizing decisions and political resources, an economic order of relatively independent firms gives support to the democratic process, and at any rate helps to prevent the concentration of power and resources that in the long run would probably undermine the institutions of polyarchy. The argument is, I believe, valid. But it is an argument for decentralization and not necessarily for decentralization to privately owned firms. In principle the argument would be met by decentralization to socially owned or employee-owned firms, either of which might in principle be democratically controlled . . .

It might be argued that economic decision making in a privately owned, competitive economy is reducible to private exchanges among individuals each of whom is free to agree or not agree to the exchange. This, the view of classical liberal theory, became an assumption of neoclassical economics. Under the positive principle of autonomy, it would seem to follow that every person is entitled to freedom of choice on any matter except where the exercise of free choice could be shown to be (a) socially harmful and (b) not a fundamental right. Although making judgments of this kind is notoriously difficult, in my view this orientation is nonetheless a valid one. Yet while we might imagine an economy . . . in which all transactions are reducible to voluntary exchanges among freely acting persons, when we descend from the imaginary realm to the actual world we realize how different the two are.

To begin with, if the initial distribution of resources is unjust, then the outcome of the whole network of transactions that depend on that distribution is also unjust. In a democratic country, therefore, people might reasonably choose to remedy an unfair distribution of resources by using their government to redistribute resources, or to regulate particular transactions, or both. Moreover, because wealth, income, education, information, access to organizations, and many other resources are unequally distributed among different persons, in practice the persons who are actually involved in exchanges are not equally "free" to accept or reject a proposed exchange. To make a familiar and flagrant case, in nineteenth-century mill towns, children were not "free" to work or not to work in the mills—nor, for that matter, were their parents . . .

It seems to be widely believed in the United States that the boards and managers of privately owned corporations do not actually make decisions on public matters because their control is derived from a fundamental right to property; and consequently they are merely exercising their right to decide matters in the interests of the owners. It is true, of course, that if the control of owners and managers is derived from a fundamental right in property, then the autonomy exercised by managers in behalf of owners of private enterprises would not constitute an alienation of public matters to private firms. For on this assumption what they do is a private affair.

Although this defense undoubtedly has great ideological strength, it is badly flawed theoretically. For the justification of private property as a natural, inalienable, or fundamental right provides scant justification for the existing ownership and control of large corporations. Insofar as a right to property is justified by the principle that one is entitled to use the products of one's own labor as one chooses, then surely the privileged position of stockholders is unjustified. On this principle, indeed, the employees would have an even more fundamental claim to own and control the firms for which they labor . . . The inalienable right of an individual to property might also be justified on the grounds that a freedom to acquire some level of material resources and to use them as one chooses is essential to many other freedoms . . . Like the other, this principle fails to justify an exclusive claim to ownership of corporations by stock-holders or other investors. Again, it would provide even stronger support to a claim to ownership by workers . . .

[Solution: Democratic Control of Economic Organizations]

A satisfactory solution [to these problems] would require at least two changes. First, the distribution of income would have to be fair. Second, decisions that would remain discretionary because of the inevitable looseness of regulation by the market would be subject to democratic control. But democratic control requires an appropriate demos . . . Both fundamental rights and social utility provide adequate grounds for holding that different matters should often be subject to control by different bodies of citizens—just as they are by governments of municipalities, states, and the nation . . . In determining what discretionary decisions should properly be on the agenda of a particular demos, I do not see how the conclusion can reasonably be avoided that of those decisions which most affect their lives all the employees of an economic enterprise must be included in the demos. And to satisfy democratic criteria, citizens of a firm would have to possess equal votes. I am aware that a solution along these lines is bound to encounter many objections and many genuine difficulties. Conceivably an economic order fully under democratic controls would be unacceptably inefficient. But . . . ways of achieving an economic . . .!er that is both efficient and democratically controlled are yet to be fully explored. I cannot say, of course, whether the changes in structures and in civic orientations necessary to remedy the defects in the American system of organizational pluralism will come about. To the extent that they do not, however, the United States will surely fail to achieve the best potentialities of pluralist democracy.

The Top-down and Bottom-up Construction of Democracy

Selections from the Work of
Charles Tilly

People *construct* democracy in two different senses of the word. First, they create a set of political arrangements whose effects are democratic, however we define democracy. The second sense of "construction" refers to the shared understandings, the culture that people create for themselves. Indeed, those shared understandings affect the political arrangements' operation. In the past, durable democratic institutions emerged out of repeated, long-term struggles in which workers, peasants, and other ordinary people were much involved, even where the crucial maneuvers involved an elite's conspiring in small concessions to avoid large ones. Revolutions, rebellions, and mass mobilizations made a significant difference to the extent of democracy in one country or another. Yet current theories of democratization give little place to popular collective action, emphasize instrumental maneuvers and bargains among elites, stress promulgated beliefs, and stage the critical political changes in the short run. Is the history revealed to us by Barrington Moore[1] [for instance] an illusion? Or have the rules changed fundamentally?

To Conceptualize Democracy

Before examining that question, let us do some conceptual construction. In order to get to democracy, we must work our way down a chain including state, polity, rights, and citizenship. Here is the chain:

Excerpts from Charles Tilly, "Of Oilfields, Lakes, and Democracy." Working Paper 152, Center for Studies of Social Change, New School for Social Research, November 1992, by permission of the author. Another version of the paper appeared as "Democracy Is a Lake" in *The Social Construction of Democracy*, ed. H. Chapman and R. Andrews (New York: New York University Press, 1995). Bracketed headings have been created by the editor of this volume.

State: an organization controlling the principal concentrated means of coercion within a delimited territory and exercising priority in some respects over all other organizations within the same territory. *Polity:* the set of relations among agents of the state and all major political actors within the delimited territory. *Rights:* enforceable claims, the reciprocal of *obligations. Citizenship:* rights and mutual obligations binding state agents and a category of persons defined exclusively by their legal attachment to the same state. With that conceptual chain in place, we can begin hauling up an idea of democracy as a particular form of citizenship. Democracy combines *(1) broad and (2) relatively equal citizenship with (3) binding consultation of citizens in regard to state personnel and policies as well as (4) protection of citizens from arbitrary state action* . . .

Notice what this conception does not do. It does not make general equality of means or opportunity a criterion of democracy; equality only refers to claims on and from the state in a person's capacity as citizen. The proposed quadruped conception of democracy *does,* on the other hand, declare that a polity is undemocratic to the degree that citizens' political rights and obligations vary by gender, race, religion, national origin, wealth, or any other general set of categories, that it is likewise undemocratic to the extent that large numbers of people subject to the state's jurisdiction lack access to citizenship . . .

The four criteria—equality, breadth, consultation, and protection—form continua from none (0) to complete (1). All real polities lie somewhere in between. For conceptual clarification, nevertheless, we can conveniently split each of the four dimensions into Yes (1) and No (zero). That step allows us to diagram competing forms of political organization in the same terms, as in Table 1. There, *patrimonialism* appears as 0000: narrow, unequal citizenship with little or no consultation and protection. *Oligarchy* (0010) likewise entails narrow, unequal citizenship and little protection of citizens from arbitrary state action, but involves binding consultation of the small number who possess citizenship. *Dictatorship* (1100) looks much different: equal, broad citizenship but little or no consultation and protection. *Democracy* comes out, then, as 1111, high on all four criteria . . .

Table 1 generalizes the conceptualization by [also] identifying a number of other types among the sixteen possible permutations of the

Table 1. Pure Types of Polity

Configuration	Equality	Breadth	Consult	Protect
democracy	1	1	1	1
corrupt democracy	1	1	1	0
tutelary democracy	1	1	0	1
dictatorship	1	1	0	0
patriciate	1	0	1	1
corporatism	0	1	1	1
oligarchy	0	0	1	0
paternalism	0	0	0	1
patrimonialism	0	0	0	0

four elements. A patriciate (1011), for example, looks a lot like a democracy, except that it adopts a narrow definition of citizenship. A *tutelary democracy* (1101) combines broad, relatively equal citizenship with substantial protections but has little binding consultation of citizens; state agents proceed quite autonomously. One might dispute my labels, but the main point remains: even in a simple dichotomous form, the four variables do a relatively effective job of distinguishing major types of polities, and of placing democracy among them . . .

Let us distinguish tautologically necessary conditions for democracy from contingent conditions that may produce or sustain it. My proposed definition requires two interlocked conditions: a substantial state and citizenship relating people to that state. Citizenship has no substantial meaning in the absence of a relatively powerful and centralized state. It follows that . . . we can expect democratization and democracy to proceed differently as a function of variation in the trajectories of states and citizenship . . .

[The Social Bases of Democracy: Class Coalitions and Subordination of the Military]

European experience suggests strong hypotheses concerning the social bases of democracy's components:

1. *Protection from arbitrary state action* depends on (a) subordination of the military to civilian control, (b) class coalitions in which old powerholders ally with relatively powerless but large segments of the population, e.g., bourgeois and workers, thus extending old privileges and protections.

2. *Binding consultation* depends on (a) subordination of the military to civilian control, (b) extensive domestic taxation (as opposed, e.g., to state revenues drawn directly from exports), (c) representation with respect to the assessment and collection of taxes.

3. *Equal citizenship* depends on (a) broad class coalitions including powerholders, (b) creation and expansion of electoral systems.

4. *Broad citizenship* depends on (a) extensive domestic taxation, (b) broad class coalitions, (c) direct recruitment of large military services from the domestic population.

We might reasonably hypothesize that the relative strength of these factors prior to democratization also affects the kind of democracy that emerges, for example that systems growing up chiefly through subordination of the military via defeat in war, military occupation, or some other cause will emphasize protection and breadth more than equality or binding consultation, while domestic taxation alone will promote binding consultation and breadth of citizenship while leaving equality and protection more uncertain.

An Illustration: Democracy and Citizenship in Great Britain

The case of Great Britain illustrates the ties among democratization, citizenship, changes in the state [and the social bases of democracy.] Analyses have pigeonholed Britain as an example of political transformation in the absence of a strong state. [This conception has now been demolished.] In fact, the creation of large military forces, their supply with men, goods, and services, the repression of domestic dissidence, and expansion of the fiscal system wrought great changes in British government between 1790 and 1815: not only a large net increase in military forces and government expenditures despite the demobilization of 1815–1816 and a remarkable tightening of the central bureaucracy, but also a dramatic shift of political power from the king, his clients, and other great patrons toward parliament. The state swelled in importance and parliament grew within it like a goiter.

This process of expansion had enormous importance for citizenship. Remember that by "citizenship" we still mean rights and mutual obligations binding state agents and a category of persons defined exclusively by their legal attachment to the same state. Between 1750 and 1815 such rights and obligations multiplied as a result of the state's pursuit of war. War had its most visible effects in the realms of taxation and military service. Total taxes collected rose and military service expanded enormously in scope. As Colley (1992, p. 312) sums up: " . . . it was training in arms under the auspices of the state that was the most common collective working class experience . . . "

Through the increasingly visible presence of the tax collector, the recruiting sergeant, the militia commander, and the member of parliament, ordinary British people acquired much more extensive direct contact with the state than they had experienced since the revolutionary period of 1640–1660. This time it lasted. From multiplied encounters with agents of the state, Britons acquired a growing sense of Britishness, which did not keep many of them from attacking press gangs, evading tax collectors, or joining radical movements; on the contrary, the nationalization of daily life and consciousness nationalized British struggles and resistance to authorities as well. In the process, direct obligations between subjects and state gained enough scope and intensity to merit the name citizenship.

What of democracy? As of 1750, we can plausibly describe Great Britain as a 0001, a paternalistic polity involving narrow, unequal citizenship and only partial binding consultation of those aristocrats and gentry who enjoyed something like citizens' privileges, but substantial protections from arbitrary state action for them. The narrowness of citizenship did not reside so much in the small parliamentary electorate as in the mediation of most Britons' relations with the state through local and regional notables such as the Justices of the Peace, who enjoyed great autonomy in their exercise of state-authorized positions.

By 1835, Great Britain had moved closer to 1001 or even 1011, as a broader but arguably more unequal citizenry enjoyed extensive rights to assemble, associate, and communicate their grievances directly to the state, although the exclusion of the population's vast majority from the suffrage made binding consultation questionable. The Reform act of 1832 had not greatly expanded the electorate, despite shifting the basis of representation from chartered privilege to population and wealth. But contention during the previous 75 years had significantly enlarged citizenship by establishing numerous channels, including mass associations, election campaigns, and public assemblies, through which even non-voters exercised strong collective claims to be heard directly by agents of the state. The working-class Chartist program of 1838–1848 demanded an extension of democracy by means of equalization: universal suffrage, secret ballot, annual elections, salaried members of parliament, no property qualification for members, and equal electoral districts, a call for 1111, with the unstated presumption that British citizens already enjoyed protection from arbitrary state action. The movement collapsed in 1848, but its program gradually passed into law through the acts of 1867–1868, 1885, 1918, and auxiliary legislation. Through struggle from inside and outside the polity, the breadth and equality of citizenship increased as popular consultation—chiefly in the form of periodic elections—became more binding and protections extended as well.

By the enactment of female suffrage in 1918, Great Britain edged into the category of 1111, by no means a "full" democracy, but nonetheless unusually democratic among the states of its time. Thereafter, the chief alterations in citizenship consisted of openings to residents of former colonies and extensions of the state services or payments to which citizens had a right . . . [Thus] British history of the last two centuries illustrates the truism that changes in the character of the state and of citizenship entail alterations in the extent and character of democracy.

Once we recognize the importance of military activity to the British state's transformation, British history takes on a delightful irony. In the world as a whole, autonomous militaries generally inhibit democracy, even when they seize power in the name of democratic programs. They regularly inhibit democracy by diminishing the protections of citizens against arbitrary state action, and often by blocking the definitiveness of popular consultation—annulling or falsifying elections, bypassing or intimidating parliaments, evading public surveillance of their activities. Yet in Britain militarization of the state indirectly fostered democratization. It did so through the struggle and bargaining it generated, which fortified citizenship and subordinated military activity to parliamentary control.

The process began in the 16th century with Tudor checking of great lords' private armies and fortified castles. It ended, for practical purposes, in the 19th century with the elimination of press gangs. An aristocratically led military continued to draw a major share of the state budget, retained great freedom of action in Ireland and the colonies, and enjoyed great prestige at home, yet as such never wielded autonomous power in domestic politics after 1660. But the reliance of the British military on parliament for finance and supply—still an acute issue in the struggles that led up to the revolution of 1640— eventually subordinated the army and navy to civilian, parliamentary control. In retrospect, we can see the crucial importance of that subordination to the later creation of British democracy.

Democracy Resembles a Lake

The exploration of tautologically necessary conditions for democracy—states and citizens—clears the way for thinking about contingent causes and concomitants of democracy. No one has so far succeeded in separating common correlates of democratic arrangements from non-tautologically necessary, sufficient, or contingently causal conditions. The task is difficult, first because the crucial relationships are almost certainly multiple and complex; second because democracy-promoting and democracy-sustaining conditions have most likely varied and changed from one historical setting to another . . . The problem resists solution because democracy [resembles] a lake. A lake can come into being because a mountain stream feeds into a naturally existing basin, because someone or something dams up the outlet of a large river, because a glacier melts, or for a number of other reasons. Democracy behaves like a lake: Although it has distinguishing properties and a logic of its own, it forms in a variety of ways . . .

Quick! Let's abandon the simile before it drowns us! Here is the point: We have absolutely no a priori reason to believe that only one set of circumstances produces and sustains democracy, even if during the last few hundred years' experience particular circumstances have often nurtured democracy. The most we can reasonably hope to get from scrutinizing historical cases of democratization is a map of alternative paths by which the process has occurred, an indication of sufficient—not necessary—conditions for that transformation, and a specification of general mechanisms that play a part in producing or sustaining democratic institutions.

[Class Coalitions, Subordination of the Military, and Democratization]

From their outstanding comparative study of democratization Rueschemeyer and his colleagues[2] draw important conclusions. They confirm Moore's assertion that the political power of labor-controlling landlords inhibited democratization while denying Moore's association of democratization with a politically strong bourgeoisie. Instead, they show, workers allied with others (who were often bourgeois) pushed much more reliably for democracy, sometimes over the resistance of bourgeois who preferred more limited forms of political participation.

Rueschemeyer and colleagues conclude that in general capitalism does, as often alleged, promote democracy, but not because capitalists prefer democratic government; all other things [being] equal and enemies such as landlords absent, capitalists prefer something like oligarchies of wealth: 0010, not 1111. Such oligarchies allow them to use state power to control workers. But capitalism generates both working classes and the conditions under which they are likely to mobilize, working classes then press for enlargements of citizens' rights and full inclusion of workers among citizens. Given powerful allies, they often succeed. Rueschemeyer and colleagues do not quite recognize their argument's implication: Not capitalism itself, but proletarianization constitutes the crucial conditions for democratization. To the extent that proletarianization occurs by non-capitalist means, all other things equal, it still promotes democratization.

Rueschemeyer and colleagues also understate the importance of their most powerful finding: Armed men who exercise autonomous state power inhibit democracy. The finding connects closely with the inhibitory power of landed classes. For so long as great landlords command large numbers of peasants and serfs, they provide an alternative source of military manpower. Where landlords directly supply and command military units, they retain great political power. As my précis of British history suggests, one of the more surprising and crucial effects of expanding capitalism was that it allowed prosperous states to buy off their militaries, supplying and paying them

well but subordinating them to tax-authorizing parliaments and civilian bureaucracies. Stirred by fears of armed workers, those states
also disarmed the civilian population and created demilitarized police forces specializing in control of civilians. The result was to reduce the chances for any armed group to wrest power, locally or
nationally, from civilian hands . . .

As my tale of Great Britain suggests, mass military mobilization
empowers the classes supplying the bulk of military manpower . . .
The path runs something like this:

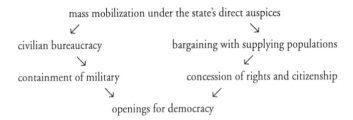

The existence of openings does not guarantee passage through
them. In the absence of favorable class configurations, the path of
mass militarization easily leads to authoritarian repression of the
populace.

[Conclusion: The Social Construction of Democracy]
The militaristic itinerary constitutes only one road to democracy.
Others pass through the federation of small-scale democracies, the
defeat or self-destruction of authoritarian regimes, and the imposition of constitutions by outside powers. Each historic journey left
its mark on the travelers; Swiss, Canadian, and Japanese democracies operate in quite different ways. In most of them, bottom-up
action, unintended consequences, and long-term transformations
play a fundamental part. But in all of them, social construction
matters greatly.

How, then, does social construction matter? It matters because
all four components of democracy—equality, breadth, consultation,
and protection—concern the past and present less than the future.
They concern the expectation that agents of the state will in the
future honor the relatively equal rights of a broad citizenry, that they
will yield to citizens' collective decisions and protect citizens from

arbitrary state action. Of course past and present performance in these regards provides much of the evidence from which citizens project these futures. But the secret of democracy lies in the expectation that one's day will come.

Even in a smoothly operating democracy, a lost war, a deep depression, the formation of an authoritarian mass movement, economic dependency on an outside power, or the acquisition of autonomy by military forces sometimes undermines that expectation rapidly, as the experiences of Italy and Germany after World War I illustrate vividly. Expectations, however much based on realistic observation, depend heavily on social construction, and remain subject to social deconstruction. That is why democracy, once formed, does not stay in place forever. That is why the site of democracy always carries the sign *under construction.*

Notes from the Editor
1. See Moore in this volume.
2. See Huber, Rueschemeyer, and Stephens in this volume.

References
Colley, Linda. 1992. *Britons.* New Haven: Yale University Press.

The Third Wave

[Economic Development, Expansion of
the Middle Class, Elite Compromises, and
Democratization in the Late Twentieth Century]

*Selections from the Work of
Samuel P. Huntington*

The Waves of Democratization

A wave of democratization is a group of transitions from nondemocratic to democratic regimes that occur within a specified period of
time and that significantly outnumber transitions in the opposite direction during that period of time. A wave also usually involves liberalization or partial democratization in political systems that do not
become fully democratic. Three waves of democratization have occurred in the modern world. Each wave affected a relatively small
number of countries, and during each wave some regime transitions
occurred in a nondemocratic direction. In addition, not all transitions
to democracy occurred during democratic waves. History is messy
and political changes do not sort themselves into neat historical boxes.
History is also not unidirectional. Each of the first two waves of democratization was followed by a reverse wave in which some but not
all of the countries that had previously made the transition to democracy reverted to nondemocratic rule. It is often arbitrary to attempt to
specify precisely when a regime transition occurs. It is also arbitrary to
attempt to specify precisely the dates of democratization waves and
reverse waves. It is, nonetheless, often useful to be arbitrary, and the
dates of these waves of regime changes are more or less as follows:

First, long wave of democratization	1828–1926
First reverse wave	1922–42
Second, short wave of democratization	1943–62

Second reverse wave   1958–75
Third wave of democratization   1974– . . .

The Third Wave of Democratization

In the fifteen years following the end of the Portuguese dictatorship in 1974, democratic regimes replaced authoritarian ones in approximately thirty countries in Europe, Asia, and Latin America. In other countries, considerable liberalization occurred in authoritarian regimes. In still others, movements promoting democracy gained strength and legitimacy. Although obviously there were resistance and setbacks, as in China in 1989, the movement toward democracy seemed to take on the character of an almost irresistible global tide moving on from one triumph to the next . . .

This study does not attempt to predict [the] future . . . Its purpose is the more modest one of attempting to explain why, [and] how . . . a group of roughly contemporaneous transitions to democracy occurred in the 1970s and 1980s and to understand what these transitions may suggest about the future of democracy in the world . . .

[Why: Economic Development and the Expansion of the Middle Class]

The [first] question to be answered is: What changes in plausible independent variables in, most probably, the 1960s and 1970s produced the dependent variable, democratizing regime changes in the 1970s and 1980s? [Several] such changes seem to have played significant roles in bringing about the third wave transitions [The following discussion focuses on economic development] . . .

Why did economic development and the movement of countries into the upper-middle income levels promote democratization? The evidence suggest that sheer wealth itself may not have been a crucial factor. Iran and Iraq were in the transition-zone but did not democratize. Three small-population oil producers (Saudi Arabia, Libya, Kuwait) were undemocratic, although they had 1976 per capita GNPs over $4,000, ranking well up among the wealthy countries . . .

In contrast to patterns in the oil states, processes of economic development involving significant industrialization lead to a new, much more diverse, complex, and interrelated economy, which becomes increasingly difficult for authoritarian regimes to control. [First], economic development creates new sources of wealth and power outside the state and a functional need to devolve decision making. Second, economic development increases the levels of education in society. Between 1960 and 1981 the proportion of the relevant age group attending secondary school in developing countries increased dramatically. More highly educated people tend to develop the characteristics of trust, satisfaction, and competence that go with democracy. Third, economic development makes greater resources available for distribution among social groups and hence facilitates accommodation and compromise . . .

Finally, economic development promotes the expansion of the middle class: a larger and larger proportion of society consists of businesspeople, professionals, shopkeepers, teachers, civil servants, managers, technicians, clerical and sales workers. Democracy is premised, in some measure, on majority rule, and democracy is difficult in a situation of concentrated inequalities in which a large, impoverished majority confronts a small, wealthy oligarchy . . . A substantial middle class is normally, however, the product of industrialization and economic growth. In its early phases, the middle class is not necessarily a force for democracy. At times in Latin America and elsewhere, middle-class groups acquiesced in or actively supported military coups designed to overthrow radical governments and to reduce the political influence of labor and peasant organizations. As the process of modernization continued, however, rural radical movements had decreasing leverage on the political process, and the urban middle class increased in size compared to the industrial working class. The potential threats democracy posed to middle-class groups thus declined, and those groups became increasingly confident of their ability to advance their interests through electoral politics.

Third wave movements for democratization were not led by landlords, peasants, or (apart from Poland) industrial workers. In virtually every country the most active supporters of democratization came from the urban middle class. In Argentina, for instance, the choice in the 1960s and 1970s had been between an elected Peronista government based on the working class or a coup-originated military regime with middle-class support. By the 1980s, however, the middle class had become sufficiently numerous so as to provide the core element in the victory of the Radical party under Raúl Alfonsín and to induce the Peronista candidates to be sensitive to its interests. In Brazil the middle class overwhelmingly supported the 1964 coup. By the mid–1970s, however, it was precisely those sectors which benefitted most from the years of the "economic miracle" which were the most vocal in demanding a return to democratic rule: the population of the large and developed cities, and the middle class . . .

In Spain economic development had created a nation of the modern middle classes, which made possible the rapid and peaceful process of bringing the political system into line with society. In Taiwan the main actors for political change were the newly emerged middle-class intellectuals . . . In Korea the movement for democracy in the 1980s only became a serious threat to the authoritarian regime after the emergence by the 1980s of a flourishing urban middle class, and middle-class professionals joined the students in demanding the end of authoritarianism . . .

Reporting the 1987 demonstrations against the authoritarian Chun regime, the *Economist* asked, "What happens when tear gas meets the middle class in Seoul?" The answer was soon clear: tear gas loses. In several countries, including Spain, Brazil, Peru, Ecuador, and the Philippines, the business community, which had previously supported the creation of authoritarian regimes, played crucial roles in promoting the transitions to democracy. In contrast, where the urban middle class was smaller or weaker, as in China, Burma, the Sudan, Bulgaria, and Romania, either democratization was unsuccessful or democracy was unstable . . .

[How: Elite Compromise and the Participation-Moderation Trade-Off]

[The second question is:] how were democracies made? . . . They were made through negotiations, compromises, and agreements. They were made through demonstrations, campaigns, and elections, and through the nonviolent resolution of differences . . . They were made by leaders in both government and opposition who withstood the provocations to violence of opposition radicals and government standpatters. They were made by leaders in government and opposition who had the wisdom to recognize that in politics no one has a monopoly on truth or virtue. Compromise, elections, and nonviolence were the third wave democratization syndrome . . .

The leaders of the key political forces and social groups in society bargained with each other, explicitly or implicitly, and worked out acceptable if not satisfying arrangements for the transition to democracy. Negotiation, compromise, and agreement between reformers and moderates were, of course, the central elements of transplacements. In transformations the process was often implicit, as the reformers in the government opened up the political process and opposition groups modified their demands and moderated their tactics to take part in that process. At times also explicit agreements were reached between reformers leading the transition and opposition moderates, whom they wished to coopt. [Also], democratic opposition groups negotiated agreements among themselves. Once in power, former opposition moderates normally steered middle courses making concessions as needed to reformers, standpatters, and radicals. Whether the initiative for democratization came from the government, from the opposition, or from both, at some point the key players reached agreements on the crucial aspects of the democratization process and the new system that was to be created.

The agreements on introducing democracy took many forms. The transitions in Brazil, Peru, Ecuador, and Bolivia were generally characterized by tentative understandings between the opposition and an official caretaker coalition . . . These understandings usually only involved tacit agreement on some procedural . . . ground rules for the transition. In other instances, regime changes resembled the second wave transitions in Colombia and Venezuela in 1957 and 1958 in which very explicit pacts were negotiated among the interested parties. In Spain, the government under Juan Carlos and Suárez dominated the transition, but government and opposition engaged in the politics of compromise in reaching agreements in the constituent assembly on the constitutional framework for the new democracy and in the so-called Pact of Moncloa in October 1977. In this pact all the relevant political parties, including the Socialists and Communists, agreed on a comprehensive economic program . . .

In Poland Solidarity and the Communist party negotiated the Round Table agreements in March and April 1989. In Hungary government and opposition leaders negotiated the "triangular" agreement during the summer of 1989. Later that fall government and opposition leaders arrived at arrangements for the transition in Czechoslovakia. In Uruguay the military and party leaders reached agreement in the Club Naval Pact of August 1984. In almost all cases the principal participants were the leaders of government and opposition political parties. In many instances, implicit or explicit agreements were also reached with the leaders of key social and institutional forces in the society, including, besides the military, the business community, labor unions, and, where appropriate, the church . . .

The collapse of authoritarian regimes was almost always exhilarating; the creation of democratic regimes was often disillusioning. Few political leaders who put together the compromises creating those regimes escaped the charge of having "sold out" the interests of their constituents . . . That, however, may be the most effective way. In the third wave, democracies were often made by leaders willing to betray the interests of their followers in order to achieve that goal.

A central compromise in most cases of democratization was what might be termed "the democratic bargain," the trade-off between participation and moderation. Implicitly or explicitly in the negotiating processes leading to democratization, the scope of participation was broadened and more political figures and groups gained the opportunity to compete for power and to win power on the implicit or explicit understanding that they would be moderate in their tactics and policies . . .

The ruling groups in authoritarian systems often found particular opposition leaders and political parties especially anathema. Democratization required accepting these groups as legitimate participants in politics. For decades the military establishments of Peru and Argentina used force to prevent the Apristas and the Peronistas from achieving or exercising power. In the democratization processes in those countries in the 1980s, the military accepted not only the participation in politics of their old opponents but also eventually their acquisition of power. A few months after taking office in the Greek transition, Karamanlis legalized the Greek Communist party.

Facing a much more difficult situation and the severe threat of a right-wing coup, Suarez also legalized the Spanish Communist party in April 1977 . . . In Uruguay the Club Naval agreement legalized the leftist Broad Front. In the Brazilian transition the ban on the old pre–1964 political leaders was lifted in 1979 and in 1985 the legislature legalized previously outlawed Marxist parties and gave illiterates the vote. In 1989 Chilean voters amended their constitution to legalize the Communist party. In 1987 in Turkey first the parliament and then the electorate revoked the military-decreed bans that prevented one hundred politicians from engaging in politics. In South Africa in 1990 the African National Congress was unbanned, imprisoned political leaders were freed, and exiles were allowed to return to their country.

The other side of the democratic bargain was moderation in tactics and policies by the included leaders and groups. This often involved their agreeing to abandon violence and any commitment to revolution, to accept existing basic social, economic, and political institutions (e.g., private property and the market system, autonomy of the military, the privileges of the Catholic Church), and to work through elections and parliamentary procedures in order to achieve power and put through their policies.

In the Spanish transition, the army accepted the socialists and communists as participants in Spanish politics, the socialists accepted capitalism, and the communists abandoned their republicanism and accepted the monarchy as well as special arrangements for the Catholic Church . . . In Portugal, Mário Soares similarly led the socialists to the center . . . In Greece Papandreou distanced himself from the more extreme and polemical positions he had espoused in the past and acted with restraint in office. In Peru APRA moved to the center; in Argentina the Peronists moved to the right; in Poland Solidarity moved first to the center and then to the right. In Brazil, the opposition party, the MDB, cooperated with the government's political game [and] was extraordinarily moderate . . . In the referendum campaign on Pinochet in 1988 in Chile the opposition coalition similarly pursued a consciously and explicitly moderate course. Transitions were thus helped by the deradicalization of new participants and former leftists . . .

[Conclusion: The Prospects for Democracy]

Formidable obstacles to the expansion of democracy exist in many societies. The third wave, the "global democratic revolution" of the late twentieth century, will not last forever. It may be followed by a new surge of authoritarianism constituting a third reverse wave. That, however, would not preclude a fourth wave of democratization developing some time in the twenty-first century. Judging by the past record, the two key factors affecting the future stability and expansion of democracy are economic development and political leadership. Most poor societies will remain undemocratic so long as they remain poor. Poverty, however, is not inevitable . . . Economic development should create the conditions for the progressive replacement of authoritarian political systems by democratic ones. Time is on the side of democracy.

Economic Development makes democracy possible; political leadership makes it real. For democracies to come into being, future political elites will at a minimum have to believe that democracy is the least worse form of government for their societies and for themselves. They will also have to have the skills to bring about the transition to democracy against both radicals and standpatters who inevitably will exist and who persistently will attempt to undermine their efforts . . .

For a century and a half after Tocqueville observed the emergence of modern democracy in America, successive waves of democratization washed up on the shore of dictatorship. Buoyed by a rising tide of economic progress, each wave advanced further and ebbed less than its predecessor. History, to shift the metaphor, does not move forward in a straight line, but when skilled and determined leaders push, it does move forward.

Class Inequalities, Elite Patterns, and Transition to Democracy in Latin America

Selections from the Work of
Larry Diamond and Juan Linz

Of the "new nations" that have broken free of European colonial rule in the past two centuries (excepting the United States), the countries of Latin America are by far the oldest. Thus . . . [their analysis] presents us with distinctive opportunities for explaining why democracies emerge, mature, break down, and reemerge; and why some countries have greater overall success with democracy . . .

[Our] cases include the seven most populous countries in Latin America and three of the most theoretically interesting smaller ones—Uruguay, Costa Rica, and the Dominican Republic. They encompass the most stable, democratic regimes in the region, the most successful cases of democratic development historically, and also the longest standing undemocratic regime—Mexico. But it is important to appreciate that they are not representative of the full range of political historical variation in Latin America, and that this skewing of our sample may give an overly optimistic impression of the future of democracy there . . .

[Elite Competition as Precursor to Democracy]

One of the features that distinguishes some of our Latin American cases from the others is their evolution during the nineteenth century of competitive, representative political institutions, which became increasingly inclusive and democratic over time. Chile, Argentina, Uruguay and Costa Rica all began, by the mid-nineteenth

Excerpts from L. Diamond and J. Linz, Introduction to *Democracy in Developing Countries*, vol 4, *Latin America*, ed. Larry Diamond, Juan J. Linz, and Seymour Martin Lipset (Boulder, Colo.: Lynne Rienner, 1989), 1–15, 37–41, 51–52. Copyright © 1989 Lynne Rienner Publishers, Inc. and the National Endowment for Democracy. Used with permission of the publisher. Bracketed headings have been created by the editor of this volume.

century, evolving some form of competitive oligarchy. In Colombia this process was delayed and truncated by recurrent civil strife but flowered in the early twentieth century, while in Brazil an even more limited parliamentary monarchy developed during the period of the Empire (1822–1889).

The early development of a partial, elite democracy, however tentative and flawed, contributed to the ultimate development of full democracy. Of those countries in Latin America that have had the most overall success with democracy, or that now have stable democracy, only Venezuela failed to develop an early constitutional system based on elite competition. By contrast, those countries that have had the least success with democracy in the past few decades—notably Mexico and the Dominican Republic—are also those that were unable to develop and institutionalize some kind of partial, oligarchical democracy in the nineteenth century.

The protodemocracies of the nineteenth century were hardly exemplary models of free and fair competition for power. Fraud and force figured more or less prominently in each electoral system, diminishing more quickly and substantially in some cases (such as Chile) than in others. But these experiences involved the establishment of important democratic institutions—elected presidents and congresses; political parties—and at least some degree of meaningful competition for and rotation of state power. And the most successful of these experiences—in Chile, Argentina, Uruguay, and Costa Rica—also involved the gradual and continuous expansion of the boundaries of competition, incorporating ever larger proportions of the population (first middle-class groups, then workers and peasants) through peaceful political reforms extending suffrage and access to public office.

This path of political development had several positive implications for democratization. First, even where (as in Brazil) they did not produce lasting democratic institutionalization, elite settlements on peaceful competition for power at least resolved (or preempted) the violent, chaotic conflict of the early postindependence period, permitting state building to proceed. Second, even where (as in Costa Rica) they were frequently interrupted, the oligarchical democracies produced political parties and other democratic institutions that took root in the society and provided the political infrastructure around which democracy could grow and mature.

Third, regular elections through constitutional procedures gave competing elites valuable experience with democratic competition and permitted the gradual evolution of trust among contending parties and factions. Over time, the integrity of political competition improved, and its arena widened to incorporate more and more social groups. Fourth, because this process of incorporation was gradual and regulated by elites, mass political participation—signaling the transition to a fuller democracy—could be accommodated, as socioeconomic pressures for it crystallized, without elites fearing mortal damage to their interests. Thus, wider democratic competition, when it came, was more subdued and less polarized than it would otherwise have been . . .

[Elites, Mass Participation, and Democracy]

One of the most crucial historical variables in our Latin American cases is the way in which ruling elites responded to pressures for increasing mass participation in the polity. Where the elite made room gradually for autonomous institutional expressions of new popular interests, democracy developed. Where it resisted incorporation and inclusion, adaptation and political reform, the result was the radicalization and polarization of mass politics, as in Peru.

Where reform through brief, democratic experiments failed or was blocked, and elites later pursued strategies of mass incorporation from above in the absence of existing democratic institutions, the result was the most stable undemocratic regime in independent Latin America: Mexico. Where ruling elites panicked in the face of the challenge of mass political incorporation, abandoning democratic institutions for either exclusionary or corporatist strategies, the result . . . was the tragic and sweeping reversal of development that plunged Argentina into decades of praetorian instability . . .

[Elite/Public Political Culture and Democracy]

Political culture involves a number of different psychological orientations, including deeper elements of value and belief about how political authority should be structured and how the self should relate to it, and more temporary and mutable attitudes, sentiments, and evaluations concerning the political system . . . At some historical junctures, elite values and beliefs may differ sharply from those of the public, and these differences may have crucial implications for democratic development . . .

[Our] cases strongly suggest a reciprocal relationship between political culture and political system. Democratic culture helps to maintain and press for the return of democracy, but historically, the choice of democracy by political elites clearly preceded, in many of our cases, the presence of democratic values among the general public or other elites. This elite choice of democracy was no doubt influenced by values, including those induced by international diffusion and demonstration effects. Admiration for the political dynamism of the United States was reflected in the degree to which new democracies in Latin America modeled their constitutions after that of the United States.

However, to a considerable degree, the option for a democratic regime was a matter of pragmatic, calculated strategy by conservative forces who perceived that representative institutions were in their best interest . . . Even at the elite level, deep normative commitments to democracy appear to have followed these rational choices. In Chile, Uruguay, and Costa Rica (and much later in Venezuela), values of tolerance, participation and commitments to democratic principles and procedures developed as a result of practice and experience with democratic institutions . . .

The development and maintenance of democracy is greatly facilitated by values and behavioral dispositions (particularly at the elite level) of compromise, flexibility, tolerance, conciliation, moderation, and restraint. The early development of oligarchical democracy in Chile, Argentina, Uruguay, and Costa Rica clearly was advanced by the evolution of these values among elites. Indeed, it was precisely when violent struggle began to be replaced at the elite level by conciliatory, accommodating behavioral norms that liberal, competitive regimes began to develop and endure. And as these democracies evolved, broad belief in the intrinsic desirability of democracy became an important underpinning of their stability. By the same token, where these beliefs in democratic legitimacy and in compromise and accommodation weakened or were highly contingent on continued elite hegemony, as in Argentina, democracy was much more vulnerable to breakdown . . .

We see in our cases of Costa Rica and Venezuela that democratic culture contributes to democratic stability. In these two most stable of Latin America's democracies, popular and elite belief in democratic legitimacy remains high, despite prolonged, severe economic crises . . . In both countries, pronounced elite dispositions toward compromise, consensus-building, inclusiveness, restraint, and respect for democratic procedures and principles reinforce legitimacy by avoiding political crisis and polarization, focusing political discontent on individual governments rather than the regime, and incorporating new groups into the political process. Democracy in these two countries is also culturally sustained at the mass level by broad and deep normative commitments to tolerance, moderation, and civil liberties, and by unusually high levels of citizen participation in associational life outside the state, motivated and structured by democratic norms . . .

[Inequalities, Class Structure, and Democracy]

Issues of socioeconomic inequality and class structure figure prominently in the experiences with democracy of many of our cases. This is not surprising, given the well known levels of inequality in Latin America. But our analysis suggests that the relationship between inequality and democracy is considerably more complex than a simple negative correlation.

Historically, countries with the most rigidly stratified and severely unequal class structures proved least successful in developing any kind of democratic polity in the nineteenth and early twentieth centuries. Quasi-feudalistic patterns of land tenure and labor exploitation, and enormous concentrations of land and other forms of wealth, were forbidding obstacles. The failure to implement even moderate redistributive reforms heightened political instability, giving rise to violent revolution in Mexico and to polarized, politicized class cleavage in Peru.

However, the impact of inequality on the possibility of democracy was mediated significantly by political leadership and choice . . . Agrarian society in Chile during the nineteenth century was also rigidly stratified, with great concentrations of land ownership and semifeudalistic landlord-peasant relations, persisting well into the twentieth century. What was most different in Chile was that economically privileged elites judged a gradual opening and democratization of the political system (and later, socioeconomic reform) to be in their interest. A similar judgment by the landed upper class in Argentina also led to experimental democratization, despite substantial inequality in land ownership . . .

While substantial inequality was not necessarily incompatible with the development of democracy, it can certainly be argued that it was *less* conducive to democracy than was a more egalitarian social structure. The historic absence of *hacienda* agriculture and large landholdings in Costa Rica, and the shortage of agricultural labor that kept rural wages high, bred an egalitarian social culture and interdependence among classes that clearly helped to foster the development of democratic political institutions. As the political system continued to open in the late nineteenth and twentieth centuries, social reform attenuated the effects of newly increasing inequality and so enhanced democratic legitimacy. In Colombia, Uruguay, and Costa Rica, the absence of a large class of landless laborers diminished the potential for radical class mobilization, just as the control of the major export crop (coffee) by an indigenous agrarian bourgeoisie reduced the potential for radical nationalist mobilization; both trends facilitated the emergence of oligarchical democracy.

The role of an emergent bourgeoisie in pressing for democratization and the limitation of state power in Latin America is an obvious and important issue for investigation. The case of Chile cautions against any simplistic analogies between the rise of democracy in Europe and its development in Latin America: In Chile, as elsewhere in the region, democratization preceded the emergence of a substantial urban bourgeoisie and was spawned instead by landed elites. In some cases, however, the rural elites who pushed forward democratization were not really aristocrats but more properly an agrarian bourgeoisie, as were the coffee planters in Costa Rica.

An equally rich area for comparative analysis concerns the rise of the working class and the way in which it became excluded from or incorporated into the political process. We have already cited the response to new social mobilization as a crucial factor in shaping the trajectory of political development in Latin America; the response to working class mobilization was often the most fateful. In Chile, open politics combined with repressive employment circumstances to produce class-based parties, the Communists and the Socialists, oriented to the electoral process.

A similar development was probably aborted in Argentina by the 1930 coup, and subsequently by Perón's drastic reordering of the whole class structure through his dual strategy of state corporatism and radical protectionism. But the failure of his policies turned his strategy on its head, creating a highly mobilized and organized labor movement with great political autonomy and an undemocratic character. With its political role crystallized in this way, labor became a major player in the political and economic stalemate and instability that bedeviled Argentina during the 1950s, 1960s and 1970s.

By contrast, in Colombia and Uruguay, with their established two-party structures, initial organization of the working class did not lead either to a corporatist or an independent unified labor organization, facilitating the tendency of the party system to cut across and diminish class cleavage. It was only later, as real wages declined precipitously during the 1960s and radical ideology flourished, that labor militancy and government repression polarized into a crisis that contributed to democratic breakdown in Uruguay.

It is notable that the major political parties in Venezuela and Costa Rica also tend to cross-cut and soften class cleavages. To the extent that this does not result in the effective exclusion of strategic social forces from the political process, it seems to be conducive to democracy. We do not wish to advance the proposition that more clearly class-based parties, as in Chile and Peru, are incompatible with democracy, but the tendency of such party systems to fractionalization and polarization argues strongly for the flexibility and coalition-inducing features of a parliamentary system.

To conclude with some more contemporary evidence, our cases suggest a tension between extreme inequality and (or) class polarization on the one hand, and stable democracy on the other. The urgent need for "deconcentration" is a crucial element . . . of the democratic prospect in Brazil, where inequality became especially severe and politically destabilizing during the country's rapid, post-World War II transformation from a predominantly rural and agricultural to a predominantly urban, industrial, and service economy. The marked failure to reduce inequality was an important structural factor underlying the breakdown of democracy in 1964, as it denied the established parties strong bases of popular support and eroded the overall legitimacy of the political system, while at the same time subjecting that weakened system to a combination of pressures—tenacious rural clientelism and emerging urban radicalism and populism—that it could not manage.

As Brazil has become even more urbanized and socially mobilized in the past two decades—while income inequality and, by some accounts, even absolute poverty have worsened despite the stunning economic growth under military rule—deconcentration for democratic consolidation has become imperative. And yet policies to reduce inequality, such as land reform, carry serious political risks in the short run, while the reduction of absolute poverty requires sustained policy commitment over the long term that may be equally difficult to achieve politically . . .

What is [no less] telling is that in Costa Rica and Venezuela, and Colombia as well, substantial, persistent and even increasing inequalities of wealth and income [form] serious challenges to the maintenance (or for Colombia, reconsolidation) of stable democracy. Similarly . . . the enduring legacy of extreme inequality [is] one of the most disturbing obstacles to democratic consolidation in the Dominican Republic.

The overall degree of inequality is not the only measure of the problem; our cases also urge attention to two other, interrelated factors. First, there is some indication that expansion of the educated middle classes may also improve the social and cultural base for democracy, while softening and even perhaps mediating between the extremes of wealth and poverty. Our [cases] of Peru and the Dominican Republic suggest that the growth of urban professional and business classes, and even a middle peasantry in Peru, has shifted values and perceived interests in a democratic direction.

At the same time, however, the cases of Argentina and Uruguay call for careful attention to the actual and perceived interests of middle-class groups, and to the rate of social mobility . . . Non-elite groups in general and perhaps middle-class groups in particular may assess social equity not so much in terms of equality of outcome as equality of opportunity. Where mobility aspirations become blocked by prolonged economic stagnation, this may result in radicalization of strategic groups, such as the intelligentsia, and sapping of legitimacy among the middle classes and the more well-to-do elements of the working class. This argument . . . [applies], we think persuasively, for Argentina, and it seems to apply to Uruguay as well. It also points to the fluidity in Brazil's class structure, and its high rate of spatial mobility among the lower classes, as safety valves that relieve somewhat the pressure of acute inequality . . .

[Conclusion: Prospects for Democracy in Latin America]
At this juncture, democracy in Latin America is everywhere in pain . . . All of the newly restored democracies remain vulnerable . . . The prospect of new democratic breakdowns in Latin America during the 1990s cannot be dismissed. Yet, there are also reasons for cautious optimism about the prospects for new democracies such as Argentina, Uruguay, Brazil, and Chile. The performance of the authoritarian regimes, particularly in Argentina, has weakened the potential appeal of military rule. In contrast with that rule, democracy has gained renewed legitimacy, even when it confronts serious unsolvable problems and shows low efficacy . . .

Democracy might not be the ideal regime and it might not be able to solve all problems, but we suspect the fate of most of the new democracies of Latin America will be to make their present democratic institutions work as well as possible. Our perspective, which is probabilistic, assumes that people have the opportunity and the choice to make institutions work, to improve them, and to make necessary social changes within a peaceful democratic framework. However . . . politics is only part of the life of a society, and its success in facing the economic and social problems and the technological and scientific revolution in changing societies depends ultimately on the society, not exclusively on political institutions. Neither the state nor the political process—nor, obviously, democracy—can assure a good life for everyone. That sobering realization should contribute to the stability of democracy in the Iberoamerican world.

Capitalism by Democratic Design in East/Central Europe

Selections from the Work of
Claus Offe

Under the label "transition to democracy," an important and successful research branch in the social sciences has concerned itself over the last decade with comparative studies of political modernizing processes since the Second World War. Three groups of countries stand at the center of these investigations: the "postwar democracies" Italy, Japan, and West Germany; the Mediterranean democratic processes of the '70s (Portugal, Spain, Greece); and the collapse of the authoritarian regimes in South America (Argentina, Brazil, Uruguay, Chile, Paraguay) during the '80s. The suggestive temptation to add a fourth group to these—i.e., that of the Central and East European states—and to analyze them with the proven instruments supplied by this tradition, turns out, however, to be unsuitable and misleading. The revolution taking place in the former socialist countries is, indeed, basically different from the countries mentioned above . . .

In the above-mentioned cases of "transition to democracy," the modernizing processes are of a strictly political and constitutional sort, i.e., they concern the *form of government and the legal relationships between state and society*, whereas at the end of socialism the additional task of *reforming the economy* is the order of the day. In the countries that underwent a transition to democracy, capital remained in the hands of its owners, and as a rule the owners remained in charge of their capital. On the other hand, the Soviet Union and its former satellites are faced with an acute and altogether different as well as more demanding problem: the transfer of the hitherto

Excerpts from Claus Offe, "Capitalism by Democratic Design? Democratic Theory Facing the Triple Transition in East/Central Europe," trans. P. Adler, *Social Research* 58 (1991): 865–892. Reprinted by permission of the journal. Bracketed headings have been created by the editor of this volume.

state-owned productive assets to other forms of property, and, to this end, the creation of an entirely new class of entrepreneurs and owners in a way that has to be decided and justified in a political way and through politically visible actors. The revolutionary installation of an entrepreneurial class (i.e., of a previously nonexistent category of agents who are now to partake in market competition on the basis of property rights) is a task which none of the previous transitions had to accomplish . . .

The Dilemma of Simultaneity: [Transition to Democracy and to Capitalist Class Inequalities]

In view of [this], the revolutionary transformation in Eastern Europe can be analyzed only with conceptual means whose use has not been called for in almost all of Western and Southern Europe since the First World War. In the Soviet Union and most of its former satellites are simultaneously at stake: . . . (1) the issue of democracy, i.e., the dissolution of the monopoly claims of a party and its replacement by a constitutionally tamed exercise of authority and party competition in the context of guarantees of basic human and citizen rights ("glasnost"); (2) the issue of the economic and property order and the orderly political management of pressing production and distribution problems (perestroika).

The stages of a process, which in the case of the "normal" Western European examples were mastered over a centuries-long sequence (from . . . capitalism to democracy), must thus be traversed nearly simultaneously in Eastern Europe . . . This occasions . . . a dilemma [which] may be outlined as follows: a constitutional and democratic political system finds its appropriate content of issues and cleavages, the smooth processing of which in turn continuously reproduces its legitimacy, only if a certain measure of autonomous economic development has already taken place and when interest coalitions, collective actors, and themes of conflict have—in contrast to what is the case in the forcibly homogenized societies of existent socialism— emerged from the system of the social division of labor.

Only a somewhat developed free-market society with a relatively high level of wealth enables competitive democracy to work as a procedure for the arbitration and reconciliation of interests (Lipset, 1981, ch. 2). In a society in which a labor market is unknown and where the overwhelming majority of the adult population consists of so-called "working people" (trudjascijsja) with similar incomes and uniformly regulated educational, dwelling, and living conditions, competitive democracy lacks, due to this atomized social structure of repressed "difference," sufficiently formed protagonists, collective actors, and issues considered worth processing through the machinery of democratic politics.

Or, alternatively, the lack of a developed complexity in civil society leads to the dominance of themes which, albeit suited to conflict, are not also suited to compromise. In both of these seemingly polar cases, perfect homogeneity and deep antagonism, the social structure lacks the requisite degree of differentiation, i.e., division of labor, status, interest, and cultural identity that only a developed market society will generate . . .

On the other hand, already prior to the introduction of private property and the market economy, procedures are requisite which hold the political elites accountable and enable participation on the part of the majority of the population—in other words, at least rudimentary democratic procedures are necessary at the *initial* stage of the transformation. This is so not only because democratic concessions will alone, apart from being a minimum condition for much-needed economic aid, be able to appease the indignation at arbitrariness and paternalist authoritarianism that were practiced by the old regime, but also because from a certain point of view democratization appears . . . as the precondition of economic transformation.

The Dilemma of Simultaneity: [Elite-Designed Political Capitalism]

In contrast to its Western pendant, the market economy that is emerging in Eastern Europe will be, if it in fact emerges, "political capitalism." It is a capitalism designed, organized, and set into motion by reform elites. Its driving motive is not the prepolitical datum of the owner's (Lockean) natural right to his property and its free enjoyment. Rather, the driving motive is what in the case of the Western countries was only discovered subsequently as a welcome functional side effect of an economic order based on the freedom to property, namely, the fact that an efficient economic mechanism serves at least arguably and in the long run the overall interest of society. Thus the reform elites, by taking responsibility for and helping to start a capitalist economic mechanism represent the interests of society, without, however, being able in the process to rely upon and comply with the demands of an already existing class of capitalist owners and their interests, power, and ideological propositions.

Again, the contrast to the Western pattern of the growth of capitalism is obvious. There, a class of proprietors claims rights which it bases upon moral and ideological arguments that are critical of the forces and institutions of the absolutist, mercantilistic, and feudal old regimes; efficiency, economic growth, and eventually prosperity are mere by-products of the victorious ideological initiatives taken by early entrepreneurial and commercial class protagonists. There, in contrast, privatization and marketization are not rights-driven but outcome-oriented; not class-based but elite-initiated; not creeping and halting but sudden and highly visible; not supported by moral and ideological arguments on rights and freedoms but defended in the name of vehemently and universally desired economic prosperity.

That the introduction of property rights and market mechanisms *is* actually in the interest of society as a whole is, however, typically not reliably recognized and appreciated by the empirical will of the majority of the population. Such reluctance to believe in the desired beneficial outcomes proclaimed and promised by reform elites is due to two quite sound reasons: First, the population has grounds to suspect that the privatizing initiatives of the new reforming elites might not necessarily be in the service of the universal improvement of economic conditions, but contribute in the first place to the enrichment of the members of the state apparatus and its clientele. Second, no one can guarantee that the envisaged improvement of the economic situation will in fact occur, and that it will come about without massive and at least passing absolute economic deprivation of a sizable portion of the population.

These two misgivings—i.e., that the powerful will enrich themselves and that the powerless will fall victims to the market—can be cleared, and their destructive potential restrained, only if the elites in charge of reform secure a solid democratic mandate for their privatizing initiatives and recognize a fair accountability to the majority of the people. Such a mandate can in turn be obtained only via democratic means—which leads to the paradoxical result that in the case of economies of the Soviet type, and when a state-managed withdrawal of the state from the economy is to be undertaken, democracy is a necessary precondition of economic transformation . . .

This "capitalism by design" (or capitalism without capitalists as active promoters of their class interests) depends in every detail on highly visible *decisions* which hence require justification, and its development cannot rely on blind evolutionary emergences, which has largely been the pattern in the history of pioneering Western capitalism. The new class of entrepreneurs (and, correspondingly, the new class of employees, into which the previous "working people" see themselves reconstituted) is created according to a blueprint designed by political elites . . .

A market economy . . . functions under the premise that a general increase of output can be achieved only at the price of a minority's being in a position to increase its income far more substantially and more rapidly than the majority, which, at least for an interval of unknown duration, may even lose out. The market economy produces, along with the growing output of goods, a growing inequality—a tendency which is resisted by the egalitarian resentment. As for democracy, it is reproached with burdening the decision process with frictions, uncertainties, and discontinuities which threaten to interfere with the already precariously poor level of economic performance. This constellation of expectations and fears . . . would obviously have the consequence that, precisely because the economic situation is so dire, promising attempts at economic reform—and at its democratic legitimation—are blocked by a majority of the population.

A Pandora's Box Full of Paradoxes

To summarize the propositions that I have discussed so far: A market economy is set in motion only under predemocratic conditions. In order to promote it, democratic rights must be held back in order to allow for a healthy dose of original accumulation. Only a developed market economy produces the social structural conditions for stable democracy and makes it possible to form compromises within the framework of what is perceived a positive-sum game. But the introduction of a market economy in the postsocialist societies is a "political" project, which has prospects of success only if it rests on a strong democratic legitimation. And it is possible that the majority of the population finds neither democracy nor a market economy a desirable prospect. If all of those propositions hold true at the same time, then we are faced with a Pandora's box full of paradoxes, in the face of which every "theory"—or, for that matter, rational strategy— of the transition must fail . . .

[The Political Economy of Patience and Tolerance to Inequality]

Decisive is the temporal structure of processes. This applies not only to the macroscopic level, where, as the Western model teaches us, a sufficient time interval between the three modernizing thrusts (market economy, democracy, and finally the welfare state), as well as different degrees of rigidity among the three levels fosters their cumulative success, but also to the microscopic level of individual actors. They must, if the simultaneous mastery of the three tasks of modernization is to succeed, be ready to muster a large measure of patience, confidence, and trust. As macroevents have assumed an incredible speed, the painful task of patient waiting falls upon individuals. They must quickly adapt themselves to the new circumstances and then be ready to wait long for the fruits of this adaptation.

They need this patience in order not to interfere with the "creative destruction" which will follow the price and property reform in a perfectly intended manner, although by making use of their newly won civil rights they would be quite capable of doing so. Not only must they be sufficiently disciplined to willingly undergo shock therapy, but they must also hold fast in the process, in spite of commonly available evidence to the contrary, to the (perhaps self-fulfilling) belief that the shock will actually be a therapeutic one. Requisite are therefore precisely the virtues and moral resources of flexibility, of patient waiting, of deliberating, probing, and weighing one's short-term vs. long-term and individual vs. collective preferences, and of tolerance for highly unequal distribution patterns . . .

[One] method to buy the time and to engender the moral credit and thrust requisite for the simultaneous transition to a market economy and democracy consists in an effective sociopolitical mitigation of the pains of transition by continued and fine-tuned mechanism of internal redistribution. Granted, such mitigation has thus far not even occurred under the extraordinarily favored special conditions of the former German Democratic republic. Presumably, tolerance for a transformation toward a market economy, in the course of which inequality inevitably increases (for some must do a lot better quickly in order for all to do somewhat better in the long run), will be more likely to be summoned up if the danger that a substantial part of the population will be, and for some extended period of time, absolutely worse off is ruled out.

Here, the design question boils down to whether you want to provide *status security* to the economic *core groups* or the unconditional guarantee of an adequate subsistence minimum for *everyone*. At any rate, the beneficiaries of the transformation to a market economy would have to be made to compensate the victims of the transformation with some kind of welfare-state security and unemployment benefits. This would certainly constitute an inversion of the sequence of Western constitutional development as it was postulated by T.H. Marshall (i.e., the sequence: liberal constitutional state, democratic state, and welfare state), and the welfare state would be recognized as the precondition for both the market and democracy . . .

So far this has succeeded nowhere; at best, it foundered in such a way that (as in the case of Argentinean Peronism) a kind of welfare state was designed to serve as a permanent *substitute* for liberal democracy. The difficulties are plain to see: the resources which are earmarked for the social insurance against "creative destruction" do make the latter less destructive, but they may also make it less creative. Correspondingly, the prospects for a politically successful privatizing of the system of production, and for concomitantly governing the distribution of incomes and services by means of state guarantees, are viewed pessimistically nearly without exception. This is all the more so because social security and protection can also easily be denounced as being ideas inherited from the old regime and thus as interfering with the unfolding of the new economic order and its hoped-for fruits.

[Difficulties in the Formation of Mediating Bodies]

Even more difficult to realize would have to be [another] solution to the problem of patience, which would consist in forming collective actors such as associations, federations, trade unions, parties, and local authorities within the East European "civil society." If each person could be assured of enjoying the protection of a robust representation and negotiation capacity from such mediating bodies, whose constitutions would have to make it impossible for them to form "exploitative coalitions" or "clans" which would work at the expense of excluded third parties, then at least a part of these fears would lose their weight—fears which otherwise might turn into a "democratic" blockage of the transformation toward a market economy and eventually make democracy itself, due to its allegedly adverse economic consequences, pointless.

These mediating bodies would not be allowed to be state artifacts and would have to enjoy constitutional guarantees that would make them relatively unavailable to opportunistic strategies. At least, they would be able to "deliberate" and find "synthetic solutions" to the conflicting preferences that prevail within their respective constituencies. Also, they would have to be able, due to the representational monopoly granted to them and the strength they derive from it, to explore the availability of their opponents for cooperative strategies without running the risk of ending up as the "sucker" (Bates, 1988). Third, they would have a moral basis in the feelings of solidarity and mutual obligation within "civil society." If such a combination of the institutional as well as moral patterns of "civic republicanism"—*cum* -"democratic corporatism" is a rarity even in the affluent societies of the West, how could it flourish on the soil of the atomized social structures of postsocialist societies?

Instead of that, and corresponding to the atomized state of the society, we see ahead of us, at least in some of the countries undergoing the triple transformation, a type of "charismatic" politics and presidentialist constitution-making unmediated by intermediary structures, in the shadow of which the forces of a civil self-organization beyond market, state, and ethnic "community" are having an exceedingly hard time to assert themselves.

References

Bates, R. H. 1988. "Contra Contractarianism: Some Reflections on the New Institutionalism." *Politics and Society* 16: 387–401.

Lipset, Seymour M. 1981. *Political Man*. Baltimore: Johns Hopkins University Press.

Elites and the Working Class
On Coupling, Uncoupling, Democracy, and (In)equalities in the West

Eva Etzioni-Halevy

Can democracy encourage progress toward greater equality? Given that democratic countries today are blatantly inegalitarian, can we nonetheless detect a positive relationship between (political) democracy and (economic) equality in the West? My thesis is that we can.

Working within a combined class-elite[1] theoretical perspective, I contend that there are some democratic arrangements whose development leads to greater equality. These include the empowerment of the working class through its coupling with elites, which depends on and implies those elites' relative autonomy from the state and their accountability to their working-class constituencies. Conversely, the erosion of such arrangements—the disempowerment of the working class through uncoupling of its ties with elites, a weakening of those elites' accountability to the working class, and of those elites' relative autonomy—leads to greater inequality.

To some extent, the said democratic arrangements developed in the West in the late nineteenth and early twentieth centuries, and this led to decreasing inequalities. By contrast, recently, a partial uncoupling of the working class's ties with elites and some weakening of their autonomy led to increasing inequalities.

As can be seen in this volume, democracy has been analyzed and reanalyzed from many perspectives; yet the issue of how it may encourage greater equality has been neglected. Much of class theory has been concerned with the persistence in democracy of economic inequalities, and much of elite theory has been concerned with the persistence in democracy of power inequalities. Neither has had much to say about the other side of that coin. In this paper I show how a combination of these theories can help fill this void. Also (apart from Michels's work[2]), so far, neither of the theories has paid sufficient attention to the relationship between the working class and "its" elites. This paper also explores that particular relationship.

Some Basic Notions on Classes and Elites

In order to explore the relationship between classes and elites we need to go "back to basics" and note that classes and elites are partly overlapping at the top of the class ladder, but nowhere else. In Western capitalist societies, the capitalist class is roughly coterminous with the economic/business elite. But all other classes do not coincide with any elite and vice versa (although higher class background may form an advantage for recruitment into an elite). Because, below the top, classes and elites do not coincide, their interests are not identical either. However, some elites (*no matter what their members' own class background may be*) and some classes may mutually empower each other by an exchange whereby each promotes the other's interests.

Classes have identifiable interests: primarily those of maintaining and increasing their resources, frequently at the expense of other classes. But, apart from the capitalist class, classes are large, amorphous categories of people, and as such cannot act as entities. Hence classes need elites (leaders and activists) to devise and disseminate ideologies that legitimize their interests. Also, they need elites to head their organizations and to spearhead action in their name. Whether elites establish organizations, or organizations generate elites, is but a chicken-and-egg problem. The important thing is that (to paraphrase Michels), who says organization says elites. And the working class requires organizations and elites at their head.

For their part, elites require resources in order to obtain and retain power and influence. These include chiefly material resources, organizational resources (control of organizations), and political/electoral support. And they may need social classes to supply those resources to them. The higher and more advantaged a class, the more it can supply an elite with material resources; and the lower the class, and the larger it is numerically, the more important is the political/electoral support it can supply.

The Interesting Relations Between Classes and Elites

So, depending on their respective interests and beliefs, elites and classes may develop some interesting relations with each other. Some elites may draw their resources from sources that are unrelated to classes, hence stand aloof from classes, and may (so to speak) be celibate with respect to classes; but others may not be. Requiring class-supplied resources, while classes require leadership, the elites and classes in question may symbiotically nourish each other, or (metaphorically speaking) couple with each other.

Elites coupling with classes, may adopt one of several strategies. They may enter into a monogamous relationship with one class; or they may enter into bigamous or polygamous relations with two or more classes, gaining resources from all of them, and juggling their interests. They may even be promiscuous and shift from one class to another. Or else, they may be monogamous, but maintain extra-marital relations with other classes, which they make greater or lesser efforts to camouflage. Conversely, classes may have one or more elites to promote their interests.

The Relationship Between the Working Class and Elites

In this context, a coupling may occur between certain elites and the working class. The working class—like other classes—has an interest in increasing its resources. To the extent that its interests are in doing so at the expense of more advantaged classes, these are also interests in decreasing inequalities; and it needs elites to promote those interests. Some potential or actual elites may require political support from this class, on which to base their elite positions. And they can gain such support by creating and heading certain movements, organizations, and parties that present themselves as defenders of working-class interests. These elites may be termed working-class elites. They are not necessarily scrupulous in confining their relations to the working class alone, but they are limited in their extracurricular activities by their need to placate the working class.

The coupling between elites and the working class depends on and implies certain democratic arrangements, in particular the relative autonomy and accountability of working-class elites.

The Relative Autonomy of Working-Class Elites

The autonomy of elites that are not part of the state may be said to exist when they are not repressed by the state and when there is an absence of state control over the organizations they head; that is to say, when those organizations' economic resources, and the positions within them, cannot be affected by the state. Such autonomy of elites is (tautologically) dependent on two of the most central principles of democracy in the state: freedom of speech and freedom of association. For without such liberties there could be no associations—or organizations—that are exempt from state control, and therefore no elites or leaders at their helm. Since even in a democracy the state has ultimate authority, such autonomy can never be absolute, only relative, relative, that is, to the situation in autocratic regimes.

The coupling between elites and the working class depends on their relative autonomy. This is so since, even if an elite wished to couple itself with the working class, it could do little to champion its interests if the state could simply crush it or control its organizations' economic resources and its positions within them. For in this case, the elite would have to fashion its actions to suit the interests of its controllers, financiers, or appointers, more than to those of the working class in its capacity as rank and file members of the organizations headed by the elite.

There are cases in which elites have championed working-class interests even in the face of the state's determination to crush such action. This was the case, for instance, with respect to labor movement, union, and party elites in Imperial Russia. But the coupling of such elites with the working class being clandestine, their action in its favor could come about only intermittently, and only when state repression failed or was temporarily relaxed. A long-term, institutionalized union of elites and the working class depends on a degree of elite autonomy and the civil liberties with which it is intermeshed. Only when these exist can the elites in question freely disseminate counterideologies and lead their organizations to sustained industrial, oppositional, and protest action and thereby press for a redistribution of resources in its favor.

The Accountability of Working-Class Elites

The coupling of elites with the working class also depends on and implies another democratic arrangement—this time within their organizations: a degree of accountability of those elites to the working class as members of these organizations. For only when they are accountable to the working class for their actions do the elites in question have any real motive to promote working-class interests. Elites' or leaders' accountability may be said to exist when the leaders are dependent on rank and file approval of their performance in order to maintain their positions. Ideally, such approval—or lack thereof—should be expressed through intraorganizational free elections. It should also be expressed through internal freedom of speech and of association, making it possible for elections to be contested by organized opposition, by which leaders can be periodically replaced, and through some mechanisms for members' control over leaders.

Failing this, leaders' accountability can also exist when members are free to "vote with their feet," to signify approval or disapproval by either maintaining their membership in the said organizations or leaving them, thus withdrawing the resources of political support which the elites require in order to maintain their positions. Assuming that it is not invariably possible for leaders to hoodwink the working-class members of their organizations, the latter's approval is likely to hinge on the leaders' ability to deliver at least some achievements to them, in line with their interests in a redistribution of resources in their favor.

The Thesis and Its Illustration

This brings us back to the thesis, that there are certain democratic arrangements whose development leads to greater equality and whose erosion leads to greater inequality: (1) working-class empowerment through a more or less monogamous coupling of elites with it, which depends on and implies (2) those elites' relative autonomy from the state and (3) their accountability to their working-class constituencies. Illustrative support for this thesis will be drawn from the fact that, to some extent, the noted democratic arrangements developed in the West in the late nineteenth and the beginning of the twentieth centuries, and that this development was among the main factors that led to decreasing economic inequalities at that time.

If, however, democracy furthers progress toward equality, why has it not done so in recent years? A further illustration for the above thesis comes from recent developments in Western—postindustrial, postmodern—societies, which spell a partial reversal of the previous trends. This reversal entails a degree of disempowerment of the working class through a partial uncoupling of its ties with elites, implying a lessening of these elites' accountability to the working class, a weakening of working-class elites, and (in some countries) a weakening of those elites' relative autonomy. These are among the main factors that (in the midst of affluence) have led to increases in economic inequalities. Thus, not democracy, but deficiencies in democracy, go some way toward explaining recent inegalitarian trends.

Illustration of the Thesis from Previous Developments in the West: On Coupling and Decreasing Inequalities

Turning back now to the previous developments, these were the outgrowth of complex historical processes (which are beyond the scope of this paper): the breaking of Church power, the Renaissance, the emergence of liberalism, the decline of absolutism, and the partial checking of state power combined with the development of capitalism, the industrial revolution, and the flock into the cities.

The Empowerment of the Working Class: Its Coupling with Elites

Industrialization and urbanization led to the growth of the working class, while the dismal conditions under which it was forced to subsist focused attention on its plight. Growing liberalism and tolerance made it possible for various elites to take up its cause. This championing included some members of intellectual elites, who exposed the inequities of capitalism and generated the ethos of proletarian collective action to counteract them. This intellectual work provided the ideological base for the elites that expressly coupled themselves with the working class, first and foremost the elites of social movements.

The Working Class and Social Movements' Elites

Throughout the nineteenth century, especially in Western Europe, a variety of social movements arose that concerned themselves with the plight of the working class. They included the Utopian Socialists in France and later in Britain, the Chartists in Britain, the Marxian Socialist movement in various countries, the Syndicalist movement in France, Democratic and Revisionist Socialism in Germany, and the Fabian Socialists and the Guild Socialists in Britain.

Having recourse to a variety of socialist ideologies, these movements all called for socioeconomic redistribution and/or universal suffrage and democratic government—measures designed to favor the disadvantaged, who were also excluded from the franchise, in particular, the working class. Thus these movements' leaders coupled themselves with the working class by focusing their activities on the advocacy of changes that tallied with working-class interests. In return, they required working-class support for those movements and for their leadership positions within them.

The Working Class and Trade Union Elites

Eventually these movements were institutionalized in, or replaced by, other organizations, first and foremost, by labor unions. Labor unions began to emerge during the first half of the nineteenth century, and since the late nineteenth century they have greatly expanded. Their expansion reached its peak after the middle of the twentieth century, when union affiliation in some countries (e.g., the United States and The Netherlands) comprised about one-third of the workforce and in others (e.g., Britain, Italy, and Australia) reached about half of the workforce (Pontusson 1992, p. 11; Visser 1992, p. 19).

Like the development of social movements, that of unions spelled the creation of a symbiotic relationship between their elites and the working class. The union leaders had to rely on working-class backing to build up and bolster their positions, while they gradually became more adamant in promoting a working-class ethos and struggling for workers' democratic rights, increased wages, and improved working conditions.

The Working Class and Labor Party Elites

One achievement of labor movements and unions was the extension of the franchise to the working class. From the late nineteenth century, in most Western countries, the acquisition of the franchise went hand in hand with the emergence of sizable labor/socialist/communist parties. In the United States, of course, there were never sizable labor parties. This situation, however, was the exception rather than the rule. Not only did labor parties emerge, but in most Western countries they drew their electoral support overwhelmingly from the newly enfranchised working class. Their relationship with the working class was expressed in the fact that they reciprocated working-class support by advocating socialist ideologies and pressing for at least some economic redistribution in its favor.

The Attainment of the Elites' Relative Autonomy

Unions and their leaders fought for immunity from state repression, and they made significant gains in this respect toward the end of the nineteenth and the beginning of the twentieth centuries. In countries such as Britain and France at that time, they achieved successively greater freedom to organize, and attempts to suppress them gradually diminished. In the United States attempts to repress unions and discourage unionization persisted well into the twentieth century, but eventually developments followed the same direction. Also, because the unions subsisted on their expanding membership's fees, the state had little control over their financial resources.

Even in the West, union elites' autonomy never became absolute. Governments were able to tame the union elites and dissipate their threat. But since governments could not suppress or control them, they had to use indirect strategies to this end, especially cooptation. In several West European countries this took the form of corporatist arrangements—whereby heads of union federations joined employers' associations and governments in forging economic policies. Collusions with the capitalist class made it impossible for union leaders to preserve their unflagging fidelity to the working class. But because of their initial relative autonomy and consequent ability to countervail state power, they could exact a certain price for their willingness to enter into such collusions. This price included government acceptance of some of their demands for redistribution of resources in favor of the working class. Thus, these elites were not entirely faithful to the working class. But in the very act of betrayal, they also affirmed their commitment to it.

The labor parties' leaders, too, had some autonomy. For, relying on working-class support as their power base, they were neither repressed nor financed nor controlled by the state. The evolution of labor parties also signaled the emergence of a relatively independent opposition to existing governments. This opposition was institutionalized and its leaders entered parliament, joined the establishment, and eventually gained a share of government power. Yet, like union elites (with whom they were occasionally intertwined) its leaders achieved a degree of success in promoting working-class interests. They did so by utilizing their newly gained share of government power or, indirectly, by causing conservative leaders to forestall radical action on their part through the introduction of nonradical, limited, piecemeal, but still significant socioeconomic reforms. Thus they, too, used their power, at least to some extent, to affirm their alliance with the working class.

The Elites' Accountability

As Michels has convincingly shown, many newly emerged labor parties and unions developed oligarchical tendencies. But, while they rarely met stringent standards of internal democracy, many nonetheless developed certain mechanisms of accountability of leaders to rank and file members. In the United States, for instance, although some unions have been autocratic, others have had oppositional activists, occasionally leading to leadership turnover. In Britain, in some unions, the most important functionaries have not been elected; in others, once elected, they have continued until retirement; in still others, they have been elected periodically. In some British unions there have also been oppositional factions, although widespread member-apathy has assisted incumbent leaders to maintain their positions. In unions and parties in various Western countries, even oligarchical leadership-groups occasionally—especially at times of internal crisis—have been ousted by a sporadic opposition.

Furthermore, in a wide variety of settings working-class people have had the ability to signify disapproval of union leaders by withdrawing from unions, and to indicate their disapproval of labor parties by voting for their rivals (see below). Thus, although mechanisms of accountability have been partial, deficient, and variable, they have not been absent. So, they, too, help explain the propensity of working-class elites to put up some struggles in testimony of their commitment to their union with the working class.

Decreasing Inequalities

The period in which labor unions and parties gained more power, that is, the late nineteenth century and the first half of the twentieth century, was also an era of rapid economic development, which made it possible for workers' wages to rise while profits for reinvestment in economic enterprises, and for consumption by the upper classes, remained high. But the push for increasing wages and decreasing inequalities undoubtedly came from the working-class–coupled elites. Not surprisingly, during this time span income inequalities declined virtually all over the Western world. Economic cleavages remained formidable, but they became considerably smaller than they had been before.[3]

Illustration of the Thesis from Recent Developments in the West: On Uncoupling and Rising Inequalities

Recently, the earlier trends were partly reversed. The causes of the reversal are to be sought in an accelerated globalization of the economy, which has rendered capital more mobile and has made it easier for it to escape from costly wage claims. Also, those engaged in white-collar, financial, and other services, and in knowledge- and information-related occupations grew from less than half of the workforce in the postwar era, to between two-thirds and three-quarters of the workforce today. At the same time the blue-collar industrial sector declined to only slightly above one-quarter of the workforce. Together with the aftermath of several economic recessions, all these changes spelled rising unemployment: despite various ups and downs, unemployment in the West is generally higher today than it was in the postwar era. Concomitantly, there has been a growing fragmentation of the labor market into a core and a marginal workforce, the latter of which includes growing numbers of unskilled, part-time, casual, and temporary employees, many of whom periodically withdraw from the labor market (Offe 1985a).

Thus, the industrial working class has been nibbled away from "above," by the swelling numbers of the new middle class, and from "below," by the unemployed and those leaving the workforce altogether. It has become more internally divided and has less of a commonality of interests than previously. In addition, the growing numbers of lower-level white-collar workers spell a growth in the category of people who stand with one foot in the working class and the other in the middle class; and so the boundaries of the working class have become fuzzy.

The Partial Uncoupling of Working-Class Ties with Elites

The shrinking of the working class, as well as general affluence, has also led to its receding visibility. Just as the previous coupling of the working class with elites found its justification in working-class-centered socialist ideologies, so now there has been a rise to prominence of ideologies that no longer focus on the working class, or even on redistribution of resources among classes. These include not merely the ideologies of the new right, but also communitarianism, feminism (which, however, may have some indirect implications for class redistribution), environmentalism, and postmodernism. This change in the intellectual climate, too, has paved the way for the partial uncoupling of the ties between the working class and elites, beginning with the ties of the working class to the labor unions.

The Working Class and Union Elites

The now shrinking industrial working class is the class that had traditionally formed the stronghold of unionism. By contrast, there was less of a tradition of unionization in the now-growing white-collar service sector. Also, there are obstacles to the unionization of marginal workers, whose concerns are different from those of the core workforce. The result has been that, since the 1970s (and despite sizable differences among countries), union membership has declined in almost all countries of the Western world (Visser 1992, p. 19; Central Statistical Office 1994, p. 147). Alongside a general decline in union membership, there has been an even steeper decline in the union membership of blue-collar industrial workers. The nucleus of the working class, which once formed the majority of the union movement, has thus become a shrinking minority within it. Inevitably, this means that union elites have become less tuned in to the demands of the working class, which further weakens the motivation of working-class people to belong to unions.

Moreover, union-led industrial action, which had increased substantially throughout the West in the late 1960s and early 1970s, subsequently took a beating. In most Western countries strike activity was less extensive in the 1980s and even less so in the 1990s, than it had been before (Shalev 1992). Thus (for reasons spelled out below) union elites have no longer been as aggressive as before in their struggles for improved working conditions.

The combination of these developments manifests the working class's declining confidence in union elites, those elites' declining accountability to the working class, and their declining steadfastness in representing working-class interests. In other words, it represents a partial waning of the previous attachment between union elites and the working class.

The Working Class and Labor Parties' Elites

Because of its contraction, the working class, from which labor parties and their leaders have traditionally drawn most of their support, has now become a minority of the electorate. Also, leaving aside the United States, where the situation was different from the outset, in many Western countries the previous support of the working class for labor parties has been greatly attenuated. So the working-class electoral basis of labor parties has been eroded, and their leaders have had to shift their targets: in several countries these leaders have broadened their appeal so as to attract votes from other classes as well. Turning their parties into "catch-all" parties, they have muted their previous socialist, egalitarian ideologies. Also, their advocacy of policies aimed to advance working-class interests has been replaced by a stance that is equally suited (or unsuited) to all classes. For instance, in Britain the Labour Party leadership has abandoned the working-class concerns of nationalization and redistribution in favor of community, responsibility, and cohesion. The Socialist Party in France, which previously advocated nationalization, now no longer does so. In Germany, the Socialist Party leadership has moderated its socialist ideology.

In various countries across the West, then, there has been a partial uncoupling of the previously more monogamous link between the working class and labor party elites. While, even earlier, these elites have had an eye to other classes as well, they have now become manifestly class-promiscuous.

The Working Class and Social Movements' Elites

This change in orientation would be of less import had there been other elites, such as those of social movements, to take up the cause of the working class. Such, however, has not been the case. Unlike the "old" labor/socialist movements, the new movements that have appeared since the 1970s focus on "postmaterialist" issues, such as the quality of life or the environment. Hence they attract support from those most concerned with these issues, the new middle class, not from the working class, which remains concerned with economic redistribution (Offe 1985b).

Thus, elites of social movements, whose unique role lies in spearheading social change, and who previously professed their fidelity to the working class, now no longer do so; there has been a veritable divorce between the working class and the movement elites, and the working class has been supplanted by the new middle class as chief partner in the marital relationship with these elites.

The Weakening of the Elites and of Their Relative Autonomy

Of the elites whose ties with the working class have been loosened, the elites of trade unions have maintained closer ties with the working class than the other elites. Hence it is especially significant that the trade union elites have recently been weakened and that (in some countries) their relative autonomy has been impaired. Shrinking union membership and higher unemployment, along with the fact that, more and more, employers have been able to move their plants into Third World countries, have dealt a blow to unions and eroded their leaders' bargaining position. So, too, have the fragmentation of the labor market and the divisions within the working class, which have led to greater divisiveness between and within unions. This, in turn, has undermined the role of central labor leaders in peak-level negotiations (Golden 1992).

The erosion in the unions' bargaining position also explains the decline of the unions' industrial militancy. This further exacerbates their weakness. In the United States unions have been attacked by employers; their right to collective representation has been rejected; and they have suffered demoralization and defeat (Edwards and Podgursky 1986). In Western Europe unions are still accepted as legitimate workers' representatives, but employers there have gained greater control over employment conditions and unions have been on the defensive (Visser 1992).

These developments were interspersed with the rise of right-wing governments in the United States (under presidents Reagan and Bush), in Britain (under prime ministers Thatcher and Major), in Germany, and now in France. In some countries, particularly the United States and Britain, right-wing governments made deliberate attempts to subjugate unions and their elites, for instance through restrictive legislation, dismissal of strikers, and the like (Etzioni-Halevy 1993).

So, working-class elites have been weakened and their monogamous relationship with the working class has been impaired or replaced by another partnership, and thereby the accountability of the elites to the working class has been weakened as well.

Rising Inequalities

The labor elites' weakened bargaining position and (where it occurred) their weakening autonomy, further sapped the vitality of their relationship with the working class. This enfeeblement further detracted from their ability and motivation to struggle for working-class interests on both the industrial and the political front, which has made it easier for governments to pursue policies beneficial for the affluent but disadvantageous to the working class. Since the 1970s and 1980s, such policies—encouraging high corporate profits, tax cuts, and the like—thus came to be more widely entrenched. As could have been expected, therefore—and despite growing affluence—this period has also seen a reversal of the previous trend of decreasing inequalities and a formidable rise in inequalities.[4]

Conclusion

Transcending the traditional divisions between class and elite theories, this paper analyzed the manner in which democracy may lead to greater equality. It brought into relief what both class and elite theories have tended to neglect: that, although the very existence of elites implies inequality, their coupling with the working class, involving certain democratic arrangements, may lead to decreasing inequalities, and vice versa.

The paper clarified that historically in the West, there has in fact been some empowerment of the working class through the basically monogamous (though not totally exclusive) coupling of elites with it, those elites' growing autonomy from the state, and their partial accountability to the working class. These were among the main factors that led to decreasing inequalities. These historical developments were contrasted with recent developments: Paradoxically, it is precisely in the present-day "postmodern" society—which has become more open and variegated, where the political importance of classes has declined, where the working class has become diversified and shrunk, and class boundaries have become hazier—a society which thus is becoming more of a "classless" society—that inequalities have increased. This reversal of the previous trends was seen as related to the partial uncoupling of the former ties between elites and the working class, which also implied the weakening of their accountability to that class.

All this lent support to the paper's thesis that the coupling of elites with the working class (or with other subordinate classes) and the class-based democratic arrangements this entails are of prime importance in pushing society toward greater equality, and vice versa. It follows from this, that when governments first enfeeble working-class-based organizations and elites and then initiate paternalistic, remedial "social policies" designed to favor the disadvantaged, the latter can only imperfectly make up for the former.

Rather, if it is to come about, progress to greater equality is likely to be the result of initiatives from "below." These are initiatives by working-class or other subordinate class-based organizations or movements, in which elites or leaders are "tuned in" to a disadvantaged class and are relatively independent from the state, and members hold leaders accountable to themselves. Parties or governments that delegitimize such struggles from below in the name of overall cohesiveness are unlikely to further equality in today's inegalitarian societies. A struggle for greater equality, then, must first and foremost be a struggle for a more genuine, working-class- (or other subordinate-class-) based democracy.

Notes

1. For a definition of classes and elites, see the Introduction to this volume. By this definition elites also include leaders of organizations and movements.
2. See Michels in this volume.
3. This is indicated by a great variety of research and statistics. See, for instance, Chirot 1977, p. 189; Williamson 1991, pp. 57–63; Brenner et al. 1991, pp. 52–53.

4.   This, too, is indicated by numerous research projects and statistical data. See, among others, Green et al. 1992; Fritzell 1993; Cutler and Katz 1992; Dye 1994, pp. 19–21; Central Statistical Office 1994, p. 77.

References

Brenner, Y. S., Hartmut Kaelble, and Mark Thomas (eds.) 1991. *Income Distribution in Historical Perspective*. Cambridge: Cambridge University Press.

Central Statistical Office. 1994. *Social Trends* 24. London: HMSO.

Chirot, Daniel. 1977. *Social Change in the Twentieth Century*. New York: Harcourt Brace Jovanovich.

Cutler, David M., and Lawrence F. Katz. 1992. "Rising Inequality?" *American Economic Review* 82: 546–551.

Dye, Thomas. 1994. "Elite Autonomy and Mass Disaffection." Paper presented at the XVIth World Congress of the International Political Science Association, Berlin, August 21–25, 1994.

Edwards, Richard, and Michael Podgursky. 1986. "The Unraveling Accord" in *Unions in Crisis and Beyond*, ed. Richard Edward, Paolo Garoma, and Franz Todtling. Dover, Mass: Auburn House, 14–60.

Etzioni-Halevy, Eva. 1993. *The Elite Connection*. Cambridge: Polity Press.

Fritzell, Johan. 1993. "Income Inequality Trends in the 1980s: A Five-Country Comparison." *Acta Sociologica* 36: 47–62.

Golden, Miriam. 1992. "Conclusion" in *Bargaining for Change*, ed. Miriam Golden and Jonas Pontusson. Ithaca: Cornell University Press, 307–333.

Green, Gordon, John Coder, and Paul Ryscave. 1992. "International Comparisons of Earnings Inequality for Men in the 1980s." *Review of Income and Wealth* (March): 1–16.

Offe, Claus. 1985a. *Disorganized Capitalism*. Cambridge: Polity Press.

———. 1985b. "New Social Movements," *Social Research* 52: 817–868.

Pontusson, Jonas. 1992. "Introduction" in *Bargaining for Change,* ed. Miriam Golden and Jonas Pontusson. Ithaca: Cornell University Press, 1–37.

Shalev, Michael. 1992. "The Resurgence of Labour Quiescence" in *The Future of Labour Movements*, ed. Marino Regini. London: Sage, 102–132.

Visser, Jelle. 1992. "The Strength of Union Movements in Advanced Capitalist Democracies," in *The Future of Labour Movements*, ed. Marino Regini, London: Sage, 17–52.

Williamson, Jeffrey G. 1991. "British Inequality During the Industrial Revolution" in *Income Distribution in Historical Perspective*. Cambridge: Cambridge University Press, 57–63.

Conclusion

This collection of readings has creamed off the upper class of class analyses, and the elite of elite analyses, from the classical and modern literature on democracy. It started by presenting two points of view: one, which includes both class and elite perspectives on democracy, depicted actual democracy (as distinct from its ideal) as better, but not incomparably better, than a sham. In this view, the ruling class—or elite—rules in a democracy no less than in any other regime (Marx; Pareto; Mosca). While democracy is not completely without merit, its various mechanisms (including elections) merely determine "which members of the ruling class are to misrepresent the people in parliament" (Marx); they serve merely to "bamboozle king demos" (Pareto); as a façade for oligarchy (Michels); to aid dominant class hegemony (Gramsci); to reproduce the capitalist relations of production (Althusser) to justify the power elite's power and help manipulate the masses into apathy (Mills); to promote or camouflage the state's (the state elites' or the state managers') promotion of capitalist interests (Miliband; Poulantzas; Block). Elections and other democratic arrangements have mainly symbolic value (Dye and Zeigler); even the tolerance they create serves as an instrument of repression (Marcuse); they are there to obscure vicious micromechanisms of power (Foucault). In short, democracy, which is basically incompatible with the economic inequalities of capitalism (Manley; Bowles and Gintis) serves mainly as a fig leaf, to cover the nakedness of that same capitalism, and of ruling class/elite power.

In contradiction to this has been the second view, according to which democracy—though it is not ruled by the people—is still distinctive in that its competitive elections make it necessary for leaders to pay at least some attention to the wishes of the public

(Schumpeter; Sartori; Dahl), in that its various elites are differentiated and relatively autonomous from each other, thus countervailing each other's power (Weber; Mosca; Schumpeter; Aron), in that it creates a diffusion of power (Sartori), and a variety of links between leaders and the public (Polsby), all of which are important mechanisms for restraining the power of rulers and increasing the liberty of the ruled.

While the advocates of these two viewpoints were still busy disputing the merits and demerits of democracy, and just as it seemed that the adversaries had exhausted their arsenal, and that interest in the very topic of their dispute was slackening, some new developments occurred. Countries all over the world—from Southern Europe to South Africa—began voting on the merits of democracy with their feet, by taking at least some steps on the road toward it. This has not merely brought democracy "back in" as a topic of academic analysis, but has restored it to the center stage of intellectual attention. Concomitantly, it has led to a shift in the focus of this attention. The limelight has now turned to the factors and actors that are responsible for either blocking or generating and sustaining democracy.

On this topic, too, there has been a controversy, as certain class theorists have convincingly ascribed to classes and class relations both the role of blocking and the role of fostering democracy, and several elite theorists have done the same for elites and their relations. In class theory, the role of obstructing democracy has been imputed mainly to the landowning class (Moore), while the role of fostering democracy has been assigned to the bourgeoisie (Moore), the middle class (Lipset), the working class and its allies among the other classes (Therborn; Huber, Rueschemeyer, and Stephen), or to compromises between them (Przeworski).

No less convincing have been the arguments of elite theorists, who have imputed the role of impeding democracy to divided or, conversely, to ideologically unified elites, while assigning the role of promoting democracy to consensually unified elites (Field, Higley, and Burton), to elite pacts, or to elite imposition (Karl and Schmitter). At the same time, members of this school have also developed a variety of analyses tracing the role of elites—for better or for worse—in actual democratic transitions in various parts of the world (Burton and Ryu; Morlino; O'Donell; Reis and Cheibub; Wesolowski).

Since the two strands—that assigning the key role in (either blocking or furthering) democratization to classes, and that assigning that role to elites—are both convincing, this should certainly be the case for the strand of analysis in which the two lines are brought together. This strand includes the excerpts from Huntington and from Diamond and Linz that bring into relief the roles of classes and elites in democratization. To these must be added the contributions that explore certain relations between classes and elites in extant democracies. They endeavor to show that despite democratic mechanisms that ostensibly accord electoral power to the working class, class-elite relations are skewed in disfavor of that class (Michels) and in favor of the capitalist class (Miliband, Block). Or else it is shown that some democratic mechanisms (the relative autonomy of organizations), though necessary for the fair election of leaders, indirectly exacerbates economic-class inequalities (Dahl).

In addition, there are the analyses that view class-elite relations as either fostering or creating a problem for democratization. The weakening of the landholding class, which encourages the submission of the military elite to state control in Britain, is seen as one important factor in fostering democratization (Tilly). And the creation of a new entrepreneurial class by state elites is seen as causing a severe dilemma of democratization in Eastern Europe (Offe). These latter analysts all ask what classes and elites—and class-elite relations—can (or cannot) do for democracy, leaving it for Etzioni-Halevy to ask what democracy can do for class-elite relations. And while Michels, Miliband, and Dahl ask how class-elite relations in a democracy may preserve or increase economic inequalities, Etzioni-Halevy asks how they may decrease such inequalities.

All this does not add up to even the beginnings of a coherent theory on class-elite relations and democracy. All that could have been hoped for is that this collection of readings would bring together some tenuous ideas on these relations and democracy and (still more tenuously) on how they may block or favor democratization. If it has done so, it has fulfilled its, largely exploratory, mission. If it were found to have laid the groundwork for further exploration of this topic in the future, this would be an added bonus.

This, then, brings us to the end of our journey through the land of democracy. We have witnessed its drama; we have followed its tribulations; we have cheered its heroes and booed its villains. One thing we have not done is predict its future. This is not because the drama of democracy has been played out and the end of its history is nigh. Rather, it is because the scenario for the drama of the future still remains to be written, and it is for the main actors of democracy—the elites, the classes, the public, and their members—both to write and to enact it. This includes you, the reader; so please get on with the job.

Name Index

Althusser, Louis, vii, xxviii, 4, 5, 24, 240, 327
Aron, Raymond, viii, xxix, 44, 45, 86, 328

Block, Fred, xi, 239–240, 259, 327
Bowles, Samuel, ix, xxviii, 93, 95, 111, 327
Burckhardt, Jacob, 71, 77
Burton, Michael G., x, xv, 152–153, 174, 194, 230, 232, 328

Carnegie, Andrew, 122
Cheibub, Zairo B., 153, 222, 329
Chun, Doo Hwan, 195–197, 199
Chung, Ju Young, 201
Colley, Linda, 279
Crèvecoeur, J. Hector St. John, 122

Dahl, Robert, xi, 152, 168, 171, 239–242, 267, 328–329
Diamond, Larry, 239, 241, 293, 329
Durkheim, Emile, xxxiii
Dye, Thomas, 151–152, 155, 327

Engels, Friedrich, vii, 7
Etzioni-Halevy, Eva, xii, 239, 242, 308, 310, 321

Field, G. Lowell, 151–153, 174, 230, 232
Fonseca, E. Giannetti da, 229
Foucault, Michel, viii, 93, 103, 327
Franklin, Benjamin, 122–123
Friedrich, Carl, 170
Fukuyama, Francis, 121

Gintis, Herbert, ix, xxviii, 93, 111, 327
Gonzalez, Felipe, 211
Gramsci, Antonio, vii, 4, 12, 25

Hamilton, Alexander, 123–124
Hegel, Georg, W.F. 125
Higley, John, x, xv, 152–153, 174, 230, 232
Huber, Evelyne, 96, 142, 328
Hunt, Gaillard, 124
Huntington, Samuel, 239, 241, 285, 328

Jefferson, Thomas, 121, 123, 125–126

Karl, Terry Lynn, 153, 185
Kim, Byung Kook, 194
Kim, Dae Jung, 197–199, 201
Kim, Jong Pil, 201
Kim, Young Sam, 197–199, 201–202
King, Martin Luther, xiii

Labaree, Leonard W., 123
Lazarus, Emma, 121
Lincoln, Abraham, xxiii
Linz, Juan, xv, 239, 241, 293, 328
Lipscomb, Andrew A., 123
Lipset, Seymour Martin, vii, xv, 4, 6, 37, 96, 223, 328

Macridis, Roy C., 184
Madison, James, 123–124
Manley, John F., ix, 93, 95, 120, 327
Marcuse, Herbert, vii, xxviii, 4, 5, 18, 327
Marx, Karl, vii, xxviii, xxxiii, 4, 5, 7, 31, 94, 136, 327
McCoy, Drew, 123
Meisel, J.H., 168
Meyers, Marvin, 124
Michels, Robert, x, xxix, xxxi, 170, 175, 239–240, 242, 243
Miliband, Ralph, xi, xxv, xxvii, 239, 240, 242, 251, 327, 328

Mills, C. Wright, viii, xv, xxix, xxx, xxxi,
    44, 71, 88, 91
Moore, Barrington, vii, xv, 4, 6, 30, 96,
    184, 328
Morlino, Leonardo, 153, 205, 328
Mosca, Gaetano, viii, xv, xxix, 43, 44, 45,
    46, 53, 88, 91, 168, 169, 170, 239,
    327

Nader, Ralph, 165

O'Donnell, Guillermo, 153, 214, 328
Offe, Claus, 241, 302, 321, 329
Orwell, George, xxv

Papandreou, Andreas, 291
Pareto, Vilfredo, viii, xv, xxix, 43, 44,
    45, 47, 88, 91, 170, 176, 239, 327
Park, Chung Hee, 195, 196
Pateman, Carol, xxxi
Peron, Juan, 147
Polsby, Nelson, 151, 152, 160, 328
Pontusson, Jonas, 316
Poulantzas, Nicos, xxviii, 93, 94, 97, 240,
    327
Przeworski, Adam, xxviii, 96, 128, 328

Reagan, Ronald, 126
Reis, Elisa, 153, 222, 328
Rhee, Syngman, 195, 196, 199
Riesman, David, 173
Roh, Tae Woo, 197, 198, 199

Rueschemeyer, Dietrich, ix, xv, 96, 142,
    282, 328
Ryu, Jai, 153, 194

Sartori, Giovanni, 152, 168, 328
Schmitter, Philippe C., x, xv, 152, 185
Schumpeter, Joseph, viii, xv, xxix, 44, 78,
    170, 328
Shalev, Michael, 320
Smyth, Albert H., 123
Soares, Mario, 291
Stephens, John D., 96, 142, 328
Suarez, Adolfo, 131

Therborn, Göran, 96, 134, 328
Tilly, Charles 239, 241, 275, 329
Tocqueville, Alexis de, 124, 292
Turner, Frederick Jackson, 125

Veliz, Claudio, 177, 184
Verou, P.L. , 133
Visser, Jelle, 316, 320

Walesa, Lech, 234
Weber, Max, viii, xv, xxix, xxxiii, 44, 45,
    63, 122, 328
Wesolowski, Wlodzimierz, 153, 230,
    328
Wrobel, David, 125

Zeigler, Harmon, ix, xxix, 151, 152, 155,
    327

Subject Index

Aristocracy, 30, 32–36, 48
  and democracy, 5, 31, 137–139, 142–
    144, 146, 149

Bourgeois, bourgoisie, 8–10, 13, 33–36,
    99, 100, 101, 103, 105
  and democracy, 5, 6, 9–10, 30–31,
    94, 96, 106, 134, 136, 137, 144–
    146, 148–149
  and democratization, 34, 136–141

Capitalism, 28, 29, 65, 97, 118–119,
    266
  and bourgeoisie, 98–99, 134, 137,
    139, 254, 261, 264
  and democracy, xxviii, 4, 21, 25, 94–
    98, 101, 111–115, 131–132, 134,
    136–138, 140, 145–146, 254–258,
    261, 263–264, 266
  and democratization, 4, 26, 94, 111,
    116, 119, 137, 145
  and elites, 12, 27, 31, 97
  in Europe, 4
  in the United States, 74
Capitalist class (see also Bourgeois,
    bourgoisie)
  and democracy, 97, 255
  in Eastern and Central Europe, 303
  in Europe, 114
  in Latin America, 148
  in the United States, 73–74
Capitalist democracy. See Democracy,
    and capitalism
Class, classes, xxv, xxviii, xxix, xxxii, 7,
    12, 19, 32, 105
  and democracy, xxv, xxvii, xxix, 5, 6,
    19, 31, 36, 41, 44, 89, 93, 99–101,
    115, 244–245, 284–285, 297, 329
  and democratization, xvi, 6, 36, 91

and economic development, xxv, 24,
    36, 99, 113, 117–118, 132
  and elites, xxv, 14, 22, 44–45, 57, 89,
    223, 311–312
  struggle, xxviii, xxix, xxxii, 5, 8, 20–
    21, 23–25, 31, 140, 264–266

Democracy, democracies, democratic,
    xxiii, xxiv, 12, 16, 18, 22–24, 30–
    31, 33–34, 36–38, 39, 44–45, 53–
    58, 66, 70, 75–81, 83–85, 87–90,
    96, 98, 103, 108, 110, 113, 120–
    123, 128–130, 135, 136, 168,
    170–171, 178–179, 188–189,
    214–217, 243–244, 247, 254,
    266–269, 275–277, 281, 310,
    327–328
  and aristocracy (see Aristocracy, and
    democracy)
  and bourgeoisie (see Bourgeois,
    bourgoisie, and democracy)
  and bureaucracy, 45, 57–58, 60–61,
    65, 66–68, 249
  and capitalism, 4, 24, 26, 35, 40,
    93–94, 97, 100, 111–115, 128–
    135, 137, 252, 270, 282, 303,
    304
  and charisma, 63, 64
  and classes, xxv, xxix, 23, 31–36, 40,
    54, 73, 91, 93–95, 97, 98–99, 128,
    145, 154, 239, 297–298
  and economic development, 34, 36,
    38, 40, 41, 96, 115, 142–143,
    148–149, 151–152, 223, 271, 274,
    286–288, 303–304
  and elites, xxv, xxx, xxxi, 30, 36, 44–
    46, 50–53, 55, 91, 151, 155–159,
    169, 239, 244–247, 282, 304–306,
    328

and middle class (*see* Middle class, and democracy)
threats to, xx, xxi, 17, 21, 50, 56, 154, 171
transition to, xv, 144–147, 152–153, 215, 231, 280–281, 302–303
and working class (*see* Working class, and democracy)
Democratization, 49, 64, 69, 93, 96, 106, 109, 128, 130–134, 138–140, 143, 185, 187, 192–193, 198, 206–207, 212–213, 281, 289
and bureaucracy, 63, 69–70
and capitalism, 98–99, 138, 291
and classes, xxvi, 3–4, 41, 45, 88, 94, 131, 191–192, 241, 282–283
and economic development, 41–42, 144, 149, 219–220
and elites, 45, 93, 136, 151, 156, 196–197, 227, 289–290
waves of, 51, 63, 185–186, 205, 285–286
Dominant class. *See* Ruling class

Eastern and Central Europe (*see also* Europe)
capitalism in, 302–303
classes in, 41, 231
democracy in, 230, 234, 303
democratization in, 41, 230–234, 241, 287, 289–290, 302, 307–308
elites in, 230–232, 234–237
middle class in, 234–235, 287
working class in, 234–235
Elite, elites, 33, 47–50, 155–156, 174, 177, 182, 311–312, 322, 324
autonomy of, 45–46, 59, 82–83, 86, 88–91, 312–313
circulation of, 44, 47–49, 90, 155–156, 251
and classes, xxv, xxxii, xxxv, 43, 90, 230, 240, 311–313, 315–316
consensually unified, xxxiv, 153, 176–177, 179, 181, 183, 194
and democracy, xxv, xxix, xxxi, xxxii, xxxv, 41, 43, 45–46, 49–50, 57, 80–81, 86–87, 96, 151, 156–159, 175, 182, 222, 224–226, 233, 235, 240, 249, 252
and democratization, xxix, 43, 82, 97, 143, 146, 151, 153, 196, 199–204, 227–228, 235–236

divisions in, xxxii, 47, 153, 175–176, 179–181, 195
ideologically unified, 153, 176, 179–181
Europe
capitalism in, 28, 31, 255
capitalist class in, 37, 146, 255
classes in, 31, 48, 137
democracy in, 27, 38, 59, 61, 63, 108–109, 133, 137, 144–146, 278
democratization in, 37, 133, 137, 189, 205–213, 278–281, 289
elites in, 253, 318
middle class in, 36, 108
working class in, 11, 33, 36, 117, 133

Higher circles, 71–74, 82, 146

Intellectuals, 12–17

Latin America, 40, 146
capitalism in, 299–300
capitalist class in, 146, 300
classes in, 146–147, 228, 298–300
democracy in, 40, 147, 153, 192, 224–225, 294–298, 301
democratization in, 146–148, 188–189, 218, 220, 223, 228, 289–291, 293–294, 301
elites in, 147, 153, 222–224, 226–229, 294–297
middle class in, 146, 300–301
working class in, 145–146, 262, 300

Mass, masses, mass society, 69–70, 74–77, 91, 140, 152, 156, 157, 158
Middle class
and democracy, 40, 96, 142, 143, 145–149, 286–288
and democratization, 143, 145, 288
in Latin America, 287–288

Oligarchical tendencies, oligarchy, 52, 91, 243, 250
Organization
conservative basis of, 249–250
need for, 244, 250

Power elite, 44, 71–74, 88, 103–105, 288
Proletariat. *See* working class

Ruling class, 5, 7, 12–16, 44–45, 53–54,
    98–102, 105, 259–261
  in democracy, 54–56, 88–90, 94, 97,
    135, 139, 156

Theory, theories, theorists, xxxiii, 3, 43–
    44, 75, 90, 98, 104, 108, 109, 152
  of classes, xxvii, 4, 93, 95
  of classes and elites, xxxiv, 103
  of democracy, xxvii, 78–80, 93, 151–
    152
  of elites, xxix–xxxi, 43–46, 78, 151–
    152, 155–158, 169, 311, 323

United States, 114
  capitalism in, 95, 110–112, 124, 125,
    272

capitalist class in, 37, 123
classes in, 113
democracy in, 95, 120–127, 136,
    160–163, 165–166
elites in, 120–122, 124
middle class in, 272
working class in, 121, 123, 126, 316–
    317

Working class
  and democracy, 10, 24, 40, 96, 131–
    132, 135–141, 143–149, 253,
    265–266, 310–311, 314–317,
    319–320, 324
  leadership of, 239, 241, 246–249
  organization of, 249
  in the United States, 115–116, 316–317